FRONTIERS OF JUSTICE

Volume 1: The Death Penalty

Edited by Claudia Whitman & Julie Zimmerman

BIDDLE
PUBLISHING
COMPANY

PO Box 1305 #103, Brunswick, Maine 04011

Copyright © Biddle Publishing Company 1997

"Managing Death Row: A Tough Assignment" by Morris L. Thigpen is reprinted from the July 1993 issue of <u>Corrections Today</u> with the permission of the American Correctional Association, Lanham, MD.

PUBLISHER'S CATALOGING IN PUBLICATION DATA

1. Frontiers of Justice, Volume 1: The Death Penalty
2. Whitman, Claudia, Ed.
3. Zimmerman, Julie, Ed.
4. Capital Punishment
5. Death Penalty
6. Prisons & Prisoners
7. United States, Criminal Justice
8. United States, Corrections

Library of Congress Catalog Card No. 97-71031
ISBN 1-879418-26-6

Published in the United States of America by
      Biddle Publishing Company
      PO Box 1305 #103
      Brunswick, ME 04011
      207-833-5016

Cover design by Billy G. Hughes Jr., Death Row, Huntsville, TX

"The frontier is the outer edge of the wave—the meeting point between savagery and civilization...the line of most rapid and effective Americanization."

Frederick Jackson Turner, 1894
The Significance of the Frontier in American History

ACKNOWLEDGEMENTS

The editors would like to say thank you, thank you so very much, to...

Our essayists and artists, truly men and women of reason and conscience, for the gifts of their time and talent to make this project not only possible, but breath-takingly powerful. The words, images and support from each of you have inspired and strengthened us throughout this process.

Charlie Sullivan from CURE for his encouragement as well as for his numerous helpful suggestions which made this book better and broader than we could have imagined.

Tekla Miller who uses her professional experience and wisdom and her energy, enthusiasm and laughter to advance the message of humanity in corrections through her own writing and onward to <u>Frontiers of Justice, Volumes 1, 2 and 3.</u>

The many friends, both incarcerated and free, who encouraged us with both practical advice, research assistance and all the kind words that make doing the work of abolition less lonely: **Jim Allen, Scott Antworth, Kathy Cox, Judy Cumbee, Noelle Hanrahan, Shelby Heath, Jane Henderson, Irene Howe, Sheila Maroney,** and **Will Quay.**

Our husbands, **Laird Carlson** and **Sandy Zimmerman**, for listening, coping, supporting and being proud of us.

Brian Baldwin who will always be a part of this book.

Steven Ainsworth, John Connolly, Gene Hathorn, Billy Hughes, Mumia Abu Jamal, Ricky Langley, and **Blake Pirtle** for teaching us that creativity, generosity, humor and friendship can bloom on Death Row. And especially to **A.J. Bannister** who has spent the last year facing the threat of imminent execution. May all of you live to see the end of capital punishment in America.

Claudia Whitman and Julie Zimmerman

IF YOU SUPPORT CAPITAL PUNISHMENT...

In a system run by humans and therefore prone to human error, if you support capital punishment, you accept the fact that some of the people executed will be innocent.

As more and more teenagers are being tried as adults, if you support capital punishment, you accept the fact that some of the people executed will be children.

Because "knowing right from wrong" disqualifies an offender from using an insanity defense, if you support capital punishment, you accept the fact that some of the people executed will be mentally ill or mentally retarded.

In a society that clamors for victims' rights and compassion for the innocent, if you support capital punishment, you accept the fact that pain and suffering will be inflicted on those who have committed no crime, the family and friends of the offender.

In an age when more and more Americans distrust "the system," if you support capital punishment, you accept the fact that you have granted that system the right to decide which of its citizens deserve to die.

In a nation that prides itself on its criminal justice system, if you support capital punishment, you accept the fact that it is the poor who are executed and that the race of the victim does more to determine who gets a death sentence than the crime itself.

In a country that seeks to decrease violence on television, on the streets and in the family, if you support capital punishment, you accept the fact that our children will learn that killing is the solution to society's problems.

In a world that cries out for peace and understanding, if you support capital punishment, you have made a judgement that thousands of incarcerated Americans, (about whom you know only what the media has told you), are no longer human, are no longer children of God, and are incapable of change, reconciliation or redemption, and that the family of the murder victim are incapable of forgiveness.

Seven years ago, my uncle was murdered. My uncle's killer is still alive, serving a life sentence. I thank God that the brutal, irrational crime that ended my uncle's life did not result in another senseless killing.

J.Z.

THE CONTRIBUTORS

Steven King Ainsworth - Death Row Inmate, CA
Lindsay Graham Bannister - Wife of Death Row Inmate, MO
Stephen B. Bright - Attorney, GA
Noel Bruno - Student, NY
Robert R. Bryan - Attorney, CA
Anne Coleman - Mother of Murder Victim, DE
Pamela Crawford - Sister of Executed Inmate, NC
Mario Cuomo - former Governor, NY
Mike Farrell - Actor, CA
John Gaffney - Journalist, ME
Henry B. Gonzalez - U.S. Congressman, TX
Abdullah T. Hameen - Death Row Inmate, DE
Shakeerah Hameen - Wife of Death Row Inmate, DE
Gene Hathorn - Death Row Inmate, TX
Shelby Heath - Widow of Death Row Inmate, AL
Joe Ingle - Minister, United Church of Christ, TN
Marietta Jaeger - Mother of Murder Victim, MI
Benjamin Jimenez - Student, NY
Perry Johnson - former Commissioner of Corrections, MI
Adria Libolt - Deputy Warden, MI
Robert Lopez - Student, NY
Tekla Dennison Miller - former Michigan Warden, CO
Bill Pelke - Grandson of Murder Victim, IN
Matthew Regan - Catholic Priest, CA
Jessica Scannell - Teacher, NY
Harley O. Staggers - former U.S. Congressman, WV
Armond H. Start - Physician, WI
Morris L. Thigpen - former Alabama Commissioner of Corrections, DC
Margaret Vandiver - Professor, TN
Tony Vaello - Student, NY
Eugene G. Wanger - Attorney, MI
Charmaine White Face - Writer, SD
Gershon Winkler - Rabbi, NM
John Yarbrough - former Police Officer, former Death Row Inmate, TX

TABLE OF CONTENTS

ILLUSTRATIONS

10

Louis Osei Cotton - "The House That Crack Built"

MARIO CUOMO

Speech for Death Penalty Focus of California
Annual Awards Dinner

For over thirty years I have studied the death penalty. It is a subject that has been familiar to me for a long time, long before the Pope chose to speak on the subject.

I've heard all the arguments, I've analyzed all the evidence I could find. I've measured public opinion when it was opposed, when it was indifferent, when it was passionately in favor, and always I've concluded that the death penalty would only make things worse than they are. After twelve years as governor, on the basis of more and more cumulative hard evidence, I continued to conclude that it makes things worse.

It doesn't deter. That used to be the argument. Does it deter? Doesn't it? You would come with your records, they would come with their books. They would cite authorities. You would cite other authorities...No more. There's not even a pretense any more. Nobody seriously says, "Well if you do this, the crime rate will go down," because all the evidence is the other way.

It's much worse than that now. Now it is simple revenge. "I want it! He killed her, I'm going to kill him! And I'm not going to have to dress it up. I'm not going to have to make any elegant case for you." I've seen it, it's different now than it used to be.

It's worse now than it used to be. It's clear it's been applied mostly against those unable to afford the best legal defense. There's no question that it's been applied erratically. There's no question that it is inherently unfair. It is certainly true that it has never brought back a single life, and it has cost us recklessly, cruelly, needlessly, more than one innocent life. It seems absolutely plain that in the end, it is an instruction in brutality, when we need lessons in civility more than we need anything.

It has debased us. And it gets clearer and clearer that it debases us. I lost the election in 1994. I was not happy about that, although we knew it was going to be difficult. I had been offered an opportunity to sit on the Supreme Court of the United States, and told President Clinton, "Thank you very much. . ." You know, the notion that I could say no to this seems almost an absurdity to me, coming from where I come from. The idea that I got to be a lawyer was a big deal for Poppa. He couldn't read or write English. He was proud of the fact that, "Mario, you got through school and became a lawyer." If I could tell Pop that I was on the Supreme Court of the United States it would mean everything. "But Mr. President, that's not where the issues are now. The Constitution is important indeed, but what I could do as one of nine in what's left of my life is not enough to justify giving up what we could do with the socio-cultural, the fiscal and philosophical issues that are out there now. We're in trouble in this country." So I said, "I'm going to take a shot and even if I lose, I'll be around, I'll be free. I'll be free to make the case, I'll be free to help you. We need a lot of help." And the death penalty was one of the things I was thinking about, because it's symptomatic of the situation in this society—callous, negative, retreating, regressing.

I lost. I was very unhappy about losing. But Matilda and I were invited to the inaugural of the new governor, who's a good fellow, an old friend of mine, but a Republican who thinks a little bit differently than I do—a lot differently on the death penalty. And I sat on that stage for his inaugural and we applauded at the proper moments, and it was going pretty well. There were maybe fifteen thousand people in the audience, and they were kind to Matilda and me. When we were announced, they applauded--that felt good. And then he started to speak, the new governor, and it wasn't going so hot for him—he didn't say a whole lot—but then he got to a really great line that brought the house down. "And the first thing I will do is bring back the death penalty!" Fifteen thousand New Yorkers stood up, and they cheered, and their arms went up, and their fists went up. They were punching one another with their elbows...gonna have the death penalty! And then you sit down and you're a little shaky. Wow. What are they thinking? What is it that made them so happy? All right, you're going to have the death penalty, all right it's something you wanted, okay, I can understand that. You disagree with me, you made your case, I understand that. But my God, the joy in you, the delight at the notion that finally you're going to kill somebody! Now if you thought that it was going to make your daughter safe from the rapist, that it was going to make you safe from the attacker, that's something else, I can see you being joyous. But you know it doesn't deter, we don't even argue that anymore.What is it that you're cheering?

Oh, it's worse now than it's been for a long, long time...the death penalty used as an applause line by a new Governor of the great State of New York, the place where America began, the place we boast of as the place where civility began in this country. The Big Apple, the Empire State—back to death.

What is it exactly that produces the hunger for this bloody version of justice?

In the end I believe it is, ironically, not just a lust for revenge but a desperate expression of a longing for a safer world, a world free of fear. Californians, New Yorkers, Americans everywhere are appalled by the new madness created by drugs, the calculated murders committed by twelve year olds, the audacious atrocity of the crimes they hear about, or may even have seen with their own eyes. When it appears to the people that crime is rampant, when criminals are seen as immune from adequate punishment or even apprehension, well then people get angry and they try to find a short-hand answer. I understand their frustration, I understand their fear. I have been with the victims and their families, I've made a point of that. I've felt the anger myself more than once. I know what it is to be violated, to have one's close family violated.

How would I react if someone took the life of my daughter or even just touched her. . .or Matilda? Anger? Surely. Terrible anger, probably. Violence? Perhaps. I'm no saint. I might not be good enough to suppress it, despite the better angels. So I understand the cry for retribution, for vindication, even for revenge. But I do know something else—and it is worth saying over and over. I know that this society should strive for something better than what we are in our worst moments.

If this great nation hopes to fulfill the great promise of our civilization, the constant struggle for greater fairness and intelligence, then we cannot build the fortress of our law on the surging tide of those emotions. We need to respond more effectively to the new violence. Of course we need law enforcement. But we need to make our justice system not more severe, but more certain. To the extent that law enforcement can help, you don't need Cesare Beccaria to tell you as he did a few hundred years ago, that it isn't the severity of the punishment that will deter, it is the sureness of it. There's no point in telling someone you're going to kill them or hang them or put them away for thirty years, if the likelihood that they're going to get caught, convicted, and serve time is nil. You have a law enforcement system that's not effective because most people who commit crimes don't get caught. If they get caught, they don't get prosecuted; if they get prosecuted, they don't get convicted; if they get convicted, they don't get imprisoned. That's an immense problem. How do you solve it? More judges, more prisons, more...nobody wants to do that. So what do you do...? Death penalty! As though that were going to make up for law enforcement that's ineffective. It won't. It's just a cop-out by the society, at the prodding of the politicians. And even if you had a really effective law enforcement system, that wouldn't do it. The only thing that will really work is prevention.

You want to know how to end crime, go back to my neighborhood, South Jamaica, where I was born—the hundred and third precinct. When I was born, it was a tough neighborhood, a really tough neighborhood. There were a lot of poor people, and we were among them and you had all kinds of fights, and there were gang wars and they would cut your cheek if you touched somebody's sister. They wouldn't kill you, it was a different time—we're more callous and brutal now. But go back to that neighborhood and see it now. A toddler emptied out into the street at the age of two in these tenements, surrounded by pimps, prostitution, degraded every conceivable way you can be. I have said about these kids in those communities, they become familiar with the sound of gunfire before they've ever heard an orchestra. How do you think they grow up? Why do you think she has a baby when she's fifteen or sixteen years old? Because she grew up in that community, she went to P.S. 50, where I went, but now the ceiling is falling down, now nobody is getting taught anything. There was a story in the papers yesterday that says a corporation, instead of giving them computers, took a look at the schools and bought them furniture and books, and said, "This is ridiculous."

There's no point in going to school there. If she did, where would she get a job? You've stacked them all into communities, piled them on top of one another, created such enormous density. There are no jobs. You don't try to help them to get jobs. She's fifteen. "I have no shot, I'm going to make a baby, because it's mine. . .this is something that allows me to fulfill myself." And the guys are in jail, they're all doing drugs—no, not every one of them...miraculously one will survive, or two will survive out of a dozen. Would my kids have survived, my beautiful five who are setting records everywhere? I'm not sure. Would I have survived? I don't think so. Instead of these streets to despair, give them avenues to dignity. Give them a place to live where there's a little air. Give them an education. Give them a chance to do a job!

One thing is absolutely for sure. There is no reason to believe that returning to the machinery of death will be any wiser now than it was for all the times in the past when we had it, used it, regretted it, and discarded it. Or that it will work any better in this country than in all the other nations of the industrialized world which rejected it long ago, led by our beautiful neighbors to the North, Canada. Even South Africa, our last partner in punishment, gave up executing its people last year.

In the end, I believe there are no persuasive arguments for capital punishment. The impulse to kill the killer, however it is disguised, is more emotion than thought.

This is clear, even from the advocacy you hear. You should have heard the arguments in New York State when I was governor. I would go and listen, always I'd sit upstairs and listen to the Senate, and then go over to the Assembly and listen to the Assembly. You should have heard the arguments. Here's the quote: "Whatever the studies show, the people in my district believe that the taking of a life justifies the forfeiting of a life."' No matter what the proof is, no matter what intelligence says, no matter what the truth is, all I can tell you is, if my people are dumb enough to think it works, I'm gonna give it to them! An eye for an eye, a tooth for a tooth.

"An eye for an eye..." (Genius of a legislator, happened to be a Democrat.) "An eye for an eye—the governor ought to know that, he reads books. I understand he even read the Bible. Ho Ho Ho." I waited for him.

"Tell me, Pal, about this eye for an eye, tooth for a tooth, I may have missed that. Tell me about that, where is that?"

"Well, it's an eye for an eye, tooth for a tooth."

"Really, do you read the Sanhedrin, do you read the Torah, did you go to the Sanhedrin, look this up, what it says, what the rabbis said about that?"

"What the hell does that have to do with anything, the Sanhedrin?"

"It's not to be taken literally. Even Israel gave up the death penalty, saying it was barbaric, except for crimes against the State. How can you say an eye for an eye, a tooth for a tooth; what are you telling me, that revenge works?! He rapes you, you rape his daughter, they mutilate you, you mutilate them? They kill you, you kill them back? That's as primitive a rule as I can imagine. It's never worked. We've been trying to outlive that for thousands of years!"

But those were the arguments they were making. Think of it. Where would it end?

Not so many years ago in New York, the instrument of that brutality was a chair designed to, in effect, burn out the life of a human being. In California, as you know, it was a chamber that filled up leisurely with cyanide gas. A classic American skeptic once defined justice as a system of revenge in which the state imitates the criminal. The imitation is harder to detect now. We pad the tender places in our conscience with the comfortable fiction that lethal injection, presumably painless, is therefore essentially humane. But then, just in case somebody up there is watching after all, we still make sure we do it in the middle of the night.

And we continue to put people to death despite the lack of evidence that it will protect us, despite the copious irrefutable evidence that past recipients of our official barbarism have occasionally been innocent, and there's no good reason to believe we could avoid killing innocent people in the future as well. At least twenty-three people are believed to have been wrongfully executed, eight of them in my great state of New York. Quite a record.

I thought about this a lot in office. I tried to imagine myself as a governor who had asked for and approved of the execution of a person who was later found to be innocent. You put yourself in that position. What would you have done, what would have happened, when the family of the innocent man came to you and said, "Governor, why did you do it, why did you have to kill him?" What would you say? You couldn't say, "Well I had to do it in the interest of deterring others from murdering people. I had to kill him—even though there was a chance that he might be innocent, there's always that chance."

"But if you were sure it didn't deter anyone else, then why would you have to do it?" What would you say? They made me do it? The people want it? It's popular? We can't think of anything else? It makes me feel good? I feel like I'm getting even? What would you say? I couldn't think of anything to say. And that's why I was against the death penalty.

It's distressing to see the administration that replaced mine make its first major accomplishment the return of death to New York. I have volunteered to be an attorney in the first death penalty case in my state; I hope to have the chance to participate in that as a lawyer, so that what I couldn't do as a governor, maybe I'll be able to do as a lawyer.

But having the death penalty come back to New York is a little discouraging, I have to admit that to you...but only a little. I find it helpful to remember that the real story of human progress has always been a tale of progress, retreat, and then progress again. We're constantly moving in slips and slides, but constantly moving forward.

I take great comfort in the fact that the history of this nation in particular has for all of its fits and starts essentially been a tale of inexorable advances forward and upward toward the light, toward greater fairness, toward greater intelligence, toward a better approximation of real justice. Those are good things to hang onto in moments when it seems too hard to imagine that we or anybody could reverse the tide of public desire for seeing killers put to death. Don't be discouraged.

An American statesman once reminded us that all progress has resulted from people who took unpopular positions, not so much because they were courageous, but because they have been given this great gift of something to believe in passionately. Passionately! And because they had the ability and the generosity to share that gift, those people will continue to raise their voices, louder if they have to, speeding the time when civility replaces harshness, intelligence overwhelms anger, and we return—all of us—to the path upward.

And I hope to be there with you when it happens.

Mario Cuomo was the Governor of New York State for 12 years, beginning in 1982. Known as one of the best orators of our time, Governor Cuomo is in demand as a speaker from coast to coast. Two highlights of his speaking career were as a radio show host, and at the 1984 Democratic National Convention where he gave the nominating speech for President of the United States. He is now a practicing attorney in New York City.

Steven King Ainsworth - "1996–America: The Land of the Imprisoned, Condemned and Executed"

STEVEN KING AINSWORTH

"A Relic of the Past"

I

The power to kill is awesome. Why do we allow those ruling in our names to use it against us? Why did we carry capital punishment across the Atlantic when we were escaping the bloody excesses of monarchy ourselves? How has capital punishment been used by the powerful to quash the less powerful in our society?

These questions and others I will attempt to address in the following pages and hopefully offer you, the reader, some points to ponder while you decide if capital punishment is necessary in America today.

In this time of revisionist history, I am sure we all realize that Columbus did not "discover" America, but simply opened it up to exploitation by himself and by those people who followed him. Columbus used capital punishment to enforce an economic policy on the island that is now known as Haiti: "In the province of Cicao, Indians who brought to him a certain quantity of gold were given a copper token to hang around their necks. Those found without a copper token had their hands cut off and bled to death."[1] This was in 1495 and throughout the 1490's Spaniards took prisoners among the Arawaks, the native population of the Caribbean Islands, hanging them and burning them alive at will.

Columbus, Pizzaro, Cortes, Coronado, and all of those who wreaked havoc through South America, Meso-America, Mexico, and the Southwestern United States during the 15th and 16th centuries did not use the sophisticated cover of judicial assassination to justify the slaughter. They simply said that they were acting out the will of God, their God, in bringing the heathen savages to their knees.

The first English ship bringing colonists to America had barely set anchor in Chesapeake Bay in the Spring of 1607 before the Ruling Council of Virginia (Jamestown) acted upon their own in a tribunal of sorts. George Kendall was condemned and "put to death for attempted mutiny"[2] in December of that year. Our English forefathers had not even been in this land eight months before the judicial homicides began! Mr. Kendall may well have been the first white man to suffer capital punishment in America.

The first law recorded in Plymouth Colony on December 27, 1623, established the trial by jury system on the North American continent. Seven years later John Billington, a signatory of the Mayflower Compact, one of our nation's founding documents, "was sentenced to death in the colonies' first capital case."[3]

Justifying their use of capital punishment on the Old Testament law of Leviticus, the Puritans of New England, the same crowd that brought us Thanksgiving, put to death a teen-aged servant named Thomas Granger for bestiality. Leviticus had written: "The man who lies with an animal, he must die and the animal must be killed."[4] Young Tom could not identify the specific animals he acted lewdly with, so all "the animals were cast into a pit and killed as he watched then he was put to death, in September 1624."[5] Before you decide the Puritans were right in following Leviticus, let me hasten to add that the Old Testament also prescribes the death penalty for disobedient children.[6] Could those who gather in support of the death penalty today who use "eye for an eye" as a justification for their support stone a child to death?

The infamous Salem witchcraft trials of 1692 in Massachusetts were another legal remedy. Nineteen men and women were executed on the strength of very dubious testimony by others who may have been coerced into saying such things as: "Her yellow bird sucked betwixt her fingers." I am sure every little old lady in America today who shares her world with a canary who eats from her hand would be astonished that such behavior could be considered the work of the devil, and that they would be subjected to capital punishment for such carryings on with their feathered companions.

Oppression of the poor and capital punishment have long gone hand in hand in white America. When Maryland opened its first courts, in 1638, legislation concerning servants (indentured servants, usually poor whites from England) was one of the priorities at the time, because of the number of runaways. "Unlawful departure"[7] was punished by hanging. Quitting a low-paying job had serious consequences in 1638.

Inequality in our justice system was clearly evident as early as 1675 where in New York Colony it was declared: "According to the council ruling of 1675, there were two sets of laws, one for the colonists and one for the Indians."[8] Still separate laws governed black slaves in our early history. An early Virginia Act of 1705 declared the punishment for arson by a Negro could be having "the right hand cut off, the head severed from the body, the body divided into four quarters, and head and quarters set up in the most public places of the country."[9] Vestiges of these early examples of oppression of the poor, inequality, and racism still permeate the American justice system today.

The separation between justice for the rich and justice for the poor is illustrated at least as far back as 1710. In the case of a rich lawyer named

Thomas Macnemara, he was allowed to plead guilty to "homicide by chance medley,"[10] and was branded with the letter "M" on the right hand. A poor white man or woman, indentured servant, slave, or Indian would have suffered a greater punishment for homicide, perhaps "limbing," which entailed hitching the arms and legs of the condemned human being to the harnesses of horses and while the victim "raised his head and looked at himself . . . the four horses tugged (in different directions) . . . and carried off the two thighs after them . . . . Then the same was done to the arms."[11] Quite a gruesome form of capital punishment, but still in existence as late as 1790 when our founding fathers found it necessary to mention it in our Constitution.

Racism, public fear, and coerced testimony played an integral part in the trial and condemnation of Thomas Jeremiah (freed slave) in 1775. Public outrage prohibited then-governor Campbell from granting Jeremiah clemency despite his belief that the witnesses, "terrified at the recollection of former cruelties," had "perjured themselves to escape punishment . . . I could not save him, my Lord."[12] I would opine that many governors today face a similar dilemma in commuting the condemned, unlike Theodosius II, Emperor of Rome (423-450), who may well have been the first abolitionist of the death penalty. Theodosius "was well read, particularly the Scriptures. He fasted, he disliked capital punishment, and frequently pardoned those who had been condemned to death."[13] In the face of public outcry and political ambition, commutation or clemency is rare for the inhabitants of death row in the 20th century.

In 1750, Pennsylvania law proscribed for a second offense of "any" sort that "you were stood in a cart with a rope around your neck and driven beneath the gallows, and then the cart went off without you, leaving you to dangle."[14] House burning was punishable by death in Ohio in 1788; 350 crimes were punishable by death in the 1780's.[15] The 1705 Virginia slave code called for the punishment of runaways by dismembering (limbing). In 1723, Maryland would cut off the ears of blacks who struck whites or would hang them. The death penalty was used extensively to quash real and imagined slave rebellions and uprisings of poor whites in our early history.

In 1721, twenty-one blacks were executed for arson in New York; some were hanged, one broke on the wheel, one hung alive in chains in the town and "one was burned over a slow fire for eight to ten hours . . . all this to serve notice to other slaves."[16] Twenty years later, in 1741, after a trial full of lurid accusations by informers and of forced confessions, two white men and two white women were executed along with eighteen slaves, thirteen of whom were burned alive. Informers, paid or otherwise, have served the hangman well. Going back to 1661, in an "imagined" slave conspiracy in Gloucester County, Virginia, four blacks were executed on the word of a paid informer who received his freedom and 5,000 pounds of tobacco for his testimony.

Just as the colonists used capital punishment to put down and/or respond to rebellion, Charles II used it against whites rebelling against crown rule in the colonies. In 1676, a benchmark act of American independence, "Bacons's Rebellion," was put down by hanging the rebels in accordance with private instructions from the Duke of York who swore, "By God, Bacon and Bland should die!"[17] Bacon died before he could be caught and hanged, but 23 of his followers felt the royal noose, including Bland.

For those who still are under the delusion that capital punishment serves as a deterrent, we should recall that our independent America was founded on an act of rebellion, criminal treason in the face of certain hanging! On June 12, 1775, the British general, Thomas Gage, issued a proclamation that all persons who would lay down their arms would be pardoned. Those who did not would face the gallows. Both John Hancock and Samuel Adams were singled out by Gage for this Englishman's right—death by hanging. Luckily, neither was captured. In fairness, the prospect of a royal rope did not go unnoticed by the patriots. One diarist wrote, "If I should fall into the hands of the British, the gallows will be my fate. The terrors of the gallows are not to be conquered, but I must indulge the hope that I may escape it."[18] In 1776, on the day the Declaration of Independence was being signed, Mr. Harrison, a portly man of Virginia, commented to Mr. Gerry, a lanky man of Massachusetts, "When the hanging scene comes to be exhibited I shall have the advantage over you on the account of my size. All will be over with me in a moment, but you will be kicking in the air a half hour after I am gone!"[19] I think the issue of deterrence can be put to rest with their signatures on our historical document, and it can be said that the death penalty was not a deterrent to criminal action in 1775, nor is it in 1997.

All of this maiming and hanging was taking place in a land full of people who, for the most part, did not practice a form of capital punishment amongst themselves, as is illuminated in this Native American response to the Governor of Maryland in 1635, who was demanding that Indians who kill Englishmen face English law. The Indian said, "It is the manner amongst us Indians, that if any such accident happen wee doe redeeme the life of a man that is so slaine, with 100 armes length of beads and since you are heere strangers, come into our country, you should conform yourselves to the customes of our country, than impose yours upon us."[20] We did not conform and we did not respect the Native American population. We exacted violence for violence and introduced vengeance to the land! "In 1642, when Claes Rademaker was murdered in Albany (New York), the Indian who did it said that as a small boy, he had come with his uncle to trade beaver, but that some of the Swannekins [Dutch traders] had robbed his uncle and killed him. The boy swore revenge, which he nursed until he was grown."21

II

Three events mark the closing of the 18th century in America: the end of the Revolutionary War, the writing of our Constitution, and the opening of the first penitentiary. It was at this juncture in our history when we should and could have rid ourselves of the terrible vestige of European monarchial power—capital punishment.

Heretofore, "the one punishment that can easily be inflicted by a state which has no apparatus of prisons and penitentiaries is death,"22 and it could be said that "our social authorities relied on the ritual of Execution Day to promote civil and religious order."23 I have often pondered if it is not the fact that Christianity was founded upon and depended upon the very act of [Roman] capital punishment for its faith which has made it so easy for our Judeo-Christian nation to accept it. In my mind, Christ's words on the Mount, "You have heard that it was said, an eye for an eye, and a tooth for a tooth, but now I tell you do not take revenge on someone who wrongs you"24 would at least give pause to those of the Christian faith.

This was not to be. The new foundling government of the United States acted against dissidents to their rule in the same manner as their British masters did before them! In 1787, just four years after Britain and the United States signed the peace treaty that ended the Revolutionary War, Daniel Shays and a group of angry farmers rose in armed protest against the new Massachusetts government's economic policies, and were defeated. Several members of Shays' rebellion were tried and condemned. Samuel Adams, once a candidate for bloody Britain's noose, had this to say in opposing clemency for Shays' followers: "In monarchy the crime of treason may admit to being pardoned or lightly punished, but the man who dares to rebel against the laws of a republic ought to suffer death." Daniel Shays was pardoned, but many others were hanged.

In the fall of 1787, the United States Constitution was signed and, despite its opening line, "We the People . . .," it carried with it the stench of racism and oppression with the decree "excluding Indians" and counting servants and slaves as "three-fifths of a person" in determining a state's number of representatives in Congress.

The main body of the Constitution did have in its composition one very important provision, that being: "The privilege of the writ of habeas corpus shall not be suspended, unless when in cases of rebellion or invasion the public safety may require it."26

The placement of the right to habeas corpus in the main body of the Constitution signifies its importance to the citizenry. Congress first codified the writ as a judicial remedy in the Judiciary Act of 1789, which gave federal courts the power to issue relief to prisoners "in custody under or by colour of law of the authority of the United States." The statutory precursor to the present day writ is found in the Habeas Corpus Act of 1867 and presently codified in 28 U.S. Code Sections 2241-2256 (1982). The writ gives the accused and convicted the right to present new evidence—in some cases actual evidence of innocence—or to show why there was a technical or real miscarriage of justice, thus allowing a new trial and/or release of a person from unjust restraint and/or execution. It is a foundation stone of justice.

By covert default, reactionary legislation and judicial politicizing, we have allowed a significant alteration to that foundation. The Anti-Terrorism and Effective Death Penalty Act of 1996 placed severe restrictions on all citizens' right to habeas corpus. It should be noted that a 1996 update to a 1993 staff report by a judiciary committee of the U. S. House of Representatives found that since 1973, 65 death row inmates were eventually cleared [via writ of habeas corpus] by the federal court system and released. It is estimated that 40% of the state capital crime convictions reviewed on writ of habeas corpus prior to 1996 were overturned by the federal courts because of violations of the constitutional rights afforded to *all* citizens.

In the late 18th century, laws were beginning to be changed to provide "milder punishments for certain crimes for which infamous and capital punishments are now inflicted,"[27] and the rise of penitentiaries to house criminals took hold in America.

Cesare Beccaria's "An Essay on Crimes and Punishments," published in Philadelphia in 1778, began to capture the minds of America's ruling elite and social reformers. Beccaria asserted that no one ever gave to any other [not even the state] the right to take away a life. He opposed capital punishment and proposed "perpetual slavery—lifetime imprisonment—as a more effective deterrent because it was a more horrifying punishment than death for the spectator to contemplate."[28]

At the same time [1789] Thomas Jefferson and James Madison were writing the Bill of Rights, the first ten amendments to the Constitution. Madison praised Beccaria's book and was a death penalty abolitionist. Thomas Jefferson gave credit to Beccaria for awakening the world to the senseless severity of capital punishment and had a copy of Beccaria's book in his personal library. Did they intend to abolish capital punishment when they wrote the Eighth Amendment phrase ". . . nor cruel and unusual punishments inflicted"?[29] Does the Fifth Amendment's clause, ". . . nor shall any person be subject for the same to be twice put in jeopardy of life and limb"[30] support the death penalty?

Obviously, as I have pointed out in this writing, capital punishment was not unusual on the North American continent up to this point. However, can any one deny that killing a viable human being is not cruel?

In the contemporary sense, is it not cruel and unusual punishment to hold a human being in a small cell at the point of a gun for "X" number of years so that at some future time, a time you tell him some days ahead, he will be physically overwhelmed, strapped down to a table, his arms out in cruciform and punctured by steel needles, his living blood pumped full of deadly drugs and he will gasp and grimace, change colors and expire—all the while 20 or 30 invited guests are looking on?

What can the participants in such a macabre ritual be thinking? It's a job? We are following orders? It's necessary for our society and state security? Sounds a lot like the defense at Nuremburg, doesn't it? As we no longer "limb" people, why can't we set aside the other relic of the past, the taking of life in an act of capital punishment?

The phrase "cruel and unusual" has a long history. It started in Britain, as most of the laws of America did. It appears in the British Bill of Rights of 1688 that the taking of life or limb is in fact a cruel and unusual punishment.

During the period of Henry II (1154-1189), in the Constitutions of Clarendon, life and limb are linked with punishment. The Petition of Right of 1628 referred to both of the documents in its proclamation that "no one man shall be forejudged of life or limb against the form of great charter and the law of the land." The modern British Bill of Rights expressly refers to these great legal doctrines and declares that punishments that take life or limb are indeed cruel and unusual and may not be inflicted without suspension of the law. England finally abolished the death penalty in the mid-1900's and reaffirmed that fact again in 1994.

We should follow them. The path is elucidated by the finest documents of law made by man:

                1162 - Constitutions of Clarendon
                1215 - Magna Carta
                1620 - The Mayflower Compact
                1628 - The Petition of Right
                1688 - The British Bill of Rights
                1765 - Declaration of Rights
                1774 - Declaration of Rights
                1776 - Declaration of Independence
                1778 - Articles of Confederation
                1787 - Constitution of the United States
                1789 - The Bill of Rights

The abolition of the death penalty is a natural evolutionary step in the development of man's law and it was brought up in the summer of 1784, when the framers of the Constitution convened a committee where the Eighth Amendment's clause barring "cruel and unusual" punishments was discussed.

Samuel Livermore told the assembled members that "the clause barred the death penalty,"[31] and shortly thereafter the members voted on the amendment and it passed by a considerable majority.

In 1792, Dr. Benjamin Rush, a leading opponent of capital punishment and a proponent of prisons, urged the new Republic of the United States to shed capital punishment as a relic of monarchial excess: "The United States have adopted these peaceful and benevolent forms of government. It becomes them therefore to adopt their mild and benevolent principles. An execution in a republic is like human sacrifice in religion. It is an offering to monarchy and to that malignant being who has been stiled a murderer from the beginning, and who delights in murder, whether it be perpetuated by the cold but vindictive arm of the law, or by the angry hand of private revenge."[32]

With the advent of prisons, executions became more and more private affairs. The days of public executions were coming to an end in the urban East as the 19th century began. "Private executions were accessible only to a selected few. They became theatrical events for an assembly of elite men who attended the execution by invitation, the elite segment of society gathered at the private execution to celebrate extinction"[33] of a human being, a V.I.P. system still extant today. Do you even wonder what motivates these people to watch someone be judicially assassinated?

There were a few victories for the opponents of capital punishment in the years before the Civil War. In 1847, Michigan abolished the death penalty. The New York Society for the Abolition of Capital Punishment was formed in 1844, the Massachusetts Society in 1845. A petition by women in the Pennsylvania Legislature contained 11,777 names and made the point succinctly that it is the "poor who are executed,"[34] while the more wealthy universally escape the penalty. By 1853, both Rhode Island and Wisconsin had abolished capital punishment.

III

The Civil War brought the discussion of abolition of the death penalty to an end for some time and the use of capital punishment continued. In 1874, authorities quashed the labor movement of the "Molly Maguires" by executing eleven of its leaders. In 1886, a bomb went off in Haymarket Square, Chicago, Illinois. Eight anarchists were put on trial for their ideas and literature. Only one was placed at the scene of the crime. All were sentenced to death, four hung within a year. Later, Governor John P. Altgeld pardoned the remaining men in the belief that they were truly innocent of the crime. In 1890, William Kemmler was the first person executed by electrocution at Auburn Prison, New York. The United States record for execution en masse was the hanging at Fort Snelling, Minnesota of 38 Lakota Sioux who were guilty of protesting violations of their treaty rights by whites in the 1890's.

In 1891, fifteen black farmers were summarily executed in Arkansas for arson and murder. In 1893, several Italian immigrants were lynched in New Orleans. In 1915, Joe Hill was executed by a firing squad in Utah for a killing in which there was no direct evidence presented in court that he committed the murder. In 1927, Nicola Sacco and Bartolomeo Vanzetti were executed as "police broke up marches and picket lines with arrests and beatings and troops surrounded the prison as they were electrocuted." It is now believed that the two were innocent.

The 1950 trial of the Rosenbergs featured coached and coordinated testimony by government witnesses, one a confessed liar! The trial judge and prosecutors conferred in secret to ensure that Ethel and Julius Rosenberg were sentenced to death. In furtherance of this artifice of justice, the Attorney General of the United States and the Chief Justice of the United States Supreme Court met in secret and the Chief Justice assured the Attorney General that no stay of execution would stand. In fact, the Chief Justice dissolved an issued stay, and on 19 June 1953 the Rosenbergs were electrocuted.

IV

Hundreds upon hundreds of human beings have been executed in the United States since the hanging of George Kendall in 1607. Men, women, children, black, red, yellow, white, criminals, political dissidents, labor activists, farmers, civil protestors, immigrants, illegal aliens, miners, and many innocents among them have met the executioner's hand. Even today, the Rehnquist court seems to believe that it may be constitutional to execute a human being for a crime he did not commit,[36] as long as his trial was fair.

In 1972, when the California Supreme Court ruled that the then-death penalty statutes were unconstitutional,[37] it began to look as if we as a society may have made a humane decision. California's decision was followed some months later by the United States Supreme Court in **Furman** v. **Georgia**,[38] which temporarily stymied the use of capital punishment by states clamoring for the blood of their own citizens. After the decisions in **Gregg** v. **Georgia** and **Woodson** v. **North Carolina**,[39] in 1976, the tide turned red again with the consensual execution in Utah of Gary Gilmore in 1977. The nation had once again resurrected capital punishment and political aspirants raced to see who could kill the most constituents.

The brief, very fleeting period of national abolition of capital punishment and the ten-year hiatus between the last execution in Colorado in 1967 and the 1977 execution of Gary Gilmore in Utah, are our only experiences in national abolition of the death penalty. Ten years of human salvation in 390 years of judicial homicide. Did we really give abolition of capital punishment a chance?

On November 21, 1993, President Clinton—praising the 1993 crime bill that expands the use of the death penalty in 60 federal statutes—noted with unintended irony, "Our disregard for life in this nation can be seen coast to coast."

What example to our youth is such unrestrained use of capital punishment? As long as the national and state governments use the law to kill individuals they deem beyond the pale, then the same rationale will continue to be used in the streets. It is analogous to blowing smoke in your kid's face and telling him not to smoke. By law or bullet, killing is killing—there is no gray area in death.

Nothing has really changed in the post-**Furman** era in the application of the new death penalty laws. Only the words have changed. Condemnation and execution are still the prizes of the poor. Almost 100% of the persons executed from 1930 until 1967 were poor.[40] Almost without exception, people on death row today are poor. Clinton Duffy, former Warden, San Quentin State Prison, says, "Only the poor and underprivileged are put to death. In the 60 years I have been around prisons I have never known of one man who had wealth or position who has ever been executed."[41] As in almost all legal matters in America, one usually ends up with the degree of justice that one can afford.

You may say, of course, given my present position on death row, that it is self-serving of me to plead poverty and point out the injustices of capital punishment. I realize that the last thing a free, law-abiding citizen wants is a lecture by a condemned killer. But it would behoove a reasonable, thinking person to study this volatile life-and-death issue before reaching a conclusion about its use as a punishment. It is the job of thinking people, as Albert Camus suggested, not to be on the side of the executioners.

V

The costs involved in the capital punishment scheme are astronomical. I am here in this death row cell now, held at the point of a gun, in order that I might be murdered in the future. I and others like me have supported a vast network of private citizens and civil servants to see us to this end—judges, wardens, guards, lawyers, district attorneys—until the final moment when the executioner executes. It has been reckoned that the good citizens of California spent approximately $5 million to eventually produce the cyanide-ridden cadavers of Robert Alton Harris (executed 21 April 1992) and David Edwin Mason (executed 24 August 1993).

Vengeance is costly because most people charged, convicted and condemned to death are poor, so the taxpayers are footing the bill for both sides. I know of no person on the row who has his own attorney for appellate purposes, and know of only one or two who could afford a private attorney at their capital trials. The forces needed to defeat a capital charge and conviction are so enormous that very few people can afford it; those that can and do are almost always not sentenced to death. The fact is, one can buy justice in America.

If everyone convicted of killing a human being were subject to the death penalty, then it might be a viable practice—but everyone is not, and it is little more than a lottery of death, a lottery operated by the county district attorney. It is at his (or her) whim and caprice that a tiny minority are chosen to participate in this ritual—choices no doubt based on racial prejudice, the economic condition of the defendant, and the district attorney's own political ambition.

> "Persons who undertake the task of administering justice impartially should not be required—indeed, they should not be permitted—to finance campaigns or to curry favor of voters by making predictions or promises about how they will decide cases before they have heard any evidence or argument. A campaign promise to be 'tough on crime,' or to 'enforce the death penalty,' is evidence of bias that should disqualify a candidate from sitting in criminal cases."
> Justice John Paul Stevens, 1996.[42]

The political career of George Deukmejian is a case in point. From district attorney to governor, his whole career was built on the trigger rhetoric that surrounded the death penalty. He left the State of California with the largest prison population in the western world, second only to Red China, and the taxpayers with a multi-billion dollar deficit. No one was executed during his tenure at the capitol. While he shouted about crime, prisons, and death, he did nothing about the roots of the problems and left the state in fiscal ruin.

The power vested in the Attorney General's office and the tax money it controls are immense. In a 1982-83 Shasta County, California death penalty case, the defendant, Mr. Proctor, was found guilty of the crime but the jury deadlocked 11-1 for death in the penalty phase. The defense attorney suggested that the defendant "might consider" accepting a life without parole sentence and forego an appeal—a move which would have saved Shasta County thousands of dollars. For some "higher reason" the district attorney would not agree, even after the County Auditor advised that the agreement would be best for the county coffers.[43]

Mr. Proctor was subsequently retried as to penalty and sentenced to death. Now the county and the state taxpayer are faced with the cost of a capital crime appeal and collateral litigation, costs which were estimated at a minimum of $600,000.00 in 1984.[44]

Factor in annual inflation and multiply that by the 450+ men and women on death row in California today and you are talking about a lot of libraries, schools, youth programs, health care, additional law enforcement officers, drug and alcohol treatment programs, child abuse prevention clinics, spousal abuse programs, jobs programs—social spending that actually attacks the roots of crime, programs that are in essence victim prevention programs.

The other glaring inequality in our capital punishment design is its racist application. The arbitrariness and caprice found unconstitutional in **Furman** v. **Georgia** still exist in the post-**Furman** application. The 1990 GAO report, <u>Death Penalty Sentencing: Research Indicates Patterns of Racial Disparities</u>,[45] well illustrates the racial disparities in its application. This report comes from an entity of our own government—can we possibly ignore it?

You might say, "Damn the Constitution—speed up the executions!" If you do, you are wrong. Curtailment or infringement of a constitutional right after conviction can lead to terrible consequences. A lot of capital cases are made with suspect evidence and false testimony, crime partners exchanging false testimony for leniency, jailhouse informants exchanging testimony for plea bargains—all accepted as truth by the whim and caprice of the local district attorney.

A fine example of enterprising jailhouse informants was brought to light by the TV program "60 Minutes," which documented the activities of snitches in the Los Angeles County Jail system. These informers would impersonate county officials via telephone to gather data from various county authorities, then manufacture evidence with little or no factual basis, presenting this bogus info as pure truth to a jury—with the zealous assistance of the case prosecutor. The problem illuminated in Los Angeles is systemic throughout the American criminal justice system. It is the nation's shame if a person is executed wrongly as a result of false testimony.

At last report, 125 men currently sentenced to death at San Quentin do not have qualified counsel to represent them on automatic appeal or in an initial collateral attack on their confinement via state habeas corpus, as is now required by a "political pronouncement" emanating from the Lucas court (California Supreme Court) and also indicated in the Rehnquist court's decision in **McClesky** v. **Zant**. Both of these "political pronouncements" were from politicized courts reacting to the hue and cry to streamline the capital appeal process by limiting habeas corpus filings to one in state court and one in federal court. The aforementioned Anti-Terrorism and Effective

Death Penalty Act of 1996 was a direct result of the **McClesky** decision of 1991.

A warning to the self-righteous: these new streamlined measures can and will be applied to non-capital cases as well.

VI

Faced with the myriad of legal machinations involved in retaining the death penalty in the post-**Furman** era, Supreme Court Justice Harry Blackmun finally threw in his towel with this comment in his dissenting opinion in **Callins** v. **Collins**:[47]

> "For more than 20 years I have endeavored—indeed struggled—along with a majority of this Court, to develop procedural and substantive rules that would lend more than mere appearance to fairness of the death penalty endeavor.
>
> "Rather than continue to coddle the Court's delusion that the desired level of fairness has been achieved and the need for regulation eviscerated, I feel morally and intellectually obligated simply to concede that the death penalty experiment has failed.
>
> "From this day forward, I no longer shall tinker with the machinery of death."

United States Supreme Court Justice Lewis F. Powell, Jr. had a similar revelation which came to light in a 1995 biography written after his retirement. In it he disclosed a response to a question about which of his court decision votes he would like to change. He said the one he would change is his vote in the majority rejecting **McClesky** v. **Kemp**,[48] in which the Court rejected overwhelming evidence of the racist application of the death penalty in America. The Court side-stepped this glaring fact by stating **McClesky** had not proven racial prejudice in his case specifically. **McClesky** was decided by a one-vote (5-4) majority.

Both Justice Blackmun and Justice Powell were in the majority block who voted to resurrect capital punishment in America in the 1976 **Gregg** v. **Georgia** case. The late revelations did not matter one scintilla to the 345 human beings executed since 1976![49]

Nineteen ninety-six was a banner year for judicial assassinations. Thirty-two had been executed by mid-September. I believe that, rather than the further destruction of the writ of habeas corpus and infringement upon our constitutional rights, we should follow the sage advice of Justice Thurgood Marshall:

> "If it is impossible to construct a system capable of

accommodating all evidence relevant to a man's
entitlement to be spared death—no matter when
the evidence is disclosed—then it is the system, not
the life of the man sentenced to death,that should
be dispatched."[50]

And that of the late Governor Edmund G. Brown, who allowed many executions to take place during his tenure in office, and who also commuted some death sentences; he said, "The death penalty has been a gross failure; beyond its horror and incivility, it has neither protected the innocent nor deterred the wicked. It is inflicted upon the weak, the poor, the ignorant."

Lift the threat of death from the heads of the 3,153[51] death row convicts. Life imprisonment will serve the same purpose at less cost, and perhaps more of the condemned will come to the point that Michael B. Ross, on death row in Connecticut, has reached. He recently said, ". . . This sense of reconciliation that I yearn for the most, reconciliation with the spirit of my victims, reconciliation with the families and friends of my victims, and finally reconciliation with myself and God—this will be the final part of my transformation and undoubtedly the most difficult."[52]

Killing is cruel no matter who is doing it, for whatever purpose. Our leaders should lead by example and abolish the death penalty. Its use has brutalized mankind for centuries and it is demeaning to our society. Now, as we enter the 21st century, it should be set aside as a relic of the past.

Haven't we killed enough?

Steven King Ainsworth has over 25 years of prison experience, the last 17 years of which have been spent on death row at San Quentin, waiting to be executed for the crime of murder with special circumstances of robbery and kidnap which took place in 1978. He is an accomplished artist, and his work appears in this publication, along with his statement of the importance of art in his life as a death row inmate.

Footnotes

1. A People's History of the United States, 1492-Present, Howard Zinn (1995).

2. Wilderness at Dawn, Ted Morgan.

3. Records of the Plymouth Colony (1855).

4. Leviticus 20:15.

5. William Bradford, of Plymouth Plantation, 1620-1647 (1987).

6. Deuteronomy 21: 20-21.

7. Abbot E. Smith, Colonist in Bondage (1947).

8. Indian Affairs in Colonial New York, Allen W. Trelease (1960).

9. NVHS Manuscript collection.

10. The Dulany's of Maryland, Ted Morgan (1955).

11. Michele Foucalt, Discipline and Punish, and the Birth of Prison,
    (Tr. Alan Sheridan, Pantheon Books 1977).

12. A Troublesome Community: Blacks in Revolutionary Charlestown, 1765-1775 (1976).

13. J. B. Bury, History of Later Roman Empire.

14. Gottlieb Mitterburg's Journey (1989).

15. T. Sellen, Ed., F. Hartung, Trends in the Use of Capital Punishment,
    Murder and the Death Penalty, p. 11 (American Academy of Political and Social
    Sciences, Philadelphia, 1952).

16. A People's History of the United States, 1492-Present, Howard Zinn (1995).

17. Beginnings, Progress, and Conclusions of Bacon's Rebellion in Virginia in the Years 1675
    and 1676, by T.M.

18. James Thacher, A Military Journal During the Revolutionary War, from 1775 to 1783
    (1823).

19. Biography of the Signers of the Declaration of Independence, John Sanderson (1827).

20. Nash, Gary B., Red, White, and Black: The Peoples of Early America, Englewood Cliffs;
    Prentice Hall (1970).

21. Wilderness at Dawn, Ted Morgan.

22. Pollack and Maitland, History of English Law, Vol. II, p. 452.

23. Rites of Execution, Louis P. Masur (1989).

24. Matthew 5: 38-39.

25. A Peoples History of the United States, 1492-Present, Howard Zinn (1995).

26. United States Constitution, Article 1, Section 9, paragraph 2.

37. Annals of the Congress of the United States, Fourth Congress (Dec. 1795).

28. Cesare Beccaria, An Essay on Crimes and Punishment, 5th Edition revised
    and corrected (London, E. Hodson, 1801).

29. United States Constitution, Eighth Amendment.

30. United States Constitution, Fifth Amendment.

31. Bill of Rights, a Documentary History, (Chelsea and McGraw-Hill, 1971).

32. Rush, Considerations on the Injustice and Impolicy of Punishing
    Murder by Death, (Philadelphia, Matthew Carey (1792)).

33. Rites of Execution, Louis P. Masur (1989).

34. Petition on Capital Punishment, January 23 to March 5, 1847, Library Company of
    Philadelphia, Manuscript Collection.

35. Toughin, Louis and Morgan, Edmund, The Legacy of Sacco
    and Vanzetti, New York, Quadrangle (1964).

36. Herrera v. Collins, 113 S.Ct. 853 (1993).

37. People v. Anderson, 98 Cal.Rptr. 825 (1972).

38. Furman v. Georgia, 408 U.S. 238 (1972).

39. Gregg v. Georgia, 428 U.S. 153 (1976), Woodson companion case.

40. Greenberg and Himmelstein, Varieties of Attack on the Death Penalty, 15 Crime &
    Delinquency, 1969.

41.   San Francisco Chronicle, 13 October 1982.

42.   Justice John Paul Stevens, address to the opening assembly, American Bar Association
           Annual Meeting, August 3, 1996, at 12; gleaned from <u>Killing for Votes: The
           Dangers of Politicizing the Death Penalty Process</u>, a report by the Death
           Penalty Information Project, Wash. D.C. (1996).

43.   <u>Protor, Death Penalty Worth the Cost?</u>, Record Searchlight, 4 Feb. 1983; **People** v. **Protor**,
           4 Cal. 4th 499 (1993).

44.   Strieb, <u>Executions Under the post-</u>Furman<u> Capital Punishment Statutes: The Halting
           Progress From "Let's Do It" to "Hey, There Ain't No Point in Pulling So Tight"</u>,
           15 Rutgers L.Rev. (1984).

45.   United States General Accounting Office, Report to the Senate and House Committees on
           the Judiciary, GAO/GGD-90-57, Racial Disparities in Sentencing.

46.   In re Clark, 93 Daily Journal D.A.R. 9671 (1993); McClesky v. Zant, 499 U.S. 467 (1991).

47.   Callins v. Collins,   U.S.   (1994).

48.   McClesky v. Kemp,   U.S.   (1986).

49.   The number executed as of 18 September 1996.

50.   Evans v. Muncy,   U.S., dissenting opinion.

51.   The number of death row inmates in the United States as of 31 July 1996.

52.   Michael B. Ross, North Coast XPress, Vol. 4, No. 5, August, 1996.

Jesse Roberts - "Decide: Life Together"

MARIETTA JAEGER

"Not in My Susie's Name"

"Wake up, Mama! There's a big hole in the tent and Susie's gone!!" With those words, the most terrible tragedy of my life sliced into consciousness and changed my world forever.

Only a week into a once-in-a-lifetime family vacation—camping for a whole month through the state of Montana with my husband and our five children—my youngest, seven year old daughter Susie, was kidnapped from our tent in the middle of the night. Though we would not know it for fifteen anguished months, a week later her life was taken from her, and this precious child was gone forever from our lives.

In the beginning, I wanted to kill the man who took her and most certainly could have—with my bare hands and a smile on my face—if only I had known who he was. He had called others involved in the case—brief calls identifying Susie by an unpublished birth defect, saying he wanted to exchange her for ransom, but never quite giving the final arrangements necessary. Finally, on the first year's anniversary of her disappearance, one year to the minute that he'd taken her from our tent in the middle of the night, the kidnapper called our home in Michigan. Suddenly I was voice-to-voice with the man who had taken my little girl.

He was calling to taunt, but something had happened that changed all our expectations. During that long year just past, I had had a major wrestling match with God, justifying my version of justice—revenge and death. But in the end, the foundation that had been laid in me as a practicing woman of God held in good stead. I surrendered to God and committed myself to the challenge of living up to those principles ingrained in my conscience.

With daily diligent discipline, I reminded myself that in God's eyes—the God I say I believe in, a God who's crazy about each and every one of us no matter who we are or what we've done—the kidnapper was just as precious as Susie. I worked hard to think and speak of him, whoever he was, with respectful terms, to remember that he was a member of the human family and had dignity as such, and I tried to pray for him every day.

To my amazement, as I was speaking to him on the phone in the middle of the night on the first year's anniversary, in spite of the fact that he was being very smug and nasty, all that I had been working for to move my heart from fury to forgiveness came to fruition in me.

That was not what he was anticipating, and he was undone by it. When I asked him what I could do to help him, he broke down and wept, and in the ensuing conversation, which lasted over an hour, the kidnapper so let down his guard in that milieu of concern and compassion that he inadvertently revealed enough information for the FBI to identify him. Three months later he was finally arrested and charged with Susie's death, which warranted the death penalty.

By this time, though, I had come to understand that God's idea of justice was not punishment but restoration. Though I did not know if this very sick young man could ever be "restored," I could not deny him that possibility. Also, I felt that to execute him in Susie's name would be to violate and profane the goodness and beauty of her life. I believed I better honored her by insisting that all of life is sacred and worthy of preservation, even the life of the man who'd taken hers.

So, the Prosecutor offered him the alternative sentence—mandatory life imprisonment with no chance of parole. The young man accepted this, and only then was he willing to confess to the four deaths he had caused in that county. So much for the deterrent value of the death penalty!

Given the fact of deterrence; racist, class and capricious applications; documented deaths of the innocent; and the outrageous costs of capital punishment, an intelligent society would be hard put to justify the value and efficacy of same. Still, there are many who claim that the death penalty is a matter of justice for the victim's family. In response, I say there is no amount of retaliatory deaths which would compensate me for the inestimable value of my daughter's life, nor would they restore her to my arms. In fact, to claim that the execution of any other person, however maladjusted, will be "just retribution" is to insult the immeasurable worth of the victim.

Loved ones who have been wrenched from our lives by violent crime deserve more beautiful, noble and honorable memorials than premeditated, barbaric, state-sanctioned killings, which only make more victims and more grieving families. Through the years since, I have kept in touch with this young man's mother, and I know how she has suffered.

If people are genuinely concerned with the victim family's plight, there should instead be a clamor for the legal and social measures which will provide the real support systems these families need in their time of anguish and irrevocable loss—financial assistance, therapeutic counsel, trial information, resolution, etc.

Victim families have every right to the normal, valid human response of rage and hatred. However, to legislate that same gut level desire for bloodthirsty revenge will have the same deleterious effect on the community as it does on individuals. It degrades, dehumanizes, and debilitates us as a society. The capacity for mercy and compassion is what sets us apart from the rest of creation. Our laws should call us to higher moral principles than the practice of primitive acts of more murders to resolve our conflicts, hatreds, fears and frustrations. We violate our own honor and dignity by unabashedly killing a chained, restrained, defenseless person, however deserving of death we deem that person to be. We become that which we deplore—people who kill people—an insult to the memory of our beloved victims.

I say, "Not in my name! Not in my Susie's name!"

Marietta Jaeger was a founding board member of Murder Victims Families for Reconciliation. At age seven, her daughter, Susie, was murdered. Mrs. Jaeger is the past director for the Michigan Coalition for Human Rights, and currently works for the Episcopal Church Publishing Co. She presents workshops, retreats and gives lectures on forgiveness, reconciliation, peacemaking and non-violence throughout the U.S. and Canada, and is the author of The Lost Child.

Louis Osei Cotton - "Into God's Arms"

REMEMBERING LARRY HEATH

Shelby Heath - "Eternity at Midnight"

Stephen B. Bright - "Indifference to Injustice"

Morris L. Thigpen - "Managing Death Row: A Tough
Assignment"

SHELBY HEATH

"Eternity at Midnight"

On March 20, 1992, my husband, Larry Gene Heath, Death Row inmate Z-425, was executed in Alabama's electric chair for hiring the murder of his pregnant wife, Becky, on August 31, 1981.

Larry hired two men to kill his wife. They kidnapped her from their home in Alabama, and took her to Georgia, where they shot and killed her. She was nine months pregnant and the baby died also. Larry was arrested on September 5, 1981, along with five other people who were involved in the crime. He was tried in the state of Georgia. Because his wife was kidnapped from Alabama, the Alabama Prosecutor's office followed Larry's case closely and was even present at his trial in Georgia. On February 10, 1982, the judge in Georgia sentenced Larry to a life sentence instead of death. When the State of Alabama learned of this, they extradited Larry to Russell County, Alabama, and began to prepare to try him in Alabama for the same crime, using the same circumstances, same evidence. Larry's attorney in Georgia told him not to pay for an attorney in Alabama—just to take the court appointed attorney—because this was clearly a case of double jeopardy and he would be back in Georgia in no time to complete his sentence there, and eventually be paroled. Larry was brought to trial in Russell County and on February 10, 1983, was sentenced to death by the State of Alabama.

Larry and Becky had a son who was two years old at the time of the crime. That little boy had become more important to Larry than anything or anyone else ever had and, in his efforts to keep his son in his life, he made all the wrong decisions. He tried to control events and control his own life and in doing so, lost everything that had ever mattered to him. Larry's deceased wife's parents took Larry to court and were successful in terminating Larry's parental rights to his son. Larry held his son on the day he was arrested, but he was never to see or hold him again.

Following is Larry's own account of the night he asked Jesus to take over his life:

"On June 25, 1982, I was in the Muscogee County Jail in an isolation cell. I had just returned from a hearing where my wife's parents were successful in terminating my parental rights to my son. After the conclusion of that hearing, I was crushed,

mentally, emotionally and physically drained. My son had meant more to me than life itself. It took that fatal blow from the court to make me get down on my knees in my cell and ask the Lord to come into my life and take it over completely. I repented and asked forgiveness for my sins. As I prayed that night for strength and peace of mind, God became very real to me. I kept thumbing through my Bible, searching out verses of Scripture that had come to mean more to me than just mere words. I found a verse of scripture in the book of Hebrews, Chapter 13, verse 8, which states, "Jesus Christ, the same yesterday, and today and forever." Nobody I knew, or had ever known, could make that claim. When all others I thought had cared, had turned their backs on me for what I had done and the mistakes I had made—my Jesus still wanted and loved me! I cried a long time that night in my solitary cell, but you see, I began to realize I wasn't alone, nor would I ever be alone again. It was as if a tremendous weight or burden had been lifted from me and I began to view every-thing from a new perspective, in a different light. His Light. I had a peace of mind which I had never known before.

I was raised in the church from the age of seven. I had always be-lieved in God, but I didn't believe He got involved in our personal lives—I thought He had better things to do than bother with me and my petty prob-lems. With head knowledge, but no heart knowledge of the Lord, I left the church when I was grown and "did my own thing."

I had always believed in the death penalty and said, more times than I can count, "If their problem is that they can't find someone to pull the switch, call me—I'll do it,"and thought I meant it. On the morning of Octo-ber 21, 1983, as I went through my morning routine of getting ready to go to work, I heard on the radio that my nephew had been arrested for kidnap-ping and murder. That night on the local news, the District Attorney an-nounced he would be seeking the death penalty for my nephew. David con-fessed to the murder, and the next night attempted suicide in the county jail. We learned later that he was heavily into drugs and alcohol and he had begun to steal to support his habit. The night of the murder, he and a friend went out to steal again, but it went way too far and wound up in murder.

I began to visit him every Saturday morning in the County Jail. He went to trial in March of 1984 and the judge handed down a death sentence for him in September, 1984. He was immediately transferred to Holman Prison in Atmore, Alabama where all of death row was housed at the time. I continued to visit him as often as I could and we exchanged letters. One night in April, 1986, I wrote a poem about freedom and mailed it to David. Death row allows one man per tier out of his cell during the day to do odd jobs such as taking up laundry and giving out food trays. The day that David received my poem, he had been talking about poetry with the inmate work-ing the hall. So when he received my letter, he called out to the man, "Speaking of poetry, read this." The man read the poem and asked David to tell me he liked it. David said, "Tell her yourself." That man was Larry Heath. So, Larry wrote a one page note and enclosed a copy of his personal testimony of what the Lord had done and was doing in his life and sent it to me with David's next letter.

I had been searching for months, but didn't know what I was searching for. I had lived in sin for years and had gone from one hurtful relationship to another, searching for love, but ultimately winding up alone. One night in December of 1985, I reached the end of my rope—I snapped, and I began to sob uncontrollably and began to cry out to God. I said, "God, if You're out there, please help me—I can't go on like this." Nothing happened (so I thought) and the next morning I was embarrassed about my outburst. But I believe that was the moment that allowed God to intervene in my life and show me a way out of my misery.

When I read Larry's first note and his testimony, I shot holes in it, called it "jail house religion" and said I was not getting involved with anyone else on death row—my nephew was enough. But something in Larry's testimony kept drawing me and I kept going back to read it just one more time. Finally, on June 1, 1986, without making a conscious decision to do so, I wrote Larry a letter, thinking, "If this man is for real, at least I can be a friend to him." On that same night, Larry wrote me again to see if I would consider corresponding with him. And so it began—the journey that would change my life forever.

We began corresponding on June 1, 1986; Larry called me for the first time on July 1; I visited him for the first time on August 1, and on September 1, 1986, he got down on one knee in that dirty visiting yard and asked me to marry him.

From the first letter Larry ever wrote to me, he never ceased to speak of Jesus. He had been a Christian for four years when I met him. Larry was bold and aggressive; painfully honest and direct, to the point of being abrasive at times—I didn't know how to take all of that at first. But as he began to teach me of the love of God, I began to see what a big heart he had and that his heart belonged to God. As he would speak to me about Jesus and what He had done in his life, big tears would well up in his eyes and he would struggle not to break down so he could finish telling me about the Lord. This man was different from anyone I had ever known before and I began to realize that Jesus was the reason for the difference. Larry made John 3:16 come alive for me. Oh, I had known the words since I was a child, but that's all it had been to me—just words. Until the day Larry asked me why Jesus cried out on the cross, "My God, my God, why hast Thou forsaken me?" I said I had always thought that God had not forsaken Him, but He must have been in so much pain that He felt as though He had left Him.

Then Larry asked me, "What is it that God hates?" I said, "Sin." He said, "And what did Jesus take on Himself on that cross?" I said, "The sins of the world." Larry said, "That's right—and not just the sins of the past, but all the sins of the present and future." He said, "God cannot look upon sin and so at that moment when Jesus took all the sin of the world upon Him, God turned His back." For the first time in my life, I saw the enormity of what Jesus had done for me, and I felt the pain of God, the Father, at the death of His son, and I saw how much He must have loved me to be willing to sacrifice His Son for me, to turn His back on Him for that moment so that my sin could be forgiven. My heart was pierced and I was broken and crying before I knew what had happened to me. From that moment on, my heart was no longer mine—it belongs to Jesus and always will. And John 3:16 is alive in my heart.

Visitation days for death row at Holman are Monday or Friday of each week. An inmate is allowed one visit per week. So, in order to see Larry, I had to take a day of vacation each visit. My employer was very understanding and considerate and allowed me to take my vacation a day at a time so that I was able to stretch it out, so that I saw Larry an average of three times a month. Although his telephone privileges varied over the six years we were together, they finally stabilized and he was able to call me every four days.

So, Larry and I fell in love. From the beginning he told me every detail of his crime and his past, not hiding anything from me, no matter how terrible it was. He took responsibility for what he had done and never denied his guilt. On September 3, 1987, Larry and I were married in the visiting yard at Holman prison. We were never allowed to consummate our marriage, but we went into it knowing that. We believed with all our hearts that it was God's will for us to be married and that He would take care of the details. Larry's love for me was unconditional. No matter what I told him about my past, his love was steadfast. If not for his unconditional love, I don't believe I would have ever come close to understanding God's love for me. Larry was my best friend and I was his. He was the head of my house, he made household decisions, he put me on a budget that eventually enabled me to pay off my bills, he designed the floor plan of my mobile home that I lived in for the last three and a half years of our marriage. We were one and our marriage was an extremely happy one despite our circumstances. My years with Larry were the happiest of my life—and Larry said the same— and we both knew it was because we always strived to put God first in our marriage and in every aspect of our lives.

Larry was enrolled in many Bible Correspondence courses and received a degree in Ministerial Studies from Berean College of the Assembly of God churches. He also completed the Bible study courses offered, and received diplomas from Rhema Bible School, United Christian Bible Institute, Israelite Heritage Institute and the Institute of Jewish-Christian Studies. In Larry's own words, "I realize that a degree or diploma is not important or necessary to God for someone to spread His word and the Good News, but I am preparing myself for whatever He has in mind for me to do in the future." He felt a call on his life to preach and teach God's word and his only complaint was that he didn't get to do it enough. Daily he talked with and witnessed to death row inmates, as well as the guards and officers, about Jesus. The chaplain and Larry were very close and the chaplain sought him out to discuss scripture and spiritual matters and topics for sermons.

Larry and I always believed that God would deliver him from his death sentence and that he would eventually be released and we would have a life together in the free world. However, Larry had told me early in our relationship that, if that should not be the case, he knew enough about the law and the appeals system that he would be able to prepare me ahead of time, if it looked as though his execution would be carried out. On November 1, 1991, during one of our visits, Larry told me that, unless God miraculously intervened, his execution appeared to be imminent and could happen as soon as March 20, 1992. Although by then I was fairly familiar with the appeals process myself and knew we were in a critical time, it hit me hard. I knew Larry would not be telling me such a thing without feeling that he had to, in order to prepare me and give us a chance to face together what might lie ahead.

The appeals process for a death sentence in the State of Alabama is a long, slow, drawn-out ordeal. The truth of the matter is that it becomes so routine, each court taking its own sweet time to rule on a case, that the inmate and his family get almost complacent. Larry and I had settled into our pattern of three visits a month, phone calls every four days and writing letters every night, waiting for the court we were in at the time to make a decision on his case—always hoping, always trusting God and believing with all our hearts that God would intervene and Larry's life would be spared. When one court would turn him down, Larry took it in stride; his faith never skipped a beat, and we moved on to the next court full of hope and faith. Larry was strong and I drew from his strength. He knew that and always told me to draw from him whenever I needed to—he knew where his strength came from and his Source had a limitless supply. Without a doubt, the Lord sustained us both, even when we weren't aware of it.

Around August of 1991, things began to escalate on Larry's case. Larry's appeal and application for rehearing in the Federal Court were denied and we began an emotional roller coaster ride that would last for months. His appeal and application for rehearing in the Eleventh Circuit Court in Atlanta were denied. We had been accustomed to a court taking anywhere from eight months to a year or longer to make a ruling, and here we were with four rulings in four months. Larry's attorneys stepped up their activities on his behalf, talking with family members, organizing a plea for clemency, preparing briefs.

One of the ministers who held church services on Death Row, Jim Britnell, was an ex-con himself and now had a prison ministry called Rivers of Living Water Ministries. Sometime in December, Jim approached another pastor by the name of Buford Lipscomb about the possibility of ordaining Larry as a minister. Pastor Lipscomb was Pastor of Liberty Church in Fairhope, Alabama at the time and was a district overseer for Liberty Church in South Alabama and North Florida. There were other ministers in the area, including the chaplain, who agreed with Jim that Larry should be ordained. Buford was taken aback at the suggestion at first and would have rejected it outright if it had not been for the fact that he knew these ministers very well, loved them, knew their hearts and respected their opinions. Only because of these Godly men, did he agree to meet with Larry and decide for himself if this was a classic case of jail-house religion, or if Larry really was a man of God.

I know I am considered by most to be prejudiced in Larry's favor because I am his wife, but you only had to meet Larry face to face to know that he was real—that his commitment to Jesus was alive and vibrant. And so it was with Buford. He said that from the first visit with Larry, God knit their hearts together as if they had known each other for years. When Larry talked about Buford to me, his eyes danced — something that normally only happened when he talked about the Lord or me. Larry and I both realized that God had raised Buford up to take a stand for Larry in these last days.

And take a stand he did. Buford made connections and arranged to meet with the governor to tell him about Larry and the tremendous change in Larry's life and the impact he was having on others in the prison—an effort to make the governor aware of Larry well before an execution date was set, in hopes of the governor making a decision to commute Larry's sentence from death to life without an execution date ever having to be set. It was suggested to Buford that if he could get the parents of Larry's deceased wife to agree to clemency, there would be a greater chance of the governor granting such a request. Buford took two other ministers with him and went to Pine Mountain, Georgia to talk with the parents of Becky about possibly agreeing to clemency. Again, he was well received. They invited the pastors in, served lunch for them, listened closely to what Buford had to say about Larry and seemed pleased to hear of Larry's salvation, although they had been made aware of that fact many times in the past. When Buford left, they said they would think about it and pray about it and would let Buford know their decision in the next few days.

Buford felt so good about the visit that he went straight back to the prison and told Larry now was the time to write a letter to Becky's parents, and Buford sat there with Larry while he agonized over the letter, poured his heart out asking their forgiveness. Larry allowed Buford to proof read the letter and asked for his advice on corrections. The letter was mailed. However, before Becky's parents had a chance to receive the letter, they made a statement to the newspaper in which they accused Buford and the other two ministers of harassing them and trying to coerce them into agreeing to clemency for Larry—something they would never agree to do. And when they received Larry's letter, they called the warden of the prison and said Larry was harassing them and they wanted it stopped immediately. The warden called Larry into his office and told him, although he could find nothing wrong with the letter Larry wrote, that these people could make things really tough for him if they wanted to. He told Larry no more letters were to go out to them, or else his final visitation rights before the execution could be jeopardized. All of Larry's hopes of ever being reconciled with his ex-in-laws were crushed. Even though they said with their mouths that they had forgiven him, they still wanted him dead.

By now, Buford was in total agreement that Larry should be ordained and, after much prayer, had decided it was God's will for him to present the request for ordination to the Liberty board of presbyters that was to meet in mid-February. Buford had just been appointed as District Overseer of the Pensacola area and this was his first meeting with the presbytery. As Buford said, it was with much "fear and trepidation" that he approached these men with his request to ordain Larry. He took about fifteen minutes to tell about Larry and the tremendous change in his life, his ministry in the prison, the many lives he had touched; then he read Larry's personal testimony. There was silence for a few moments and then Brother Ken Sumrall, founder of Liberty churches, spoke up and said, "Brothers, I believe this is the Holy Ghost." There were some questions, some discussion and it was mentioned that Liberty church would undergo significant criticism and persecution from the secular community as well as some of the Christian community for such a stand on Larry's behalf—a confessed, convicted murderer who was only a month away from the electric chair. But one of the brethren stood and said that if this was of God, that it didn't matter what men might say—the only thing that mattered was what God had done in Larry's life, and if it was God, Liberty should take a stand and forget what the world might think. And so it was agreed, unanimously, that Larry would be ordained as a minister of Liberty Churches.

Back in January, Larry and I had learned that the U. S. Supreme Court had refused to hear his appeal. Larry told me that they would send his case back to the Alabama Supreme Court, who would, in all probability, within the next two or three weeks, set an execution date. On February 10, 1992, I was visiting Larry. Around 9:00 or 9:30 that morning, one of the guards came to get Larry off the visiting yard because he had a telephone call from his attorney. Larry was only gone about ten minutes. When he came back, as he was walking towards me, he smiled and said "March 20th." Because Larry had taken time with me to make sure I understood the appeals process and exactly what steps to expect after each court, encouraging me not to lose faith in God, and because of Larry's strength, which came from God, we were able to accept our circumstances and we were determined to enjoy our time together, whether we had 40 days left or a lifetime. We still believed strongly that God had a miracle waiting for us.

On February 27, 1992, an ordination service at Holman prison for Larry was arranged. Another first in Larry Heath's life—the first death row inmate to be ordained while still incarcerated. Larry said it was a beautiful service. There were no women allowed, so I couldn't be there, although the chaplain tried to get me in. But what meant more to Larry than the ordination service were the Liberty people—God's people—who were taking a stand for him, disregarding the ridicule and persecution that were sure to come from the secular media and the world in general. That demonstrated the purest kind of love to him and he was deeply touched by it. Over the years, Larry had learned to live with rejection and with being considered lower than the lowest, as do all death row inmates. We were both over-whelmed at the numbers of God's people for him in these last days, pro-death penalty as well as anti-death penalty. All came together and put forth valiant attempts to save Larry's life.

The final week of Larry's life, the warden allowed me to visit Larry every day. I was with him from 8:00 a.m. to 5:00 p.m. Monday through Wednesday. The last day, Thursday, we were together from 8:00 a.m. until 10:30 p.m. that night. Larry's execution was set for 12:01 a.m. , Friday, March 20, 1992—one minute past midnight.

I arrived at the prison at 8:00 a.m. Monday morning with my car packed, ready to spend the rest of the week in a room at We Care which is run by the Mennonite Church and is located just three miles from the prison.

Monday was the day of the clemency hearing at the governor's office in Montgomery. Buford presented his plea to the governor which included a petition signed by more than 100 ministers state-wide from many different denominations, including pro-death penalty and anti-death penalty alike. Buford pointed out that if clemency did not apply in Larry's case, it would never apply to anyone and that they had just as well remove clemency from the books. Their request for clemency was not to set Larry free, but to spare his life—to give him life without parole so that he could continue to minister to the inmates as he had been doing for the past ten years, nine of which were spent on death row.

Larry called me and asked me to call around and see if I could get some feed-back on the clemency hearing, since we had not yet heard from Buford. Larry was preaching his last sermon that night and he was preaching on faith. He stated in his sermon that he was not concerned for himself but he was concerned for the Christians on Death Row and that their faith not be shaken by the events taking place.

The news that I learned that night concerning the clemency hearing was very positive. The governor's legal counsel told them that the governor would take everything on Larry's case home with him Wednesday night and would read every letter written on Larry's behalf, pray over the situation, and reach a decision some time Thursday. Everyone present at the hearing agreed this case was different from any other they had been presented in the past, and the governor's legal counsel agreed that, in his opinion, clemency was warranted in Larry's case.

Tuesday was a good day for us. I remember asking Larry that day, "What if the governor denies clemency?" I knew the answer—it wasn't as if we hadn't discussed it before—but I guess I just needed to hear him say it. As I knew he would, he said there was no where else to go, no one else to appeal to—that, barring divine intervention, the execution would take place. We still believed a miracle was in the making because of all the activity in Larry's favor. Too much had happened and I knew beyond doubt that God's hand was on Larry. I could not see how God could possibly allow him to die when He had poured so much knowledge, wisdom and ability into Larry.

God gave us a peace that day that passes all understanding. In the midst of all the turmoil going on around us, inside and outside the prison, concerning the upcoming execution, Larry put his arms around me, dropped his cheek against my head, and we both went to sleep sitting up. That's a precious memory that I will always treasure.

Incredibly, early Tuesday night came the first, unconfirmed rumbling that the governor had already denied clemency. Larry's attorney, Steve Bright, called me to tell me so I wouldn't hear it on the news first, if it was true; but at that point, he couldn't believe it either. It was indeed true that the governor had already gone on TV and announced that there would be no clemency for Larry.

When Larry got back to his cell after church, he called me. He already knew clemency had been denied. When I asked him what he was doing, he said, "I'm cleaning out my cell." That was when reality came crashing in on me and I began to cry and to tell him I wasn't ready to let go of him. He was so strong for me, encouraged me to cry and reminded me that we probably wouldn't be alone again until the last two hours of visiting time from 8:30 to 10:30 Thursday night. A lot of friends and relatives were scheduled to come in on Wednesday and Thursday. So we talked and cried and even laughed until around midnight. We had always written each other every night, but my Tuesday night's letter was never finished and Larry never started his. We had written our final letters to each other the night before, which was my birthday, without realizing they would be our last. We hung up around midnight, and I did sleep for a while. After all, Larry and I had two more days together and I was always fine when I was with him.

When Larry called me the next night, he told me when they took him off the visiting yard after our visit, that everything had changed in the way the guards treated him. From that moment on, their execution drill or routine went into effect and everything was stepped up and intensified. While we were visiting, they had finished cleaning out his cell and had moved him to the death cell which is near the execution chamber. When they came to get him after our visit, they took him straight to the death cell—he did not get to say good-bye to the men on his tier and was not allowed any further communication with them. Larry was disturbed about this in one way and relieved in another, knowing it would have been a gut-wrenching experience to say good-bye. Larry told me that from the time they put him in the death cell, they began to document every move he made. They handed his mail to him one piece at a time, his TV and his tape player could not be in the cell with him, but were placed outside his cell where he could see or listen and they would operate them for him. He said he was reading his Bible, lying on his back on the bunk, and he would doze off as he was reading and the Bible would fall on his face and wake him up. He said this happened several times, and the officers watching made a note of it every time. Larry found their treatment of him and their new procedures very amusing and said so to me. I said, "You know, the things that you find amusing would scare most people to death." He laughed and said, "You're probably right." He knew he had nothing to fear and so he could be amused instead of frightened. He called me again around 9:30 Wednesday night. A terrible storm was passing through the area and around 10:00 we were cut off. When Larry didn't call me right back, I knew it was because he couldn't, and I began to panic. I knew if all went as the State planned, this was our last night to be able to talk on the telephone.

The wife of the chaplain's assistant, Sarah Eash of We Care, came in my room to check on me and I just broke down in her arms, sobbing. I said I knew God was still in control but it looked like we were losing the battle. She agreed and held me and cried with me. She asked her husband to go to the prison, which was just three miles down the road, to find out what had happened to the phones. Before he could get back, Larry called me back around 10:30. The telephone line to the death cell was somehow connected to the phone lines at Fountain which is a minimum security prison down the road from Holman. Fountain turns their phones off in bad weather, and when they turned theirs off, it also turned Larry's off. I told him what happened when I realized he wasn't calling me right back. Even though he understood what I was going through, he reminded me that I did not have to react that way, because of who I was in Christ. Throughout his entire ordeal, he knew he was being watched by inmates who were waiting for him to crack under the pressure and the stress, and he was determined that they would see nothing but Christ living in him. He believed the scripture that said we can do all things through Christ Jesus who strengthens us, and Larry told me that included his execution.

The only time that fear tried to grip Larry was in the death cell in the early morning hours of his last day. At 5:30 that morning, he wrote these words:

"It's amazing how we become creatures of habit that fall into a predictable behavior pattern. I woke up this morning to find the adversary had come to visit me. Recognizing the enemy, I immediately turned to the source of my strength which has sustained me over the years. I know without God in my life, I would be nothing and no difference would have been made. I wish I could have done more for Him. Like so many others there were times when I've fallen short. God forgive me. Today I feel all eyes will be on me and that's not the way it should be. It's my responsibility to keep turning the focus back to Him. That is my duty."

I arrived at the prison at 8:00 a.m. Thursday morning, March 19, 1992, and shortly after that the visitors for that last day began to arrive. I watched Larry moving around the room trying to be sure he visited with everyone, after telling me he would rather be with me which he knew I wanted to hear. Several times during the day I saw Larry take Buford, Steve and the chaplain off to a table apart from everyone else. I knew Larry was taking care of his own final details, trying to spare me as much as he could. He had asked me to please let him do this much for me. It was good that he did because I wasn't thinking very clearly—a thought would pass through my mind, leave just as quickly, and I couldn't tell anyone what it was the next second.

Around 2:30 that afternoon, Larry and I were called into the warden's office. They handcuffed Larry behind his back and put leg shackles on him so that he could hardly walk. I walked behind him with guards on either side, in front and in back. As we went out of the visiting yard, there was a black female officer standing there and she said to Larry as he passed by her, "We love you in God." That was a special blessing for Larry and for me because I knew how much it meant to him. When Larry sat down in the warden's office, he had to sit on the edge of his seat because of his hands being cuffed behind him. The warden asked one of the guards to move his hands in front of him so he could sit back. I sat across the table from Larry and the chaplain was beside me. The warden told Larry in so many words that he did not want to be a part of this execution, but something that had happened years ago had come down to today and it was his job. He asked Larry if it was true that he had turned down his last meal so he could have more time with his family. Larry assured him this was true. He asked us what funeral home we were using and the chaplain answered that for us. He asked what Larry would be wearing that night. Larry said an old T-shirt and prison pants. He asked if Larry wanted anything beforehand, meaning drugs to help him through the execution. Larry declined, and told the warden that he knew he had a job to do and that he had no hard feelings toward him for anything that was happening. The warden thanked Larry for that and then asked me if I had any questions. I said I didn't have any questions but I wanted to thank him for the way he had treated Larry over the years, that I knew this was something he had to do and I did not hold it against him. I was crying before I finished saying it. I looked across the table at Larry. He was leaning towards me as far as he could and there were the biggest tears in his eyes. As always, his tears were for me, not for himself. The chaplain prayed for us and we left the warden's office.

At 7:30 that night, we had a communion service. Larry had told me earlier in the week that every time he prayed, immediately afterwards when he opened his eyes everything had a yellow glow around it. I will never forget that because my memories of that night from 7:30 until 10:35 have a yellowish tint or haze around them. I believe with all my heart it was the Presence of the Lord. No doubt, He was there in a very powerful way.

Jim Britnell led us in communion and as he passed the bread around, he asked Larry if he had anything to say. Earlier that day, he had told Jim the spiritual condition of everyone on the visiting yard in case he had a chance to minister to any of them in the future. So, Larry said no, he thought he had already said too much that day. However, by the time he passed the juice around, Larry had changed his mind, or the Lord had changed it for him, and he did want to say a few words. I watched Larry walk from his seat by me to the table where Jim stood. Larry was very shaken and propped himself up with both arms on the table as he stood there and told of the change Jesus had made in his life. He said the last ten years in prison had been the best years of his life and that was because of Jesus. He talked about the blood of Jesus and how it was shed not only for those in the room, but for everyone from the beginning of time until the end of time. He talked primarily to those in the room who were lost. I learned later that his brother, Rickey, wouldn't look at him because he knew he was talking to him. And Jerry, his brother he had not seen in nine years, said he looked at Larry and all he saw was "a big ole angel standing there." I watched Larry, through tears, wanting so much to make it easier for him and not being able to do so. As he talked with such passion for the Lord, it seemed to me that his eyes became flame. I'll never forget how he pointed to me and referred to me as his miracle from God and proceeded to tell of the things I'd endured because of marrying a man on death row—things I had long since forgotten, but Larry never did. He was worth it all, and much, much more.

Larry had previously decided if, in the event his execution seemed imminent, he was going to request that the last two hours of visiting time allowed him be spent with just the two of us. He did not want me to witness the execution—he wanted me to remember him the way he was. The warden had agreed that they would ask everyone else to leave at 8:30, which they promptly did. I watched Larry closely as he said good-bye to his family and it was so painful for me to see him cry.

And suddenly Larry and I were alone, if you can be alone with countless guards watching and lining the wells in the hallway outside the windows of the visiting yard. Remember, the visiting yard is a glassed-in room with a hallway surrounding it. There were guards all along the hallway and the number had tripled by now. Larry began to read to me from Psalms. He must have read 20 of the Psalms to me and as we would come across one that had been made into a song, we would sing it. I also remember singing "His Name Is Wonderful." We laughed, we cried, we prayed. Once in a while, Larry would ask me what time it was.

I remember asking Larry if there was anything I could have done that I didn't do. He said no. He had already told me if all I did was come and sit by him and love him, it would be enough. We prayed and Larry called out to God to help us during this time of parting, because we couldn't do this without Him. At one point, Larry cried out, "Where are You, Lord. Where are You, Lord?" I thought my heart would break and all I could say was, "He's right here, Darling". That really bothered me for a while until Pastor Buford's wife reminded me later that Jesus did the same thing from the cross when He said, "My God, My God, why hast Thou forsaken Me?"

Then came 10:00 and Larry took off his necklace I had given him for Christmas that he loved so much—a Star of David with a cross in the center. Then he looked away from me and took off his wedding band, slipped it on the chain with the Star/Cross and fastened the necklace around my neck. It's still there. I haven't taken it off since and have no plans to.

Larry looked at me and said, "I never meant to make you cry." I said, "But you made me laugh, you made me love and you showed me Jesus, and I'd do it all again." And then it was 10:30 and they came to take Larry from me. God does something to get you through the difficult times and by the time it came for Larry and me to part, we were pretty much composed. For myself, I have to be honest and say that I don't know if it was true peace, numbness or the first stages of shock, but whatever it was, it got us through those final parting moments. We hugged and kissed for our last time. Larry held me close for a little while, no words spoken. Finally, I whispered, "Rest in Jesus." Immediately Larry released me and said, "I've got to go," and he walked away from me like he had so many times before when they would come for him at the end of our visits. The only difference was this time Larry didn't look back. I can still see his back as he walked away from me. I know that was the only way Larry could do it, but that memory is forever emblazoned in my mind and my spirit. I waited as they searched Larry in the back room, as I always did after a visit, waiting to get a final glimpse of him as they took him back down the hallway into the heart of the prison. As they brought him out, handcuffed, Larry glanced at me and I lifted a hand in farewell. There was no smile, no verbal response from him, just a look that told me he was going to be all right now. The worst was over for him. Larry's Garden of Gethsemane was parting with his loved ones, especially me. Larry had previously told me that he had always known that he could die, but it was leaving me behind that was so hard for him.

Buford was waiting for Larry in the hallway when Larry came out of the back room and they walked together, escorted by numerous guards, to the death cell, where the chaplain joined them. Around 11:00, they took Larry from his cell to shave his head and his right leg. The experience was more difficult, seemingly, for the ones who had to do it than it was for Larry. When it was done, as Larry went back to his cell, he stopped and shook hands or hugged each guard and thanked them for their care of him over the years and assured them he did not hold them responsible for that night. Buford said there wasn't a dry eye in the place.

At 11:45, Larry held out his hands and they were steady—not shaking in the least. He said to Buford, "I knew I would have peace, but I didn't know it would be like this. Look at my hands. There's no fear in me." Shortly after that, he took his Bible, handed it to Buford and said, "Give this to Shelby. I won't be needing it anymore."

Larry's attorney, Steve Bright, had picked me up at the prison after I left Larry, and took me back to his room where I waited. Larry had hoped the warden would allow him to call me one last time so I had told him where I would be in case he could call. Around 11:45 it became apparent that he would not be able to call, and I began to shake and cry. I can't describe the panic and fear that I felt for Larry, for what he was going through. Around midnight, I ceased shaking and crying and the greatest peace came over me. A friend was holding my hands and she said when the peace hit me, it flowed to her, too. It was so real, so thick you could cut it with a knife, that there was no doubt that the source was God alone. At the time the peace came over us, I remember thinking that it must be over, Larry must be gone. I learned later that he had just begun to talk!

They took Larry to the electric chair at midnight, strapped him in and asked him if he had anything to say. He said, with a smile, "As a matter of fact, I do." Buford, Chaplain Simmons and Steve Bright, were in the viewing room and were watching him through the window. Buford said, strange as it may sound, that there was almost a lightness to that moment. They were trying to encourage Larry with "thumbs-up" signs and Larry was smiling at their efforts. Larry began to speak and talked for fifteen or twenty minutes. He first addressed each one individually, the warden, the prison commissioner and the news media. He loved and forgave everyone in the room. He told the warden he wasn't as hard as he wanted people to believe. He told the prison commissioner, Morris Thigpen, who was a Christian, that the men in that prison needed his witness and that he needed to be more involved with them on a personal basis. He told the news media that he knew they had not been able to understand the change in his life, who he had become in Christ, and he wanted them to know that was okay, that he loved them anyway.

Larry said, "I have finished the race and I can see the prize before me." Then he prayed for everyone in the room that was going through the execution process with him and he asked God to welcome him home. They put the black hood over his face, the warden stepped out of the room, the switch was thrown and Larry was gone.

There were reports that two were saved the night of Larry's execution and two more were saved at Larry's memorial service the following Monday night. Several have been saved in prisons since that night after hearing the story of what God did in his life. This is, after all , God's story—not mine and not Larry's—and any glory and any praise belong to the Lord alone. When I thank God for my blessings, I thank Him first for Jesus, who died for me and whose blood cleanses me from all unrighteousness, and secondly, I thank Him for Larry Heath, who was not ashamed of the Gospel of Jesus Christ, who proclaimed that Gospel to me with all his heart and changed my life forever, here on earth certainly, but more importantly, for all eternity. Larry Heath is the best influence that ever walked into my life, because when he walked in, he brought Jesus with him.

Shelby Heath is an active member of Cathedral of the Cross, a church of the Assembly of God. She worked for 30 years as an associate office manager for Prudential. Mrs. Heath is the widow of death row inmate Larry Heath who was executed on March 20, 1992. Her nephew is also on death row in Alabama.

STEPHEN B. BRIGHT

"Indifference to Injustice"

Larry Gene Heath was executed by Alabama for a crime committed in Georgia and for which he had already been punished by Georgia with life imprisonment.

With regard to being punished twice for the same crime—once with his life—what happened to Larry Heath was quite extraordinary. The United States Supreme Court held the prosecutions against him by both Georgia and Alabama for the same crime did not violate the United States Constitution's protection against double jeopardy.

The Supreme Court's decision offends basic notions of fairness. After all, the whole purpose of the protection against double jeopardy is to prevent the government, with all its resources and power, to continue to prosecute an individual until it wears that person down and obtains the conviction or sentence it seeks.

But in other ways, Larry Heath's case is typical of the routine injustices which occur in capital cases in Alabama and elsewhere, and of the indifference of the courts to the denial of adequate legal assistance to people too poor to hire a lawyer. The legal representation provided to Larry Heath by his court appointed lawyers was shocking. On appeal to the Alabama Supreme Court, his lawyer filed a brief that was only one page long, and then did not appear to argue the case before the Court. Nevertheless, without asking for full briefing of the issues presented on whether a human being would live or die and without the argument that normally occurs on a capital appeal, the Alabama Supreme Court upheld the death sentence and dispatched Larry Heath to the executioner.

Rebecca Heath, the wife of Larry Heath, was killed by two men on August 31, 1981, in Troup County, Georgia. Four days after the discovery of the body, Larry Heath was arrested by Georgia authorities and charged with murder. Five other people were eventually arrested and charged in Troup County, Georgia. All six were indicted for the murder, and the Georgia prosecutor announced that he would seek the death penalty for Larry Heath and the two men who carried out the murder. The prosecution asserted that Larry Heath hired the two men to kill his wife.

In order to avoid the possible imposition of the death penalty, Larry Heath agreed to give up his right to a trial in exchange for the State's agreement not to seek the death penalty. In accordance with this agreement, Heath plead guilty in February, 1982, in Georgia, and was sentenced to life imprisonment.

The following October—thirteen months after the death of Rebecca Heath and eight months after the guilty plea in Georgia—Larry Heath was extradited to Russell County, Alabama, and again charged with the murder. The local judge, who is elected, appointed two Russell County lawyers to represent Mr. Heath. He was tried just three months later.

Although the two prosecutions took place in different states, they were not very far apart in miles. Mrs. Heath was killed just a short distance into Georgia from the Alabama border. Between the date of the crime and the start of Larry Heath's Alabama trial on January 10, 1983, Russell County, Alabama, from which Heath's jury was drawn, was saturated by pre-trial publicity regarding various aspects of the case, including the plea of guilty and sentence of life imprisonment in Georgia.

The Georgia Supreme Court said the media reported "a melodrama containing all of the elements that news reporters and their editors know from experience will excite the interest of substantial numbers of their readers, viewers and listeners." By the time of the Alabama trial, the media had reported over 100 times that Larry Heath had plead guilty or was convicted and was serving a life sentence for the murder of Rebecca Heath.

Based upon all of the pre-trial publicity, the appointed lawyers moved for a change of venue or a postponement, but both were denied. Eighty-one citizens were questioned briefly during jury selection. When asked about pretrial publicity, 75 (93%) answered that they had heard about the case. Fifty-seven knew that Mr. Heath either had plead guilty or was found guilty in Georgia.

The trial judge denied motions to strike 59 potential jurors because of their knowledge of the case. Ten of the twelve people selected to decide the case as jurors knew, before they were even summoned for jury duty, that Larry Heath had been found guilty of the same crime in Georgia. The other two jurors learned of it during the questioning of jury selection. As a result, all twelve jurors selected to hear the case knew that Mr. Heath had already plead guilty to the murder of his wife.

As U.S. Supreme Court Justice Thurgood Marshall observed in dissenting from the decision allowing the Alabama trial, "With such a well-informed jury, the outcome of the trial was surely a foregone conclusion." Larry Heath's Alabama trial lasted only three days. Because the jury already knew he had admitted guilt in Georgia, his appointed lawyers could only argue that he had been punished enough by Georgia. But the jurors and the elected judge knew that the only purpose of the Alabama prosecution was to give Larry Heath the death penalty. The jury recommended death and the judge imposed it on February 10, 1983, a year to the day after Larry Heath had been sentenced to life imprisonment in Georgia for the very same murder.

Of the six people who were charged and prosecuted in the murder of Rebecca Heath, including the two people who killed her, only Larry Heath was executed.

Larry Heath was entitled to an automatic appeal of his death sentence by Alabama law. But he was denied that appeal by the lawyer who was appointed to prepare the brief to the appellate courts. The brief submitted to the Alabama Supreme Court contained only one page of argument. It cited only one case. It would not have received a passing grade in a first-year legal writing class in law school.

The brief on appeal did not even tell the appellate court of the pre-trial publicity, the judge's failure to grant a change of venue and move the trial to another part of Alabama where jurors had not heard of the Georgia guilty plea, the refusal of the judge to excuse the 59 jurors who knew about the case, and the denial of a fair and impartial jury. Because the lawyer did not raise these issues, the Alabama Supreme Court did not rule upon them and the federal court held that they had been "waived" or forfeited.

In all capital cases, the lawyers have a chance to argue the case personally to the Alabama Supreme Court, to speak directly to the justices of the Court about any legal errors which may have occurred during the trial. Larry Heath's lawyer did not even appear for oral argument.

One might wonder how any court that has to decide whether a fellow child of God will live or die could decide that question based on a one-page brief and without any argument. One would expect that a court that was concerned about its constitutional and moral duty of reviewing death cases would appoint the best lawyer it could find to file a real brief, a lawyer who would show up and argue the case. But, sadly, the representation that Larry Heath received was not all that much different from that provided in hundreds of other capital cases in Alabama and elsewhere. And courts have become completely indifferent to this poor quality of legal representation.

Judy Haney was represented by a lawyer in an Alabama death penalty trial who came to court during trial one morning so drunk that the judge sent the lawyer to jail, told the jury that he was recessing the trial for the day, and the next day produced both Ms. Haney and her lawyer from the jail; the trial resumed, and she got the death penalty. The lawyer failed to find hospital records documenting injuries received by the woman and her daughter which would have corroborated their testimony about abuse at the hands of the man she was convicted of killing.

The failure of court-appointed lawyers to present critical information can be fatal. Horace Dunkins was executed in Alabama in 1989. When newspapers reported before his execution that Dunkins was mentally retarded, one juror came forward and said she would not have voted for the death sentence if she had known of his condition. However, because the lawyer did not get school records that would have established that Dunkins was mentally retarded and in special education classes, the jury did not know of his retardation at the time of trial.

Alabama, which has one of the largest death rows, particularly for its population, provides by law that a lawyer appointed to defend a capital case is limited to payment of $2000 for time spent out-of-court preparing for trial. If a lawyer spends 500 hours preparing for a death case (which is not nearly enough—most capital cases require at least 1,000 hours of preparation), that lawyer will be paid $4 an hour. It is very difficult to find good lawyers willing to work for $4 an hour, when far less stressful legal work pays so much more.

But such shameful representation is not limited to Alabama. In Houston, Texas, a city which has executed more people than any other state except the State of Texas, three people have been sentenced to death at trials at which their defense lawyer was asleep during part of the trial. In the case of George McFarland, observers found the defense lawyer in deep sleep as prosecution witnesses testified against his client. The lawyer's mouth would fall open and his head would roll back on his shoulders. When asked how he could sleep through a capital murder trial, the lawyer said, "It's boring." When asked how he could tolerate such a mockery of justice, the judge explained that although the Constitution guarantees the right to a lawyer, "the Constitution doesn't say the lawyer has to be awake."

Calvin Burdine and Carl Johnson both had the misfortune to have attorney Joe Frank Cannon assigned to defend them at capital trials in Houston. They are among ten clients of Cannon who have been sentenced to death. Cannon has been appointed by judges in Houston to numerous criminal cases in the last 45 years despite his tendency to doze off during trial. In all three of these cases, the Texas Court of Criminal Appeals held that the fact that the defense lawyer slept during trial did not deny the constitutional right to counsel. Carl Johnson was executed by Texas on September 19, 1995. George McFarland and Calvin Burdine remain on death row at this writing.

When one city—the capital of capital punishment—has three cases involving sleeping lawyers, all upheld by the state's highest court, it speaks volumes about the indifference of courts to fairness. Wilburn Dobbs was sentenced to death in Georgia after a trial where he was called by his first name by the prosecutor and he was called "colored" and "colored boy" by the judge and the defense attorney. His lawyer has said that right up until the day of trial, he did not know he was going to be the lawyer in the case and he did not know the state was going for the death penalty.

The lawyer admitted later in testimony that he believes black people make good basketball players but not good teachers, that he uses the slur "nigger" from time-to-time, and other racial prejudice. This lawyer put on no evidence at the penalty phase, and for a closing argument, he read part of an opinion by Justice William Brennan. The state and federal courts in Georgia have held that Wilburn Dobbs was not denied his right to counsel and that the lawyer's racism was irrelevant because the lawyer did not make the decision about sentence.

That case shows two things: how indifferent the courts are to poor quality of representation and how indifferent they are to the influence of racial prejudice in these cases.

To represent a person in a case, one has to know that client and has to investigate his life and background, and has to know his family and the people he works with, etc. And if that lawyer believes those people are inferior, if he does not believe those people are really worthy of saving, then he is not going to do an adequate job. A study by the Philadelphia Inquirer in Philadelphia, which rivals Houston for its high number of capital cases, found that the quality of lawyers appointed to capital cases there is so bad that even officials in charge of the system said they would not want to be represented in Traffic Court by some of the people appointed to defend poor people accused of murder. The study found that many of the attorneys were appointed by judges based on political connections, not legal ability.

Other studies have found the same poor quality of representation in capital cases in one state after another. The National Law Journal, a weekly legal newspaper, after an extensive study of capital cases in six southern states, which account for the vast majority of executions, found that capital trials are "more like a random flip of the coin than a delicate balancing of the scales," because the defense lawyer is too often "ill trained, unprepared. . . [and] grossly underpaid."

The American Bar Association concluded after an exhaustive study that "the inadequacy and inadequate compensation of counsel at trial" was one of the "principal failings of the capital punishment systems in the states today."

Quality legal representation makes a difference. It ensures that juries and judges have critical information and that all safeguards of the Bill of Rights are employed. Gary Nelson and Frederico Martinez-Macias did not receive adequate legal representation until years after they were wrongly convicted and sentenced to death.

Gary Nelson was represented at his capital trial in Georgia in 1980 by a court-appointed lawyer who had never tried a capital case. A request for a second lawyer was denied. The case against Nelson was entirely circumstantial, based on questionable scientific evidence, including the opinion of a prosecution expert that a hair found on the victim's body could have come from Nelson. The appointed lawyer was not provided funds for an investigator and, knowing a request would be denied, did not seek funds for an expert. The lawyer's closing argument was only 255 words long. He was later disbarred for other reasons.

Nelson had the good fortune to be represented later in postconviction proceedings by lawyers willing to spend their own money to investigate the case. They discovered that the hair found on the victim's body, which the prosecution expert had linked to Nelson, lacked sufficient characteristics for microscopic comparison. Indeed, they found that the Federal Bureau of Investigation had previously examined the hair and found that it could not validly be compared. As a result, Gary Nelson was released after eleven years on death row.

Frederico Martinez-Macias was represented at his capital trial in El Paso, Texas by a court-appointed attorney paid only $11.84 per hour. The lawyer failed to present an available alibi witness, relied upon an incorrect assumption about a key evidentiary point, and failed to interview and present witnesses who could have testified in rebuttal of the prosecutor's case. Martinez-Macias was sentenced to death.

Martinez-Macias received competent representation for the first time when a Washington, DC firm volunteered to take his case. After a full investigation and development of facts regarding his innocence, a federal court set aside Martinez-Macias' conviction and death sentence. An El Paso grand jury refused to re-indict him and he was released after nine years on death row.

But for most—like Larry Heath and Horace Dunkins—the consequences of poor lawyers is execution. Inadequate legal representation does not occur in just a few capital cases. It is pervasive in those jurisdictions which account for most of the death sentences.

There are four primary reasons for the poor quality of representation. The first is lack of adequate funding; lawyers can make more money doing almost any other type of legal work than defending capital cases. The second is lack of structure. There are no public defender offices in many of the jurisdictions which sentence the greatest numbers to death rows. Third is lack of independence. Judges appoint lawyers in most jurisdictions and many lawyers are more loyal to the judge on whom they depend for future business than to their clients.

And, finally, there is indifference—indifference which allows judges to preside over capital trials at which lawyers are drunk or asleep;

indifference which allows appellate courts to look the other way and up-hold death sentences at which the accused was represented by a lawyer who did more harm than good.

As a result, the death penalty is imposed not upon those who commit the worst crimes, but upon those, like Larry Gene Heath, who have the mis-fortune to be assigned the worst lawyers.

Stephen B. Bright has been the Director of the Southern Center for Human Rights since 1982. He is a defense attorney, and teaches at Harvard, Yale, Northeastern and Georgetown Universities. Since 1979, Mr. Bright has been involved in representing people on death row.

MORRIS L. THIGPEN

"Managing Death Row: A Tough Assignment"

In January, 1993, at the American Correctional Association Winter Conference in Miami, I attended a workshop that focused on death penalty procedures. Listening to the discussions and presentations, one could have concluded that executions occur in a sterile environment, devoid of any feelings or emotions.

As one who has witnessed eight executions, I know that nothing could be further from the truth. It seems that no one wants to talk about what an execution does to the staff responsible for carrying it out. With this article, I want to try to do just that. It is difficult to transpose my feelings into words—perhaps that is why there is so little writing or discussion about an execution's impact on staff.

I often have heard individuals who have never participated in an execution say they would be more than willing to pull the switch, drop the pellet or inject the needle. On the other hand, I never have heard anyone who has participated in an execution say, "I would like to do that again." For most of the members of the execution team, the procedure is a gut-wrenching, highly emotional experience. Watching death occur under any circumstances is most unpleasant. As commissioner of the Alabama Department of Corrections from 1987 to May 1993, I witnessed eight human beings move from life to death in less than 120 seconds. Those experiences remain indelibly imprinted in my mind.

When the death penalty was reinstated in the 1970s, a circus-like atmosphere surrounded many of the first executions. In Alabama, we did our best to carry out executions in an atmosphere of dignity and respect. The condemned inmates, their families and their friends deserve that.

Every effort is made to ensure that each execution is done without mistakes. This requires the execution team to go through numerous practice sessions before the actual execution. In spite of these efforts, however, sometimes errors are made.

In at least one case in Alabama, the first attempt at electrocution failed as a result of human error. I remember the scene vividly. The warden came into the viewing room where I was standing and told me what had happened.

With the condemned man's father and his principle attorney standing less than two feet away, I remember telling the warden we would have to proceed with a second attempt. Both were commenting, "They are torturing him."

I could not find adequate words then or later to express how much I regretted what had taken place. The members of the execution team who had failed to connect the chair correctly to its power source apologized time and again for their error. Steps were taken immediately following that event to eliminate the possibility of the same error occurring again. Still, that does not relieve you of the fact that you know a mistake occurred that caused unnecessary suffering.

Some victim advocates have criticized any expression of compassion for the condemned inmate as conveying a lack of respect for the victim. That certainly is not the case. I made a point of reviewing the file of every inmate before the execution. The crimes they have committed are heinous. However, I still feel compassion for them. I wonder what events in their lives led them to commit a capital offense. Was there some point at which intervention of some type might have changed the course of events?

In the last execution performed under my leadership in Alabama, we allowed a Catholic priest to witness the execution at the inmate's request. We had made numerous concessions in allowing the priest to spend as much time as possible with the inmate. In spite of that, upon emerging from the witness room, the priest turned to several of my employees and remarked that he had just "witnessed a group of barbarians in action." His comment hurt the staff members deeply and made all of us very angry. After the media reported the priest's statement, he repeated it at the inmate's funeral. We realized there was little we could do except to accept the fact that the comment came from an uninformed person.

Another troubling aspect of capital punishment for me is the length of time inmates spend on death row. I found that the person we were executing may not be the same type of person who committed the crime. One particular case that still troubles me was an inmate who had been on death row for seven or eight years. During that time he underwent a significant change in his life. His was not a last-minute acknowledgment of Christian redemption, but one that occurred several years previously. While strapped in the electric chair just moments before the death penalty was carried out, the inmate asked permission to pray. He prayed for his own forgiveness, for those who were about to execute him and for his victim's family.

I believe that individuals do have the ability to change and that over the course of time they spend on death row some rather dramatic changes occur. I always will wonder about the good this man might have accomplished, if his sentence had been commuted to life without parole. After the media reported that I was obviously disturbed by this execution, a female death row inmate asked to speak to me. "Commissioner," she said, "you should not feel any guilt about what you have to do. We put ourselves where we are today." That is true, but I still am unable to reconcile certain questions in my own mind.

Questions also surface involving plea-bargained capital crimes. I am troubled when two or more offenders are involved in the same capital crime and one testifies against the other. One life is spared, the other is taken. Does this represent true justice? One of my own very personal conflicts centers on how accountable I will be for my role in executions at the end of my life on this earth. I fully understand that what I have done is legal under the laws by which we are governed. However, my religious beliefs cause me to question my actions. After each execution, I felt as though I left another part of my own humanity and my spiritual being in that viewing room.

Holman Prison, where Alabama's executions are carried out shortly after midnight, is about a two-hour drive south of Montgomery, where I live. I almost always drove home alone after an execution. Sleep was out of the question. I found I needed to be alone for a while. During this time I wrestled with myself. Is the world a safer, more just place because of what has taken place tonight?

(Reprinted from the July, 1993 issue of Corrections Today with the permission of the American Correctional Association, Lanham, MD)

Morris L. Thigpen is a former commissioner of the Alabama and Mississippi Departments of Corrections. He is currently the Director of the National Institute of Corrections in Washington, DC.

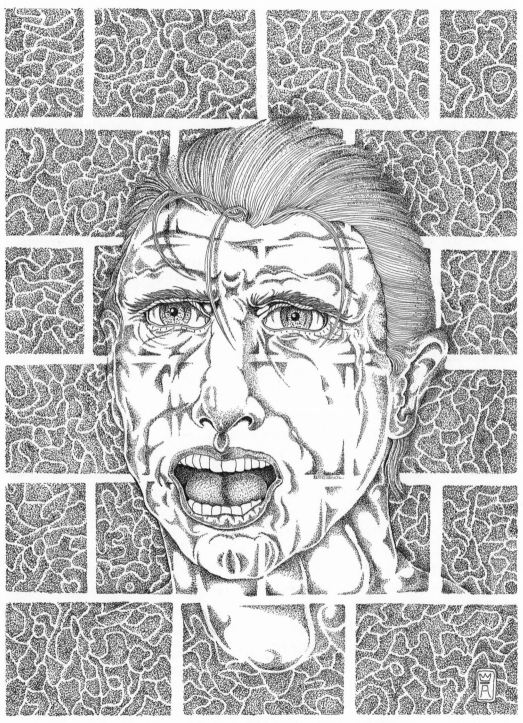

Steven King Ainsworth - "Voices From Within"

MIKE FARRELL

"To Help Mend This World"

To help mend this world is true religion.
William Penn

As we approach the Millennium, it is sad to see so much of our energy wasted, given to acting out hostility and seeking vengeance rather than striving for the "something better" that is within us as a people. As Clarence Darrow said, "There is in every man that divine spark that makes him reach upward for something higher and better than anything he has ever known."

We know, innately, that killing makes no sense. All our moral, ethical and religious precepts decry it—and something in our essential self, something at the very core of our existence, rebels at the very idea of taking the life of another. We Americans hate the idea of killing so much, in fact, that if anyone breaks the taboo and murders another, why we'll just kill that bastard good and dead. We'll show him. Or her.

Even children understand that killing people to show people that killing people is wrong is an absurd notion. That being so, the fact that we, certainly the most technologically advanced society in the world—aspiring to be the most enlightened, thoughtful and humane—continue to practice this abomination in the face of its repudiation by all other advanced industrial nations on the face of the earth, is a continuing source of consternation.

There are mysteries of human behavior, of course, but when as fundamental an issue as death-dealing becomes a social conundrum defying ready explanation, it deserves serious examination. A society that strives to improve itself, just as an individual who wants to be "better," must examine the facts and circumstances surrounding the issue in question, make an informed decision and then, usually in the face of powerful opposition, make the commitment necessary to move to a better place.

Years ago the United States Supreme Court, in a case known as **Trop vs. Dulles**, described this movement toward betterment when they referred to the "evolving standards of decency that mark the progress of a maturing society." As the Court acknowledges, the human race is growing, becoming more civilized and enlightened, toward the place to which all religious, ethical and moral teaching urges us to aspire.

As part of that natural progression, we have moved beyond barbarity and cruelty. We have come to recognize the ugliness of slavery and human bondage. We no longer celebrate the burning of witches or the stoning of women. Having people split on the rack, drawn and quartered, crushed, their limbs severed or heads cut off is no longer seen as reasonable, just or appropriate. The oppression of women, the exploitation of children, the subjugation of a race or class of people because of a manufactured notion of inferiority or the contrived superiority of others has fallen from grace, if not totally from practice.

If human progress is natural and inevitable, and both history and nature say it is despite all the salaciously revisited, media-exploited evidence to the contrary, what is it that so easily turns us away from the angels of our better nature and toward the lurid, the degrading, the vitriolic, the vengeful?

Simply put, it is fear. The key to the denial of reality, of growth, of our own value and our common human connection, is fear. We all have it; it's part of the human package. But it is the lesser-self part, the negating part. It is the part that says, "It's good where you are. Don't change." It's what doesn't want you to venture toward "better" and will whisper insidiously in your ear about failure. It's the part that says, "they are different," the part that says "other" is bad. It's the part that urges, "Hurt them before they hurt you."

Fear is one of the pieces of the human puzzle, but only one. It is as powerful as we allow it to be. Another piece, even more powerful, is love. Yet as much as we claim to recognize the power and authority of love, we too often lack the courage to make use of it. This even though we know instinctively, as Tolstoy put it so perfectly, that "All, everything that I understand, I understand only because I love."

The existence of fear in all of us, however, provides an opening, an opportunity for those who wish to exploit others for their own purposes. And exploit them they will, often in ways so subtle and ingenious they are difficult to detect.

In stressful times, when people are confused and thus more easily manipulated, fear abounds. In the midst of this fear and confusion, voices arise—in the media, in popular organizations, in churches, in business, in positions of political power—and some of these voices, honeyed, articulate, persuasive and highly seductive, cleverly exploit the worst in us by dehumanizing and demonizing others, promoting separateness and giving permission to hate. As a result of this silken cleverness, many lose their footing and grasp at easy appearing, quick-fix solutions—eliminating "the other," for one example. Those who buy into this "solution," usually without full comprehension of what is happening, deny the intrinsic value of others, frustrate the opportunity for full appreciation of themselves and forfeit their most powerful possession: the courage to love.

Today is one of those stressful times. As an increasingly disenchanted body politic is coming to realize, the primary concern of too many now in the arenas of power is self advancement rather than the welfare of the nation or its people. The accumulation of personal wealth and power has supplanted the enhancement of freedom and opportunity for all as the ultimate goal.

But in order for the Ambitious to slake their thirst, the average person's attention has to be diverted. These power-mongers have to keep waving the red flag of fear, devising clever ways to keep people off-balance so they can promote fake, self-serving solutions to "problems" they themselves have conveniently identified. They have to create an apparently worthy adversary so they can appear to be doing heroic battle as they fill their pockets with the trinkets of wealth and power.

Our history is replete with their handiwork. They've used "injuns," "niggers," "The Yellow Peril," the interning of Japanese-Americans, "The Red Menace" and now "illegals" to rally us to their cause. From Manifest Destiny to Anti-Communism, the dynamic is the same: "others" are trying to deter us from our God-given course and must be vanquished. And if the "facts" presented don' t add up to the discerning eye, they quickly dish up a heaping portion of fear and loathing to cloud the vision and justify the course taken. Only afterward, when the truth becomes known, do we experience the sense of shame the action taken in our names requires.

Today, absent any more convenient scape-goat, the target is "killers." Crime, of course, and all criminals, are legitimate objects of public concern, but today "killers" wear the bloody shirt while we, again blinded by fear, misinformation, demagoguery and sleight of hand, once again fend off shame as the powers-that-want-to-continue-to-be twist the facts to suit their own purposes.

Tomorrow, when it is understood that death is dealt in our names for political and economic reasons having nothing to do with justice—that humans die so that reputations are enhanced and careers advanced; that the innocent rot on death row along with the mentally ill and brain damaged, along with children, the disadvantaged, minorities and the impoverished who never have a chance to defend against charges brought—shame will come. Sadly, it will come too late for those innocent, ill and disadvantaged, just as it will be too late for those who made a mistake and are truly regretful; for those who came up in hopelessness, murdered in anger and returned to hopelessness, repenting as they lived, alone and in misery.

But today, in order to ward off that encroaching shame, the Ambitious have unveiled a new tactic. Not satisfied with jingoistic attempts to wrap the flag around the apparatus of killing and labeling opponents of capital punishment traitor, they have gone a step further and made the death penalty in America a secular religion. Complete with high priests, robes, liturgy, incantations and all the ceremonial trappings associated with any worshipful process based on faith and contrary to logic, state killing rolls along blessed by prelates who prayerfully gloss over the obscene costs, the grotesque cruelty, the race and class discrimination. Using shameless tricks and emotional blackmail, they glorify the execrable. As the bodies pile up, the chanting and swaying increases in frequency and decibel count as acolytes insist their litany through gritted teeth, hoping against hope that the wheels won't soon fall off.

But fall off they will as the American people, now dulled into submission by the rantings of the Ambitious and cowed by fear and confusion, begin to take in the facts and measure them against their own deeply held beliefs in fundamental principles of truth, fairness and equal justice under law.

In fact, it is these core principles, these "values" whose loss the Ambitious mourn so piously, that will eventually cause them to be driven from the temple. Americans have learned from childhood a creed that will ultimately be the undoing of the moneychangers. Revolutionary ideas—like "unalienable rights" to life, liberty and the pursuit of happiness; notions based on the value and dignity inherent in each regardless of race, creed, color or station—contain within them the seeds of personal power that, once unleashed, will reclaim this society and reaffirm its momentum toward betterment. Today's Pharisees, weeping, tearing hair and rending garments in public as they cozy up to wealth and power in private, preside over a smoldering public anger which, though now diverted into cynicism, will then become a rage even the most imaginative manipulation cannot control, stinging all with its lash in demand of a reckoning.

As with Pharisees of old, today's authoritarians have usurped people's desire to live together under agreed social limitations, called laws, and turned them to their own ends. All agree to the need for restraint of those who break the law, but the penalties imposed on the law-breaker must accord with the core values of the society. Professing, as did their Biblical counterparts, strict observance of traditional and written law, the sanctimonious declaim on crime and the need for swift and sure justice and have settled, with a little help from their spinmeisters, on death as their symbol of strength. Their willingness to kill, they piously intone, demonstrates the depth of their moral character. Those, then, who refuse to bloody their hands—to support the hooded one in his gory task—are guilty of heresy, frailty and, worse, bleeding-heartedness.

Eventually, however, facts outweigh sophistry and posturing. Truth will out. People who have been taught to believe in the fundamental value of human life can only be manipulated by their fear of "the other" for a time, after which maturity demands more than slogans. On this day the Ambitious will need more than magical incantations to keep the faithful at bay.

There is no clever turn of phrase that will explain away the innocent who have died in our chambers of horror. Were not all souls singed as Jesse Tafero's head burst into flame, electrocuted for a crime he did not commit?

Are our streets safer, our children more secure because Joe Spaziano endured 21 years of torture on Florida's death row, surviving five different dates with the executioner, before finally having his conviction overturned by an outraged judge?

Will the incantation of law and order dull the grief of Clarence Brandley, Walter McMillian, Randall Adams, Rolando Cruz, Kirk Bloodsworth, Alejandro Hernandez, Thomas Gladish, Richard Greer, Ronald Keine, Clarence Smith, Andrew Golden, Larry Hicks, Sonia Jacobs, Lawyer Johnson, Wilbert Lee, Freddie Pitts, Federico Martinez Macias, Adolph Munson, Gary Nelson, James Richardson, Johnny Ross, Dennis Williams, Willie Rainge and Kenneth Adams, who spent decades on death row for crimes of which they were innocent? Will it require the killing of countless others not defended in time to avoid the Pontius Pilates of today?

It will not do to make a sacrament of murder. Even swept under the robes of lawful authority, the blood of the brain damaged, mentally impaired, the impoverished and those singled out because of their color will seep out and stain our moral fabric. The consecration of killing as a sop to the fears of the public, fears themselves generated by the malign rhetoric of the same high priests who profit from this use of human sacrifice, confounds logic, debases principle, degrades respect for self and ultimately for life.

But history declares that life, ever insisting itself upward, ever seeking the light, will not, in the end, tolerate such degradation.

At the end of the Dark Ages, power was in the hands of a corrupt clergy and royalty who debauched, plundered and murdered at will. Claiming authority from God and from blood, they condemned as heretic anyone who questioned their legitimacy, and, smug in the belief that "all knowledge is already known," raged on. From that era, though shackled in ignorance, disciplined by fear and sheathed in superstition, the "ignorant masses," inspired by daring teachers, writers, thinkers, enlightened religious, scientists and other "Humanists," saw that a better way was possible and spawned The Renaissance.

The belief that life has intrinsic value is a thorny one for some, but human development from the depths of history presents a powerful case that people are more than the worst acts they have committed. From Spinoza's "light... uncreated and uncreatable," through Darrow's "divine spark" to

Nelson Mandela's recognition that "man's goodness is a flame that can be hidden but never extinguished," the arrogant assumption that humans can be disposed of at the whim of authority is exposed for what it is: atavistic, fear-inspired barbarism.

The Millennium approaches. With it a new dawn?

Mike Farrell is an actor, producer, writer and director, probably best known for his 8 year portrayal of Captain B.J. Hunnicutt on the television series M*A*S*H*. Mr. Farrell has traveled throughout the world over the last 20 years on various human rights and refugee aid missions. An advocate of prison reform and a life-long opponent of capital punishment, he has been active across the United States in pursuit of a more just, humane and appropriate penal system. He currently serves as co-chair of the Committee to Save Mumia Abu Jamal, is president of the board of Death Penalty Focus of California and co-chair of Human Rights Watch/California.

Jessee Roberts - "Seeds"

A QUESTION OF INNOCENCE

Margaret Vandiver - "The Execution of Arthur Frederick Goode III: A Study in the Failure of Justice"

Robert R. Bryan - "Trial By Fury: The Lindbergh-Hauptmann Case"

DR. MARGARET VANDIVER

"The Execution of Arthur Frederick Goode III: A Study in the Failure of Justice"

I often think that Arthur Goode was the most innocent person I have ever known. This is a horrible paradox, given that Arthur was the self-confessed murderer of two children, and had sexually molested many others. His actions were evil beyond comprehension, and yet Arthur was not evil. I do not mean that Arthur changed after his crimes, that he matured or reformed. I mean that there never was enough of Arthur for the concepts of good and evil to apply to him. Arthur suffered from a terrible compulsion to sexually molest young boys. He was also borderline mentally retarded. Those two disabilities, combined with his astonishing immaturity, left him unable to make moral judgments or to direct his actions according to what others told him was right and wrong. He was so incomplete, so unformed, so young, that he was incapable of understanding even simple connections between cause and effect.

Arthur Goode's case illustrates the absolute worst that the American mental health and criminal justice systems have to offer. First, the mental health system repeatedly allowed a dangerous person to go free and attack children. The criminal justice system was slow to respond, but when it finally did react, it did so with medieval savagery directed at a person who had little, if any, control over his actions. During Arthur's second death warrant, I spent many hours with him, and during his final night I stayed with him up until a few hours before his execution. My observations of him and conversations with him left no doubt in my mind that his emotional age was that of a four or five year old child.

Arthur Goode was born in 1954, the fourth child of parents 39 years old.[1] Arthur's parents began to suspect that something was wrong with him at a very early age. As an infant, the sight of leaves waving on a tree could throw him into a panic for half an hour. At the age of three, he displayed abnormal hostility, fearfulness, and extreme aggressiveness toward other children. Arthur failed the first grade, and had to repeat it. When he was eight years old, a school psychologist evaluated Arthur and recommended that he be referred to a mental health facility. That recommendation prompted a consultation, and Arthur was referred to a neurologist, who diagnosed him as having "minimal chronic brain syndrome."

At the end of second grade, a school official recommended that Arthur be placed in special education, but he was enrolled in the regular third grade class. His teacher noted that Arthur engaged in "aggressive and pestering behavior," and picked on children younger than himself. In January 1964, when Arthur was nearly ten, he was evaluated by a doctor who concluded that Arthur "probably suffers from brain damage as exhibited by his comprehension difficulty and poor fine motor coordination," and prescribed Benedril. Arthur was placed in special education the following fall, but his problems with school continued. When Arthur was nearly 11, one of his teachers wrote, with frightening foresight:

"One of the most enigmatic characteristics about [Arthur] is his honesty. He will always admit an act, and is able to fully explain whether or not it is acceptable and why... When asked why he carried out the act 'knowing' that he shouldn't, he replies, 'I don't know.' It becomes frightening to imagine him being tried under the M'Naghten rule in criminal law, which states that if a person knew what he was doing and knew it was wrong he could be indicted. Surely, though he fits in that category, he could not be fully in command of all faculties which decide on and enact the deed."

For the next several years, Arthur continued to have difficulties in school, though with some indications of improvement. He was enrolled in a special learning program in junior high school in the spring of 1968. The following fall, he became obsessed with the moon, calling weather stations, and refusing to come into the house at night, because he was watching the moon.

At 15, Arthur was enrolled in a residential facility for retarded teenagers. From the time Arthur was about 16, he repeatedly molested and assaulted young boys. His proclivities were well known: "Goode's tendencies ultimately became so notorious that local people took to warning new families in the area to keep their youngsters away from him."[2] When Arthur was 17, he began receiving weekly injections of Depo-Provera, a powerful drug that may have damaging side effects, but that can be effective in suppressing the sex drive.

During his adolescent years, Arthur was arrested a number of times and charged with offenses ranging from making obscene phone calls to assault. During this time Arthur "received a variety of treatments in Maryland and walked through a virtual revolving door of mental hospitals for sex-related crimes."[3]

At one point, Arthur was sentenced to five years probation and sent to Spring Grove Hospital for six assaults and batteries, one charge of possession of marijuana, four unnatural and perverted sexual practice charges, and two charges of attempting unnatural and perverted sexual practice. After a few months in the hospital, Arthur ran away, but returned voluntarily the next day. Several months later he "walked out of the institution and took a bus to his parents' new home in St. James City, Florida....despite warnings from a probation officer and a judge's bench warrant, no one came to collect [Arthur]."[4] On March 5, 1976, while Arthur was in Ft. Myers, a nine year old boy named Jason Verdow was murdered. Arthur became an immediate suspect; he was questioned twice by the police, but released.

A few days after Jason Verdow was killed, Arthur showed up at Spring Grove Hospital and asked to be readmitted. He was told by the admitting doctor to go to a waiting room. Arthur waited a short time, and then again asked to be admitted. After the doctor again told him to wait, Arthur left the hospital.

Soon thereafter in Virginia, Arthur kidnapped two boys and killed one of them. A woman in Falls Church, having seen television pictures of Arthur and the child he had kidnapped, recognized them when they happened to come to her house asking for work. Even then, it was not easy to get the authorities to take action. The woman called the local police, who suggested she call the Maryland State Police; the state police declared it was not their case, and told her they would call back. The woman then called the Baltimore police, and finally found someone willing to rescue a kidnapped child, and arrest the kidnapper and suspected murderer of two other children.[5]

Arthur's documented history of mental illness and mild retardation did not help him in court. He was first tried in Virginia, found guilty of first degree murder, and given a life sentence (Virginia did not have a death penalty at that time). After this conviction, Goode "gave a statement in which he demanded his return to Florida so that he could be convicted of Jason's murder and be executed."[6] In Florida, Arthur was found competent to stand trial; incredibly, he also was allowed to fire his attorney and represent himself, with a lawyer present only as supporting counsel. The court questioned Arthur to determine the extent of his legal knowledge:

THE COURT: *Define for me first degree murder. What are the elements in Florida?*

THE DEFENDANT: *First degree murder is when you plan to kill the person.*

THE COURT: *What is the voir dire examination of jurors?*

THE DEFENDANT: *The what? Pardon me?*

THE COURT: *What is the voir dire examination of jurors?*

THE DEFENDANT: *I don't understand.*

THE COURT: *Very well. Tell me, Mr. Goode, what is the purpose of opening and closing argument in a jury trial?*

THE DEFENDANT: *To get the Court to understand everything.*

THE COURT: *Who has the order of burden of proof in a criminal trial?*
THE DEFENDANT: *I don't understand.*
THE COURT: *What is the method of presentation of testimony in a criminal trial?*
THE DEFENDANT: *I don't understand.*
THE COURT: *Then you need a lawyer to explain these things to you.*
THE DEFENDANT: *But the point is, I do not want to have a lawyer.*[7]

Arthur, acting as his own attorney, was determined to be convicted and sentenced to death. He talked to the media, gave information to the prosecution, described his crimes in revolting detail to the jury, and did everything possible to ensure his own conviction and death sentence. For example, at the sentencing phase of the trial, Arthur stated before the jury:

"I have no remorse whatsoever. I'm extremely proud of knowing that I, Arthur Frederick Goode, was the last person to see Jason alive or any of the other victims which I have murdered. Also, that I was the last person who heard the sweet, sexy voice. I was also the last person who had kissed his precious warm lips before I, Arthur Goode, had murdered him."[8]

Judge John Shearer, who presided over the trial and sentenced Arthur to death, may have felt some scruples about whether Arthur was fully responsible for his condition and his actions. In his sentencing order the judge said:

"...and as you said in trial, Arthur, maybe I don't know who we blame. God forgive you of those desires or something in your environment that has made you have them, and whoever is to blame is beyond the power of this Court.

You have violated the laws, you have had your trial and I am convinced that the punishment [of death] is just and proper, and truthfully, may God have mercy on your soul."[9]

And so the circuit court of the Twentieth Judicial Circuit, Ft. Myers, Florida, allowed a mildly retarded and desperately disturbed defendant to act out an obscene charade of a trial. The judge allowed and the prosecution and media encouraged Arthur Goode, who was clearly incompetent to manage any aspect of his life, to talk his way onto death row.

Arthur was sentenced to death on March 22, 1977, and taken to death row at Florida State Prison in Starke. Conditions on Florida's death row are extremely restrictive and severe, but Arthur's confinement was even harsher than that of most condemned inmates. When Arthur first came to death row, he was housed in a single cell on a wing with other death sentenced inmates. The other men tried to attack him, however, and he was so disruptive he was moved to Q wing, the isolation area of the prison. There he was kept alone for years; he never went outside to exercise, and he had to receive his family visitors separately from other inmates. Even on Q wing other inmates sometimes teased and tormented him. David Von Drehle wrote about

Goode's time on death row:

"The men who ran the prison agreed that Goode was mad. 'I saw Arthur every month,' warden Dave Brierton said. 'He would come in for a talk, and it was always the same: he couldn't understand why society didn't allow him to have sex with boys. I tried explaining the historical development of sexual taboos, but it never sank in. He would start crying and asking why he couldn't have a boy in his cell. He was one of a kind, impossible...One time he comes in and says, 'I don't want to live here anymore...'

'I don't think Arthur ever understood that when you're executed, we can't come back the next day and talk about it,' said Richard Dugger, Brierton's successor as warden. 'It was like dealing with a child. He could make a rational appearance. He could answer your questions and appear to carry on a conversation. But he just didn't understand what you were saying.'" [10]

Arthur tried to refuse his first appeal, but the Florida Supreme Court ruled that the appeal was mandatory. In September of 1978, the court upheld Arthur's conviction and death sentence. [11] Arthur's lawyer requested a grant of executive clemency, and presented the clemency board and governor with thorough documentation of Arthur's life-long history of mental illness. The request for clemency was denied, and in early 1982, Governor Graham signed Arthur's death warrant.

Arthur, in the meantime, had requested the death warrant because he believed that he would have better television privileges if he were scheduled for execution. This type of reasoning was typical of Arthur, and illustrates the childishness of his understanding. Arthur's lawyers secured a stay of execution from the Eleventh Circuit Court of Appeals. [12] In 1983, that court ruled that Arthur's death sentence had been improperly imposed, and sent the case back to circuit court for resentencing. [13] The state of Florida appealed this decision, and in November of 1983, the United States Supreme Court overruled the Eleventh Circuit, and ordered Arthur's death sentence reinstated. In March of 1984 a second death warrant was signed.

When Arthur's second death warrant was signed, I was asked to assist his attorneys by visiting him, trying to explain the legal proceedings to him, and getting his signature on legal documents. I did this with Susan Cary, a lawyer who had many years experience working with condemned prisoners. I had worked with death row inmates in Florida for about five years, but had never met Arthur. The first visit with Arthur was a shock.

As we entered the visiting area, I saw Arthur sitting alone in one of the little cubicles set aside for legal visits. I prepared myself to greet him, but his very first words completely threw me off. He looked up at me, and held out a newspaper photograph of a popular child actor. "Hi," he said. "This is Ricky, and I'm in love with him." I reeled to my seat and tried to initiate a normal conversation. Somehow, whatever topic we began discussing, we were soon back on the subject of having sex with young boys. For the first time in the hundreds of hours I had spent with death row inmates, I found myself so upset that I had to leave the room. Excusing myself, I went into the bathroom. I turned on the cold water and let it run over my hands, while leaning my head against the cool wall and trying to breathe normally. When I had fought the nausea down, I returned to the interview room. I found Arthur trying to convince Susan that there should be a law allowing him to marry a ten year old boy. The rest of the visit remains mercifully blurred in my memory.

Afterwards, Susan and I had a long talk. We agreed that it was foolish to try to use logic with Arthur. It served no purpose but to allow him to pull us into bizarre and sickening conversations. We decided to cut off every reference to little boys; we would be gentle but absolute that we had come to discuss Arthur's legal situation, not pedophilia. And we agreed to operate on the assumption that there was some part of Arthur that was not perverted, some tiny spark of self under all the sickness. We promised each other to act toward and react to whatever tiny bit of normality we could find in him, while consistently refusing to respond in any way to his sickness. Although Arthur was difficult, we soon learned that it was not impossible to communicate with him. As I was leaving after our second or third visit, Arthur looked up at me and said, "I like you, you're nice to me." His voice and facial expression were so childlike that suddenly I understood how very young he was emotionally. Susan and I treated him as we would have treated a small child; we were firm, consistent, and as kind as we could be.

Despite our efforts, there were still many difficulties. Arthur enjoyed refusing to do things; like a very young child, he liked saying no. During one visit, I had planned to have him sign certain legal papers. This was an entirely routine process, but Arthur flatly refused. He didn't have a reason, he just wanted to refuse. But he also very much wanted me to be there and to stay with him during the visit. I tried logic, which of course got nowhere; I tried persuasion, which only made him more stubborn; I considered yelling at him, and realized I would lose the fragile emotional connection Susan and I had been able to establish with him. Arthur never signed the papers, and his appeal went into court under his father's signature, as next friend.

During Arthur's death warrant, I remained in close contact with his parents. No child was ever more difficult to rear and care for than Arthur, but his parents did everything in their power to help him and to stay close to him. Supporters of the death penalty often speak of condemned prisoners as if they were total isolates, with neither families nor friends. The experiences of the families of death sentenced inmates amount to an unmerited and horribly severe punishment. In some ways, the families suffer even more than the condemned, and they certainly suffer longer. Death is the end for the prisoner, but the family has to go on, remembering all that happened and their helplessness to prevent it.

The weekend before Arthur was scheduled for execution, I spent as much time with him as the prison rules allowed. On Saturday, he came out to visit me, and he was crying. I thought that some of the reality of his impending death might have at last gotten through to him, and I asked him what was wrong. He said, "The guard was mean to me." By that time, I had begun to get a clue as to how Arthur's mind worked, and I asked him, "Did you say anything to the officer?" He brightened up and said, "Yeah, I told him what I'd like to do to his son!" And I said slowly and with great emphasis, "Arthur, if you say those things to people, they are not going to be nice to you." And he looked at me with such utter incomprehension that I realized he had no idea of how even the very simplest rules of social interaction worked.

During his final warrant, Arthur was deeply concerned with the issue of toilet paper. He felt strongly that he was not being given an adequate supply. He wrote a great number of letters about this problem to such people as the governor and the attorney general, and to various members of the media. Only a few days from being electrocuted, he focused obsessively on utterly irrelevant details.

The rules of death watch were a torment to Arthur. Something was always wrong with his television. An officer would hurt his feelings. He would feel afraid and want the superintendent to comfort him. At the time of Arthur's warrant, Richard Dugger was the superintendent of the prison. Mr. Dugger was a stern man, but Arthur had formed a strong attachment to him, trusted him, and wanted a great deal of attention from him. This was somewhat pathetic, given that Mr. Dugger was the person who would oversee the death squad strapping Arthur into the electric chair, and then would give the executioner the signal to throw the switch. Arthur knew these facts, but they did not alter the obvious sense of safety he had in Mr. Dugger's presence.

While Susan and I were spending hours each day with Arthur, the lawyers representing him were working around the clock preparing pleadings for the courts. Their principal contention was that Florida law prohibited the execution of the insane, and that Arthur Goode was insane. Dr. George W. Barnard, a psychiatrist who had evaluated Arthur twice before, interviewed Arthur during the final death warrant. In part Dr. Barnard's report read:

"It is my medical opinion that [Arthur Goode] has a mental disorder of long-standing and that as a result of his mental disorder, although he has cognitive understanding, he lacks affective understanding of the nature and effect of the death penalty. In many ways he is as a small child who can say words which seem to make

some sense, but in reality he lacks appreciation of their meaning. When he discusses the execution process it is like hearing a child talk about a pretend or make believe situation .... It is my medical opinion that Goode has a factual but not a rational understanding of the execution process and therefore he is not presently competent to be executed."

Dr. Barnard's opinion was powerfully confirmed for Susan and me during our final visit with Arthur. We were allowed to spend four hours with Arthur the night before his execution. We were joined by one of Arthur's lawyers and by Father Maniangat, a Catholic priest. Even at that late hour, even as our last hope for a stay disappeared, Arthur continued to miss the point. His main concern for the first hour or so of our visit was the order in which he should eat the things we had brought for him from the canteen. Was it better to eat the ice cream first, or drink the chocolate milk, or start with the roast beef sandwich, or maybe the potato chips?

As the night wore on, Arthur expressed concern about the details of the process of electrocution. Susan very calmly and gently described to him everything that would be done to him, step by step: the shaving of his head, the final shower, the special handcuffs that would clamp down and break his wrists if he resisted, the walk to the chair, how he would be strapped in, the last statement. Arthur listened intently, and then asked us, "What if my nose itches when I'm strapped into the electric chair? What if I cry?" Stunned by the innocence of the question, all we could think to say was, "Mr. Dugger will be right there with you. He can wipe your tears for you."

At 7:00 the next morning, Arthur Goode was led into the execution chamber and strapped into the electric chair. Richard Dugger stood by him and held the microphone for Arthur's final statement. Arthur said, "I'm very upset. I don't know what to say. How much time do we have? I want to apologize to my parents. I have remorse for the two boys I murdered. It's hard for me to show it."[14] Dugger gave the signal, the executioner threw the switch, and Arthur was electrocuted. Years later, reflecting on all the executions he had supervised, Dugger said: *"Arthur Goode was the hardest. . . . I had some real reservations about that one. Let's face it—he was a nut. Geez, he didn't trust anybody but me. And I was the one who was gonna make sure he was gonna die. He was sure I would take care of him."*[15]

Arthur Goode was a kind of person none of our systems of control seems capable of handling: an extremely dangerous repeat violent offender who was so impaired as to be beyond the reach of reason, fear, or punishment. None of the assumptions underlying our concepts of punishment and justice applied to him. He fit in no category. His actions were evil, yet he was not responsible for them.

To punish a person like Arthur is not remedial; it does not instill any sense of responsibility or remorse or even regret. It does not respect the integrity of the punished or the punisher. Punishing such a person is only the infliction of pain, nothing more. Punishing Arthur Goode was useless in every practical sense, and had no moral meaning at all. He could feel pain, but he could not understand the reason for it. He could recognize the dislike, anger and loathing with which people regarded him, but he was unable even to begin to change himself in any way to be more acceptable.

Perhaps a day will come when people will reserve their revulsion for the disease, and not for those who suffer from it. It may be that in fifty or a hundred years, the Arthur Goodes of the world will be securely confined and cared for, and moral condemnation will be reserved for those who deliberately hurt the helpless to make themselves feel stronger and safer. But at the end of the twentieth century, in a country that considers itself advanced and humane, we took a desperately sick child, strapped him into an electric chair and threw the switch. Whether death was worse than life for Arthur none of us can answer. But by killing him we diminished ourselves forever.

With thanks to David Giacopassi and Gordon Haas for helpful comments on earlier versions of this manuscript. This chapter is dedicated to Arthur and Mildred Goode with admiration and affection.

Margaret Vandiver, PhD, is an assistant professor of criminology at the University of Memphis. She worked throughout the 1980's with lawyers defending condemned prisoners in Florida. Her principal research interest is state violence, including genocide, war crimes, and capital punishment. She has written about various aspects of the death penalty, with a focus on the impact of death sentences and executions on prisoners' families.

Footnotes:

1. The information that follows comes largely from a summary of a report written by Alan M. Wilner at the request of the Governor of Maryland who wished to "assess what, if any, deficiencies there were (and are) in the State's criminal justice and mental health systems that may have allowed Mr. Goode to escape incarceration or effective treatment..." summary of the Wilner Report was presented to the Florida clemency board byArthur's attorney. In what follows, I have also drawn from reports and testimony of Dr. George W. Barnard, who evaluated Arthur on three separate occasions.

2. Godwin, 1978, p. 319; see also Sherrill, 1984, p. 553.

3. Article from The Washington Post, no date, quoted in Sherrill, p. 553.

4. Godwin, 1978, p. 320.

5. Godwin, 1978, p. 321.

6. Goode v. State, 365 So.2d 381, at 382

7. Transcript of hearing quoted in Goode v. State, 365 So.2d 381, at 383.

8.   Quoted in Sherrill, p. 553.
9.   Trial transcript at 1280-81, quoted in Goode v. Wainwright, 704 F.2d 593, at 604.
10. Von Drehle, 1995, 230.
11. Goode v. State, 365 So.2d 381.
12. Goode v. Wainwright, 704 F.2d 593.
13. Goode v. Wainwright, 670 F.2d 941.
14. Gainesville Sun, April 6, 1984.
15. Von Drehle, 1995, 235.

Published Sources

Bayliss, George (April 6, 1984). "He offered an apology and remorse." Gainesville Sun.

Godwin, John (1978). Murder U.S.A.: The ways we kill each other. New York: Ballantine Books.

Sherrill, Robert (November 24, 1984) "In Florida, insanity is no defense." The Nation vol. 239, p. 537, 552-6.

Von Drehle, David (1995). Among the Lowest of the Dead: The Culture of Death Row. New York: Random House.

Legal Decisions

Goode v. State, 365 So.2d 381 (1978), judgment and sentence affirmed by the Florida Supreme Court on direct appeal.

Goode v. State, 441 U.S. 967 (1979), United States Supreme Court denied petition of certiorari.

Goode v. State, 403 So.2d 931 (1981), Florida Supreme Court affirmed circuit court's denial of motion for post-conviction relief.

Goode v. Wainwright, 410 So.2d 506 (1982), Florida Supreme Court denied petition of habeas corpus.

Goode v. Wainwright, 670 F.2d 941 (1982), Eleventh Circuit Court of Appeals granted motion for stay of execution.

Goode v. Wainwright, 704 F.2d 593 (1983), Eleventh Circuit Court of Appeals granted petition and vacated death sentence.

Wainwright v. Goode, 464 U.S. 78 (1983), United States Supreme Court reversed the Eleventh Circuit and reinstated the death sentence.

Goode v. Wainwright, 725 F.2d 106 (1984), Eleventh Circuit Court of Appeals affirmed lower court judgment in accordance with United States Supreme Court ruling.

Goode v. Wainwright, 731 F.2d 1482 (1984), Eleventh Circuit Court of Appeals denied motion for stay of execution.

Goode v. Wainwright, 466 U.S. 932 (1984), United States Supreme Court denied application for stay of execution.

ROBERT R. BRYAN

"Trial By Fury: The Lindbergh-Hauptmann Case"

Sixty-one years ago Richard Hauptmann was executed in New Jersey for the kidnap-murder of Charles A. Lindbergh, Jr. The modest German immigrant maintained his innocence to the end: *"I am dying an innocent man. Should, however, my death serve for the purpose of abolishing capital punishment, I feel that my death has not been in vain."*

The Hauptmann case continues to raise disturbing questions regarding society's voracious appetite for the death penalty. The legal system is composed of people, and people err. The result is that inevitably innocent people die at the hands of the state.

At 8:44 p.m. on April 3, 1936, 2,000 volts of electricity shot through Mr . Hauptmann. His shrunken frame snapped violently, the clenched fists pounded against the arms of the chair, and his mouth opened in a silent scream. Twice more the current was turned up sending the victim slamming back against the chair. Wisps of smoke rose from his head and leg. At 8:47 and 30 seconds doctors proclaimed the man dead.

Mr. Hauptmann did not have to die. There had been an offer to spare his life if he admitted some involvement in the crime. The proposal was spurned, with the response that he would not live with a lie.

On the night of March 1, 1932, the 20-month old Lindbergh child was kidnapped from the home of his parents near Hopewell, New Jersey. By the next day newspapers around the globe featured front-page pictures of the child and stories of the abduction. The Crime of the Century shocked the country.

Just five years earlier the baby's father had become a living legend— the first person to fly solo across the Atlantic. Then the hero married Anne Morrow, whose father was the Ambassador to Mexico, a former member of the United States Senate from New Jersey, and a partner of J.P. Morgan. The storybook romance captured public imagination.

The kidnapper met twice with an eccentric representative of the Lindberghs. A ransom of $50, 000 was paid. Later, a badly decomposed body was found in a shallow grave five miles from the Lindbergh estate. Everyone assumed it was the child, and the remains were hastily cremated.

For over two years the authorities hunted for the kidnapper. Public

Robert R. Bryan

pressure demanded that the case be solved. If the Lindbergh family could be so easily invaded, no one was safe.

With the arrest of Mr. Hauptmann in 1934 as he was driving from his Bronx home, desperate officials at long last had someone to prosecute. In their eyes he had to be the kidnapper because he possessed some of the marked ransom money. The New Jersey State Police, FBI and New York Police quickly proclaimed that they had caught the kidnapper.

Mr. Hauptmann said he was innocent, that he knew nothing about the abduction and killing. A box of papers had been left with him for safe-keeping by a friend who died while visiting relatives in Germany. Only a short time before being arrested, Mr. Hauptmann discovered money in the box. He unwittingly used a Lindbergh ransom bill to buy gas. At that moment his fate was sealed.

An end-justifies-the-means attitude controlled police actions. Witnesses were told Mr. Hauptmann was the culprit, and then they were ushered in to view him. A circumstantial case was woven. All evidence pointing to innocence was concealed. Even the kidnapper's fingerprints, which could have cleared Mr. Hauptmann, were suppressed. The Lindbergh family's go-between, who had met with the kidnapper during the ransom negotiations, told the police they had the wrong man. But by the time of the trial he had succumbed to enormous pressure, and from the witness stand dramatically identified Mr. Hauptmann.

The trial began January 2, 1935, in the sleepy little town of Flemington, New Jersey. For the next six weeks the attention of the world was focused on the fate of the German itmmigrant.

At the outset Mr. Hauptmann pleaded, "I am just a human being." That simple notion was lost in the fury of the moment. The man was doomed before he ever set foot in the courtroom.

The amount of attention paid to the Hauptmann trial was incredible, even by present-day standards. H.L. Mencken called it the greatest story since the Resurrection. The media coverage exceeded any other comparable event in history including the 1918 Armistice ending World War I. Over a half million words poured daily out of the hamlet.

Damon Runyon and Walter Winchell were part of the greatest array of newspaper talent ever assembled. The public's right to know evolved into an unquenchable thirst for entertainment. Even celebrities like Jack Benny, Ginger Rogers and Jack Dempsey were there.

Strong anti-German feelings prevailed in an atmosphere of mass hysteria. The jury ran a gauntlet through the mob of spectators to get into the courthouse. Charles Lindbergh daily sat close to the jury, staring at the accused. The roar of the crowd outside, crying for the blood of Mr. Hauptmann, could be heard inside the courtroom. In court, cameras rolled and flashbulbs popped.

Nearly everyone seemed caught up in the swirling storm of exploiting the case. On the radio lawyers daily picked apart the proceedings, throwing fair trial rights to the wind. Personal aggrandizement and profit ruled the day. For some it was a once-in-a-lifetime career opportunity. The lead defense attorney prepared stationary featuring a red kidnap ladder in the margin and the words, "The Lindbergh-Hauptmann Trial—Chief Defense Counsel." The Attorney General of New Jersey could not resist personally taking over from the local district attorney.

The guilty verdict and death sentence amidst the roar of the mob brought little relief. People would not be satisfied until the hated defendant was dead. The following year they were outside the prison in Trenton, New Jersey, cheering when Mr. Hauptmann was executed and yelling the next day as a hearse took his corpse away.

Anna Hauptmann, the widow whom I represented for over a decade until her death in 1994 at the age of 95, never gave up the dream of seeing the name of her husband cleared. Exposing the truth will not bring Mr. Hauptmann back. He is long dead. But it will help erase a blot on the American judicial system, and, I hope, save others from suffering a similar fate.

If we can learn from the travesty of the Hauptmann case, then it will give purpose to an otherwise senseless death. The increased use of the death penalty has brought us full circle to those bygone days in a small New Jersey courtroom where the quest for justice was obscured by a lust for vengeance.

Will we ever learn?

(A modified version of this article appeared in the <u>San Francisco Examiner</u> on April 3, 1996, the 60th anniversary of the execution of Richard Hauptmann in New Jersey.)

Robert Bryan is a San Francisco attorney who has appeared in major cases throughout the U.S., including over 100 murder trials. A member of the bars of California, New York, Alabama and the United States Supreme Court and a Fellow in the American Board of Criminal Lawyers, he specializes nationally in death penalty litigation at the trial, appellate and postconviction levels. Mr. Bryan was Chair of the National Coalition to Abolish the Death Penalty 1987-90, Vice-Chair 1991-3, and served 10 years on its Board of Directors. He is the legal commentator for the ABC network affiliate in San Francisco, appearing regularly on the Evening News. In 1981 Mr. Bryan began representing Mrs. Anna Hauptmann, the widow of Richard Hauptmann, the man executed in 1936 for the kidnap-murder of Charles A. Lindbergh, Jr.

Anthony Papa - "Fry Chicken, Not People"

HARLEY O. STAGGERS

"The Role of Emotion In the Capital Punishment Debate"

In the movie "A Time To Kill," a young black female is brutally raped and her father then kills the two rapists. In an effort to overcome the racial prejudice, the all-white jury in the father's trial for murder is asked to visualize the brutal rape and then to imagine that the young girl was white.

In a televised debate, Michael Dukakis, who publicly opposes the death penalty, was asked to imagine that his wife and daughter were brutally raped and murdered. Then Mr. Dukakis was asked whether he would support the death penalty for those who murdered and raped his loved ones.

However, in both the movie and the real life drama, the larger question of what is best for society never gets answered. In every conflict, each of us has our own viewpoint, but when we determine the rules to govern the conflict, normally we strive to reach objective and fair rules. In the above examples, the clear message is that the situation justifies the action. Subjectively we can empathize with the oppressed and we can feel the passion of the victim. Objectively, as a society, we must strive for those rules which are fair to all.

The obvious reason to force policy makers to view emotional issues from the individual, and therefore the emotional side of the debate, is to influence the policy maker. However, with most emotional issues, the majority of our society are never confronted head-on with the issue and therefore have a less than definite position of either support or opposition to the issue.

As an elected representative to our federal government, and as an elected representative to a state government, I believed that the primary job of a representative was to represent the views of the people who elected the person. But with the use of negative political ads combined with obscene amounts of money deployed in our political process, the views of any elected representative's constituency is difficult to determine. In my experience, most people could tell you whether they support the death penalty or oppose the death penalty. But this same majority contained only about 10-20% who had definite, unchangeable opinions.

When I was a U.S. Congressman, I met and talked with parents whose

children had been murdered. These parents had a very clear a[...]
view on whether our society should impose a death penalty. To
ents, someone should pay with his/her life for the crimes comm[...]
ever, most people are not clear as to whether we, as a society, should take [...]
lives of certain criminals.

When asked why he supported the position of allowing the death penalty, officer Glen Macher, a policeman with over 18 years experience, responded that simple justice and the finality of the crime convinced him. As Glen Macher says, "simple justice," or the old "eye for and eye and tooth for a tooth," makes sense. Society's need for retribution or the survivor's need for vengeance is at least understandable to most of us. In fact, it is the only argument for the death penalty that does make sense.

~ The other argument that we often hear is that the death penalty deters crime. However, those who support the death penalty as a means of deterring crime ignore the facts. Most capital offenses occur when a criminal is operating at a diminished mental capacity, whether that mental capacity be voluntary or passion-induced. It is hard to imagine an enraged person who is about to inflict mortal harm considering whether he should or should not commit the crime because of a potential harsh penalty inflicted upon him if he's caught and convicted. If he is thinking at all, he may be contemplating his ability to pay a qualified attorney.

Of course the irony is that an individual with the financial wherewithal to shop nationwide for an attorney is not likely to end up on death row anyway. However, our frustration at watching wealthy people escape criminal liability can easily excite us to clamor for harsher penalties. But it is the lower economic end of our society which will bear the burden of the harsher penalties.

As a nation, we must also face up to the fact that we do not feel much sympathy for criminals from the lower end of the economic spectrum. "Simple justice" would require an equally effective defense for all criminal defendants. But it is not likely that we will agree to have our taxes increased to allow for the necessary tools to ensure this equity. The moral dilemma is certainly uncomfortable, therefore it is easy to understand why most people do not give much thought to the solution.

The flip side of the money argument is that to ensure that the harsh penalties are carried out, we need to provide funding or adequate police, prosecutors, judges and prisons. As the old saying goes, "there is no such thing as a free lunch."

Are there alternatives to our current practices that would improve the effectiveness of our system?

1. One alternative is to forfeit our rights. We could allow a handful of government officials to decide what is "simple justice." In the abstract, this

is an appealing proposition. Let's be realistic; what are the chances that we will ever be called before our justice system? Also on the positive side, if we rely more on bureaucrats, we will all be more likely to vote in our elections, because we would want to keep all of these current qualified government officials right where they are to ensure that we receive some justice. Of course, the downside is that a jury of our peers may well believe, as some currently do believe, that if we were arrested, then we must be guilty of something. Also, once we give up our rights to the government, it is not likely that we will ever get them back.

We all know that conventional wisdom holds that criminals have way too many rights. What is confusing about the argument that criminals have too many rights is the fact that all of us are potential criminal defendants. Of course, that sad reality is that it is more likely if we are poor or black. However, any one of us could find ourselves before a jury of our peers. At that point in time, the rights we so casually dismissed as being excessive, may not appear as much protection at all.

2. Another point to consider is that we are not executing people in the most effective way. Although I do not believe that capital punishment deters crime, if any deterrence value does exist, then we need to take the next step and make everyone see the execution. This would be necessary to ensure that people learn not to commit violent crimes. Also, if we are going to deter criminals, we need to make the execution hurt and let the suffering last for longer than a few minutes. We need not worry about the costs to carry out the execution. There will be plenty of private companies willing to market the mandatory showing of the execution. We could even impose extra suffering to those criminals foolish enough to attempt to exploit this national audience for their own purposes. The extra suffering would probably ensure a larger audience, but that would be the price we would have to pay. Of course, the danger associated with this strategy is that after one or two mandatory viewings, we may (1) become so sickened that we were condoning the killing of another human being that we would demand an end to such brutality, or (2) we would become desensitized to such violence and the intended deterrence would become ineffective.

3. If we are not in a rush to give up our rights or to make viewing executions mandatory, there are other alternatives. Most people equate prison reform with another way of providing additional perks to prisoners. Yet nothing prevents us from punishing some imprisoned criminals more severely than others. Some privileges in prison could be earned or subject to removal. If it is not cruel and unusual punishment to kill a prisoner, it's not logical that it's cruel and unusual to imprison a criminal with only the bare essentials available.

With the need for retribution or vengeance in mind, society perceives that imprisonment is not enough. Full access to sport facilities, libraries, and air conditioned cells furnished with cable television just does not convince the average citizen that the criminal is being punished. The concept that a criminal who chooses to break the rules of our society is fed, clothed, educated and provided with every modern convenience, at our expense, appears at times to be more than we can provide our own families. One should not be surprised then that when questioned, people support what appears to be a quick and easy solution—kill the scum.

If we as a society want these criminals to suffer, then taking their lives is the least effective way to make them suffer. Guaranteed imprisonment will punish them for much longer; death puts an end to their suffering. Therefore, the death penalty actually runs counter to the retribution purpose of punishment.

The question is not whether we should punish those who break our rules, but how best to punish criminals without sacrificing our values. Officer Macher was correct when he stated that society needs to believe that our criminal justice system is just. The implication is that we need to believe that the punishment fits the crime. Many believe that there is no such thing as too harsh a penalty on some criminals. Therefore, for those of us who oppose the death penalty, the task remains to find punishment to fit the most heinous crimes, and to demonstrate that life in prison is not equivalent to a vacation. Harsh penalties which make the worst criminal's life seem miserable are preferable to sanctioned death.

Additionally, by keeping the criminal alive, we also allow for the possibility that society may benefit from his life. I am not suggesting that the cure for cancer is likely to be discovered by an inmate, but there are other likely contributions such as spiritual, which are within anyone's capacity. Once a man or a woman is imprisoned, he or she does not cease to be human. Their potential for good remains, just as their potential for evil has been demonstrated by their action. Keep in mind that there has never been a pancake made so flat that it did not have two sides. Even if the criminal's action warrants punishment, there will always exist that "other side" which could benefit us all.

One of the greatest (if not the greatest) moral teaching is the New Testament of the Christian Religion. The "eye for an eye, tooth for a tooth" philosophy was specifically refuted. We are instructed to turn the other cheek. It stretches even the wildest imagination to suggest that had Christ been confronted with the suggestion that had violence been inflicted against his loved ones, he would have changed his mind. However, it is easy to imagine Christ's anger toward those who would inflict any senseless violence.

The fight over this issue will be won or lost in our legislatures, but those systems are not perfect. Often, when I would offer alternatives to legislation authorizing the death penalty, many of my colleagues, including members of my own state delegation, would vote with me, but only because of important constituencies. They would state their preferences not to go on record against the death penalty for fear that a future opponent may effectively paint them as "soft" on criminals.

Those who support the death penalty come armed with polling data that mandates that elected representatives support their position because it is the majority position. However, they cannot support their position by showing that mistakes are not made. Anyone familiar with our justice system will attest that it is not perfect. Mistakes do happen. Innocent people are convicted every day of some crime. These convictions occur even though we provide many rights to those accused of committing a crime. Our system usually works very well at ensuring that an accused does obtain a fair trial. However, if we allow killing convicts, and even one of those people convicted is innocent, then we all are guilty of that murder. We should not risk that sin, just to allow ourselves a small feeling of retribution against a few bad people.

Additionally, those who favor the death penalty cannot demonstrate that our society benefits in any way by imposing the death penalty. The death penalty has not magically restored the faith of the majority in our system. If anything, the death penalty only serves to remind us that we are willing, as a society, to tolerate an extreme amount of violence.

It is impossible to take the emotions out of this emotional argument. However, we can insert logic into the debate. Firstly, the death penalty does not deter criminal behavior. Secondly, there is a need to punish, but a more severe punishment is guaranteed confinement. If the debate is switched from whether some criminals deserve to live, to a debate as to how best to punish, then the proponents of the death penalty lose their most effective argument.

Within the debate as to whether we as a society should condone the killing of prisoners, we should never lose sight of the fact that our decision concerning the death penalty cannot be isolated from other social debates. If we choose life for the unborn, can we logically accept death as an alternative for those who have been born? If we are to defend our rights which were fought for by our founding fathers, will we gladly surrender our fundamental rights so that some criminals' deaths can give us the satisfaction of revenge? Contrary to the popular myth, our laws are not there to protect the criminal, but they are in place to protect the innocent. Because we underpay our law enforcement officials and our public defenders, the two main combatants in our criminal system, we invite mistakes. Add the overcrowding of our courts and prisons, and we guarantee mistakes.

Those who support the death penalty are not dim-witted barbarians. Punishment is, in fact, necessary for an ordered community. If, as a society, we have repositioned ourselves to lack confidence in our justice system, then we must be willing to propose solutions. However, if we are willing to utilize the argument that if it was my loved one who was raped and murdered, then I would want revenge, then we must also be willing to accept the argument that if we were falsely accused we would want the chance to correct the mistake. Once a prisoner is dead, we cannot correct that mistake.

If we can agree that punishment is necessary, then we have a chance to reach some other agreements. If we believe the criminals are not punished enough in our current system of confinement, then what would we propose? How severe a confinement would satisfy our sense of retribution? If we can envision such punishment, then we may be close to agreement.

I have suggested that it is possible to consider the death penalty in an emotionally neutral debate. That is not true. My experience in both the state legislature and the federal legislature is that emotions will be considered. However, we can never truly understand our emotions unless we can calmly step back and reflect upon our personal views. Even though I could never change the views of those people left behind after a brutal murder, I was able to calmly discuss our differences. Only good can come from such discussions and we should not shy away from sharing our views with those who disagree.

My opposition to the death penalty was based upon the simple premise that once we as a society decide that life can be taken, then we find ourselves on a very slippery slope. Generally, I supported individual rights over the rights of our government. For example, I opposed gun control. I also voted pro-life which is also considered a conservative issue. However, from the other end of the political beliefs, I generally supported environmental protection which protects our health and safety and essentially our lives. I also opposed the military operations with no clear, defendable national objectives.

As a society, we should measure ourselves by how much we respect life. Except for a few well-established exceptions, such as self-defense, the situation cannot justify society taking a life. Either we respect life or we do not.

The argument that some criminals lives are not worth respecting runs counter to Christ's teaching that, "whatsoever you do to the least of my brothers, so you do unto me." And of course the questions we all must ask, who will judge which lives are worth less than others, and what criteria will be used. I believe such a task is impossible.

Life is a precious gift. We should all value this gift. We demonstrate our appreciation of this gift when we declare that we will not condone the taking of life, even when our own emotional needs are fulfilled.

Harley O. Staggers

Harley Staggers graduated from Harvard University and the West Virginia University Law School. He was the Assistant West Virginia Attorney General from 1977-79, served in the West Virginia State Senate and was a member of the United States Congress from 1982-92. Mr. Staggers is an attorney and partner in the law firm of Staggers and Staggers.

"He never gives up. He's working on his post-execution appeal."

Christian Snyder - "The Optimist"

A LIVING RELIGION

Rabbi Gershon Winkler - "The Murderous Court"

Bill Pelke - "Nana's Legacy"

Father Matthew Regan - "Catholics and the Death Penalty"

Adria Libolt - "Capital Punishment: Sacred Considerations"

RABBI GERSHON WINKLER

"The Murderous Court"

> *A court that has executed someone as*
> *infrequently as once in seven years is a*
> *murderous court; others say, even once in*
> *seventy years.*
>
> Babylonian Talmud, Makot 7a

In the ancient Judaic teachings about life, emphasis is placed primarily on the sanctity of life. Therefore, it was permitted to withhold life-sustaining medicines or equipment from a patient who was dying in immense anguish. Life for the sake of life itself does not hold as much respect in Judaism as does the sacredness of life, the quality of life. Therefore, abortion laws in the Judaic tradition, especially in ancient times, were quite liberal in situations where the woman's emotional or physical life was in danger. Contraception laws were even more liberal and required no qualifications. No woman was obligated to bear children since childbearing can endanger one's life, and any woman who so chose could drink the kosikrin, an ancient potion of herbs that caused sterilization (Babylonian Talmud, Yevamot). On the other extreme, sanctity of life also means that "if the enemies of Israel come and say: 'Surrender one of you to us to be killed and we will spare all of you,' we surrender no one, for no one can say 'my blood is more red than yours'" (Babylonian Talmud, Pesachim 25b). Unfortunately, during the Holocaust many Jewish communal leaders violated this principle and surrendered hundreds in return for the promise that thousands would be spared. In the end, they traded thousands for tens of thousands, and ultimately no one was spared as the Nazi death machine overran all "deals" and agreements.

The principle of "sanctity of life" extends deeply into the severe restrictions governing ancient Judaic laws around capital punishment. It took a minimum consensus of twenty-three judges and a maximum of seventy-one to actually send someone to their death. Jewish jurisprudence did not have room for lawyers, only uninvolved judges whose job it was to interrogate witnesses individually, both those who claimed to have witnessed the crime, and those in defense of the accused. If the witnesses presented contradicting or differing stories, or one claimed to have witnessed the crime at a time when the sun was significantly distant from its position during the time claimed by the other, they are both disqualified (Babylonian Talmud, Sanhedrin 5:3). A minimum of two witnesses was required for capital cases (Torah. Deuteronomy 17:6 and 19:15), and those witnesses who were deemed by the court as living dishonestly or immorally, were also disqualified (Babylonian Talmud, Sanhedrin 3:3).

The proceedings for a capital crime would begin in a semi-circle with a minimum of twenty-three judges, and if they could not all agree on a verdict, two more judges were added, and then another two and another, up to seventy-one (Babylonian Talmud, Sanhedrin 5:5). Each time the court was in conflict about the guilt of the accused, the judges would split into pairs to discuss the case, "and they would abstain from eating excessively and from drinking wine, and they would deliberate all night, rise early in the morning and return to the court to present their opinions."If the decision of "guilty" was reached, they would suspend the verdict yet another day and deliberate during the entire period until then, again abstaining from excessive eating and from intoxicating beverages while they re-examined their decision (Babylonian Talmud, Sanhedrin 5:5). Three scribes were assigned to the proceedings, one to record the arguments of those in favor of conviction, one to record the arguments of those in favor of acquittal, and a third to record both arguments, pro and con (Babylonian Talmud, Sanhedrin 4:3).

> If twelve of the judges are in favor of acquittal and eleven are in favor of conviction, we acquit. Twelve find guilty and eleven find not guilty, and even if eleven favor conviction and eleven favor acquittal and the twenty-third is indecisive, or even if twenty-two favor acquittal or conviction, and one is indecisive, we add two more judges to the case up to seventy-one. If thirty-six favor acquittal and thirty-five favor conviction, not guilty. If thirty-five favor acquittal and thirty-six favor conviction, they discuss one with the other until those in favor of acquittal can sway those in favor of conviction (or until there is at least a majority of one in favor of acquittal).
>
> Babylonian Talmud, Sanhedrin 5:5

Once an individual judge had decided on acquittal, he could not rule differently even if he'd changed his mind. However, a judge who had decided on a conviction could change his opinion in favor of acquittal and it would count. This rule applied solely in cases involving capital offenses, further demonstrating how the ancient rabbis bent over backwards to prevent execution and to make certain of the guilt of the accused in situations calling for capital punishment. "Cases involving monetary matters are opened with arguments for both non-liability and liability; cases involving capital offenses are opened only with arguments for acquittal In monetary cases, those who argue non-liability may change their stance and argue liability; in capital offense cases, those who argue acquittal cannot change their stance and argue conviction. No cases are argued on the eve of either the Sabbath or a festival" (Babylonian Talmud, Sanhedrin 4:1). The second century Rabbi Akiva ruled that once a court has sentenced someone to death, the judges involved must taste neither food nor drink on the day of the execution, basing his ruling on the scriptural law forbidding Jews to eat anything mixed with blood (Sifra on Torah: Leviticus 19:26). The taking of life was not perceived as a light matter in the eyes of these masters of the Judaic spirit path.

Even upon conviction, the execution procedure was set up in such a way that allowed for last-minute testimonies or evidence or change of heart on the part of the judges or the witnesses. The accused was led to the house of execution, which was situated a significant walking distance from the court house, so that in the event new evidence had come up, there would be time to halt the execution. The court would also assign someone to walk the streets announcing the pending execution so that anyone who had favorable testimony to offer might step forward and prevent the judgment from being carried out.

One man was assigned to stand outside the house of judgment holding a scarf in his hand. Another was assigned to ride a horse at some distance within a range that allowed him to see the man with the scarf. Should a new witness come forward with favorable testimony on behalf of the accused, the man with the scarf waves to the man on the horse who then rides speedily to stop the execution. And even if the accused himself claims to have thought of some new evidence in his favor, they halt the procession and return him to the house of judgment.

And this they do even if it happens four or five times...And criers are sent out before him, announcing: "So-and-so the son of so-and-so has been convicted of such-and-such capital offense and is being led to the house of execution! So-and-so and so-and-so are the witnesses against him! All who have

> testimony in his favor, step forward now and
> testify!"
>
> Babylonian Talmud, Sanhedrin 6:1

These teachings do not rule out capital punishment, but they certainly made it close to impossible to sentence someone to death, did everything possible to delay execution, and leaned toward every possibility of acquittal rather than seeking conviction. In our own time, these rules would appear politically incorrect, albeit reasonably compassionate; two thousand years ago, however, they were extraordinarily compassionate, and reflect an attempt at wrestling a balance between respect for the sanctity of life and respect for the needs of society.

All of these sources clearly describe a system of jurisprudence that raises serious questions about the contention of the Christian tradition surrounding the death of Jesus. First, no rabbinic court could have condemned him for anything he did or said, since even a cursory examination of the Talmud yields narratives about rabbinic acts and teachings that virtually parallel those of Jesus. Second, even if he had been indicted for crimes deserving of capital punishment, there was no rabbinic court in Jerusalem to try him.

Anyone who examines the teachings of the rabbis in Jesus' time will discover to their amazement a Judaism that would never have tolerated crucifixion, let alone a trial that would have taken place on the eve of a festival, let alone a trial for a capital offense that would have lasted less than thirty minutes. Most importantly, they would discover a Judaism that paralleled rather than contradicted anything Jesus said or did.

Where, then, does Judaism stand on capital punishment, today? No more cut-and-dry than it did thousands of years ago, because Judaism does not seek absolute, one-size-fits-all solutions, not in its jurisprudence and not in its spiritual teachings. Life is dynamic and each situation needs to be wrestled, assessed and examined independent of any other situation regardless of similarity. This principle applies even more stringently to the question of capital punishment, as the ancient sources demonstrate.

Nobody was ever executed without trial, and trials for capital punishment, as the sources from that era clearly indicate, were extremely arduous, to the point that very few courts ever actually got to execute anyone, and those few courts who did manage a consensus for conviction that resulted in execution were called "murderous courts."

Gerson Winkler is a rabbi serving the Jewish communities of the Four Corners region of New Mexico and Colorado, and is a volunteer chaplain for several prisons in both states. Rabbi Winkler has authored 8 books, including 4 works on Jewish mysticism, philosophy and folklore. He was ordained by the late Rabbi Eliezer Bentseon Bruk and Rabbi Zalman Schachter-Shalomi, grandfather of the Jewish Renewal movement.

BILL PELKE

"Nana's Legacy"

On May 14th, 1985, four ninth grade students from Lew Wallace High School in Gary, Indiana decided to skip school during their lunch hour.

They drank some wine and smoked some marijuana. They began to think about what they would do for the rest of the day. They wanted to play video games at the local arcade but they didn't have any money.

April Beverly came up with an idea: There's an old lady who lives catercorner across the alley from me. She teaches Bible lessons and she lives alone. I think she has money. If you three go knock on her door and say you would like to take her Bible lessons, she'll probably let you in. Then you can rob her. Since she would recognize me, I'll stay outside as a lookout.

The three other girls, Denise Thomas, Karen Korders and Paula Cooper knocked on Ruth Pelke's door. She answered it. The girls told her they would like information about her Bible lessons. She invited them into her home.

Ruth Pelke was 78 years old and for all of her life had been faithful to the many services that her church offered. She also taught neighborhood children Bible lessons called Child Evangelism. I remember her telling those stories when I was a child. She used a flannel graph board and cut out pictures to represent Bible characters. I remember especially the stories of Joseph, his coat of many colors and how his jealous brothers had sold him into slavery. I remember the stories of David, the shepherd boy who slew the giant Goliath, and how he later became the King of Israel. I remember the stories about Jesus and His disciples.

Ruth Pelke was my grandmother. To our family she was known as Nana.

At the age of 78, Nana no longer had many opportunities to tell children about Jesus, so she welcomed the opportunity to witness to these young girls. As Nana turned her back to get information for them, one of the girls grabbed a vase off of an end table and hit her over the head. As Nana fell to the floor, Paula produced a 12" butcher knife and began to stab her.

Denise and Karen began to ransack the house looking for money. They weren't finding much. Then Paula began to look for money while Karen took over with the knife. Karen held the knife in Nana. April left her lookout post and joined in the search for money.

The girls ended up with about ten dollars and Nana's ten year old car. Several of the girls drove her car back to Lew Wallace High School and took other classmates joy riding.

Nana died. Two days later the girls were arrested for their roles in the crime.

July 11, 1986 was the sentencing hearing for Paula Cooper. The other three girls had already been sentenced for their roles in the robbery/murder. April Beverly, the neighbor girl who had set Nana up, received a 25 year sentence. Denise Thomas was sentenced to 35 years; she was accused of being the one who hit Nana in the head with the vase. Denise was only 14 years old when the crime was committed. Karen Korders was sentenced to sixty years. Karen was accused of turning and twisting the knife in Nana for 15-20 minutes.

The prosecution had sought the death penalty for Karen, but the judge deemed that Karen was under the influence of a dominating person, Paula Cooper, and elected not to sentence her to death. There was no jury; it was the judge's call.

Paula Cooper's sentencing hearing lasted about 4 hours. It is a day I will never forget.

I had not been to the trials of the first three girls, but for some reason I felt like I needed to take off work and be there for Paula's. If Paula received a death sentence, she would be the youngest female on death row in America. Because Paula was only 15, I didn't think the judge would sentence her to death.

The prosecution argued strongly for the death penalty. They insisted that the judge sentence Paula to death for her part in this heinous crime. Paula was accused of stabbing Nana 33 times. Paula's attorney, a public defender, argued for her life to be spared. Paula had plead guilty and there had been no plea bargain for a lesser sentence.

I watched as my father testified for the prosecution. He spoke of the circumstances of finding Nana's body. I watched as he reviewed pictures of the crime scene. What my father saw the day he discovered Nana's body is something that no man should ever have to bear. For him to live that same scene over and over again in his mind was continued torture. With God's help my dad was able to bear that heavy load through five different trials and hearings.

The bottom line for the sentencing hearing was what stood out most in the newspaper headlines the next day: COOPER SENTENCED TO DEATH.

Life goes on. By November, I had put the murder and trials on a back burner. My personal life was about to explode. My girlfriend Judy and I had broken up about six weeks earlier by mutual agreement. Although we had dated for quite some time, we were both agreeable to move on in different directions .

Shortly after the breakup, I began to realize that was not what I really wanted. I began to see that I loved her a whole lot more than I had ever realized, and I missed the relationship that we once had, and wanted it back. Judy did not see it that way. She did not feel the relationship was going anywhere and was beginning to enjoy the freedoms of being unattached.

When I drove to work on November 2, 1986, I was broken hearted. For the three weeks leading up to this day, I had been doing something I hadn't done very often for the past ten years. I was stumbling in deep depression and had been doing a lot of praying. It was the only way to find any peace. I had to pray to keep my sanity. God was the only one I could talk to, cry to and share my burdens with.

I had been working for Bethlehem Steel for over twenty years in the crane and tractor unit. When I got to work for the 3-11 shift, I was told my services as a crane operator would be needed in a certain section of the mill. I took my overhead crane to the area I had been instructed to go to, and looked for the workers who were to be there needing crane assistance. No one was there. I had some free time.

In despair over my relationship with Judy, I began to cry and pray again. I asked God why, why, why? Why my life, why this broken heart, why, why, why?

I began to think of other things in my life that had not worked out well. My childhood sweetheart Jane and I were engaged a year and a half before I was drafted. After basic training and advanced training for light weapons infantry, I went to Viet Nam. She wrote me every day for the first seven months I was there, but when I came home after a one year tour of duty, she was engaged to someone else. I thought I had pretty well forgotten about that terrible time, but now I was asking God why did that relationship end the way it did. Why, why why?

I began to think about the terrible time I had in Viet Nam. On occasions I could have easily been killed. Why didn't I die? Did I live only so I could experience the bad times which suddenly seemed to add up so quickly? Why was I only wounded and not killed. Why, why, why? Why had I seen so many others killed?

Another big one hit me.

I had married on the rebound of the Jane breakup. It was okay for a while. There were a lot of good reasons for the marriage, but there was only one right reason and I guess I didn't have it.

After about five years of marriage, I went to Bible College. After I graduated, the marriage went straight downhill. On paper the marriage lasted for fourteen years. In reality it lasted much less. The divorce was friendly, but she got custody of the children and it crushed me not being able to raise my three kids. I asked God why, why, why?

I also asked God about the bankruptcy I had to file after the divorce because my finances were in such a mess, and why I had even gone to Bible College. Why all that time and effort? After getting my degree I just continued working in the mill. Why?

And then I began thinking about the most recent and worst blow of all, my grandmother's death. It all came off the back burner. I asked God why had he permitted one of His most special angels to die such a horrendous death? Why did our family, a good family, have to suffer the pain that we all had endured?

I had been in tears since I had first started praying about my situation with Judy, and as I thought of Nana the tears were flowing down my cheeks.

While wallowing in my own self pity, I suddenly pictured somebody with a whole lot more problems than I. I pictured Paula Cooper. I pictured a young girl, slunk in the corner of her death row cell, with tears in her eyes, looking up at nothing and moaning what have I done, what have I done?

My mind flashed back to the day Paula was sentenced to death. Her parents were not even there for this most important day in her life. I recalled Paula's grandfather at the trial. As the judge was in the middle of delivering his sentence, the old man began to cry and wail, "They're going to kill my baby, they're going to kill my baby." The judge ordered the bailiff to remove him from the courtroom as it was disrupting his court. I saw the tears running down his cheeks as he was led from the proceedings.

I recalled that as the trial ended, Paula was led away to death row. There were tears running down her cheeks too and onto her light blue prison dress, causing dark blotches all over the front of her dress.

There is a very beautiful picture that was taken a year and a half before my grandmother was killed. Whenever the media did a story about Nana's murder, the subsequent trials and Paula's death sentence, they used that particular picture. As I sat in the crane, I envisioned an image of Nana, in the likeness of that photograph but with one distinct difference. I pictured Nana with tears streaming out of her eyes and rolling down her cheeks.

I had been in tears for about fifteen or twenty minutes, but when I pictured Nana's tears it deepened my pain ten fold. I knew those tears of Nana's were tears of love and compassion for Paula and her family. I knew that Nana would not have wanted the grandfather to go through the death row scene. Paula's uncle and sister were at the trial and also pleaded for the judge to spare Paula's life. I knew Nana would not want them suffering Paula's execution. And I knew Nana would not have wanted Paula put to death, even though Paula had killed her.

I began to think about Nana and her faith in Jesus. I began to think about what Jesus had to say about forgiveness. I was raised in a home and church that taught the Bible, and I immediately thought of three incidences that Jesus taught about forgiveness. I thought about His teachings from the Sermon on the Mount. He taught we must forgive. I also recalled about Jesus talking to his disciples about forgiveness and how He stated that we should forgive seventy times seven. I knew that meant don't quit forgiving after 490 times; I knew it meant forgiveness was to be a way of life. I also recalled and pictured Jesus when He was crucified. I pictured the nails in His hands and feet and I pictured the crown of thorns on His brow and pictured Him looking up to Heaven and saying, Father forgive them for they know not what they do.

I felt Paula did not know what she was doing. Anyone in their right mind does not stab someone with a 12" butcher knife 33 times.

I had to admit to myself at that point that forgiving was the right thing to do and I would try and do that for Nana's sake. I once again pictured Nana and those tears rolling down her cheeks, tears of love and compassion. I felt that she wanted someone in our family to have that same love and compassion. I felt like it fell on my shoulders. It seemed too heavy a burden to bear. My tears continued to flow.

Even though I knew forgiveness was the right thing, as far as love and compassion, I had none. After all, my grandmother had been brutally murdered. The chief of police for Gary, Indiana, Virgil Motely, said it was the most heinous crime he had ever seen in his 35 years on the force. For two years in a row, Gary, Indiana had been the murder capital of the USA. He had seen his share.

Nana's tears dictated to me that I try to generate some sort of love and compassion and so, with nowhere else to turn, I started praying again. In tears I begged God to please give me love and compassion for Paula Cooper and her family. I begged on behalf of Nana.

My next thoughts were that I could write Paula and tell her about Nana and her faith in Jesus. I thought I could also write about God's love for her, and His forgiveness for her. I even thought I could tell Paula that through Jesus I had love for her. I thought about contacting her grandfather.

It was at this point that I realized my prayer for love and compassion for Paula Cooper and her family had been answered. Two things were immediately clear to me. I realized what is the most important lesson I have learned in my life. When God granted my request of love and compassion, the forgiveness was automatic. It wasn't something I had to do, God did the work. The second was that I no longer wanted Paula to die.

When Paula was sentenced to death, I had no problem with it. I knew people were being sentenced to death and being executed around our country. I felt if they didn't give the death sentence in Paula's case, then they were telling me and my family that Nana was not an important enough person to merit the death penalty, and I felt my grandmother was a very important person.

Basically my opinion of the death penalty was whatever the law called for was okay with me. When the Supreme Court said the death penalty was unconstitutional, that was fine with me. When the death penalty was reinstated, that was also fine with me. Whatever the law called for was fine with me.

With the granting of the love and compassion, and not wanting Paula to die any longer, I began to believe that it was terribly wrong for the State of Indiana to take her life. I wanted to help her in that area, but I didn't have any idea how.

I began to think about what others would think. After all, I had just made a 180 degree turn. What would my family think? My father had testified in court that it would be a travesty of justice if Paula did not receive the death penalty. What would my friends think? What would my co-workers think? Many of the people I worked with would say as a means of condolence about Nana's death: "I hope the bitch burns." I knew some were not going to understand how I now felt. I knew it would be the same with friends outside the mill.

But I also knew the beauty of God's love and compassion and the forgiveness it brought. I knew I had done the right thing and I would just try to get the others to understand it. I was sure I was right.

From the day of Nana's murder until this moment in the crane, the thought of Nana tore my soul. When I thought of her, I pictured her laying butchered on the dining room floor.

For fifteen to twenty minutes Karen Korders had twisted and turned the knife in Nana, and in fact the carpet beneath her body was shredded and the hardwood floor under the carpet was splintered. The thought of Nana butchered tore me up.

Suddenly, after learning the lesson of forgiveness, I began to picture Nana in a beautiful way. The way she lived and what she stood for and who she was. It was such a relief to see her that way. I knew I would no longer picture her dead on the floor again.

This beautiful experience of forgiveness and peace was not something meant just for me, but it was something to be shared with others. With all of the media coverage on Nana's death and Paula's life, I began to realize that they may also be interested in why I had forgiven Paula and was wanting to help her. A white man forgiving and wanting to help save the life of a black girl who had killed his grandmother. I was sure it wasn't something that happened every day.

I began praying again and I made God two promises that I have kept to this day. I knew that I could not take any credit for forgiving Paula, that it was only because God touched my heart, so I promised God that any success that came into my life as a result of forgiving Paula Cooper, I would give God the honor and glory.

I also promised God that although I didn't know why this experience had taken place or what its results would bring, that I would walk through any door that was opened as a result of forgiving Paula.

My tears were now dry. My life had been changed in a period of 45 minutes. The workers who were to require my services as a crane operator never showed up. I walked down the stairs of my crane to the floor a new man, no longer defeated but victorious. I knew I was a man with a mission.

The four months that followed my night in the crane saw many interesting things happen. I began a letter writing exchange with Paula. I let her know that God cared for her and loved her and that I did too. We exchanged letters about every ten days and we established that we would like to visit and meet each other. I shared Nana's faith with her. It was difficult to write at first and many tears often hit the pages, tears of joy knowing that I could truly love someone who had caused our family such pain. I always prayed to God before I wrote Paula and asked Him to guide me and help me say the right things, the things that needed to be said.

I was still trying to get the relationship back together with Judy. It was very difficult, but the lessons I learned that night in the crane helped me gain strength. Forgiveness had started to become a philosophy to me as a way of life. I became a different person because of my honing of the forgiveness experience.

I also learned about determination. I had been pretty stubborn most of my life. That night I began to see the difference between the two and I chose determination. Those two lessons alone helped keep the relationship between Judy and me at the point where there was still hope.

Judy was aware of my night in the crane experience and of the letter writing relationship that Paula and I had developed. She, of course, questioned my philosophic changes; although I had an answer for every one of them, some must have seemed pretty far out to her.

I had the opportunity to meet Paula's grandfather shortly before Christmas. I took a basket of fruit to his house and spent several wonderful hours talking and looking through the old family albums. There were pictures of Paula as she was growing up. She had been a very cute little girl.

I had also informed my parents that I was corresponding with Paula. They did not understand why, but my dad did say, "Well, do what you have to do." I thanked him for that.

Few other people knew about my relationship with Paula, maybe about 10 of my co-workers and friends.

About five weeks after my crane experience, I wrote an article for the "Voice Of The People" section of the Gary Post Tribune. It talked about love, prayer and forgiveness for Paula. It stated that Nana knew that was the answer.

The reason I wrote it was because I ran into a friend I hadn't seen for some time at a restaurant in town. His first words to me were, "I hope the bitch fries." I looked at him and said, "I don't," and then I went on to tell him what had happened that night in the crane. When I had finished he looked at me and said, "I don't want her to die anymore either. You ought to write and say something in the "Voice Of The People."

There had been dozens of letters written to "Voice Of The People" after Nana's murder, the trials, and Paula's death sentence. When I sent my article in, I had hoped it might open some dialogue on either the subject of the death penalty for juveniles or on forgiveness. I read the section every day for a response. I continued to check it out for three months, and for some reason, all articles on Paula and the death penalty stopped.

There was one very important result. After the article appeared, I came home from a Sunday night church service and was told by my friend Gene, with whom I was sharing an apartment, that a lady journalist from Italy had called and would call back later that night.

Anna Guaita called me back that evening and explained that she was an Italian Journalist and that she and a colleague, Giampalo Palli, were coming to Indiana to do a story on Paula Cooper.

It was headlines in the Italian newspaper when Paula was sentenced to death. The Italians, who do not have a death penalty, could not understand why the State of Indiana would want to execute someone who was only 15 years old. With all the murders that take place in America, why was this young black girl sentenced to the electric chair? They wanted to know what punishment the parents received.

The Italian people were fascinated with this story and Anna and her friend were coming to Indiana to do interviews. Their stories would run in the three largest Italian newspapers.

Anna had called the Gary Post Tribune and asked for leads in who they should interview for their story. She was advised about Paula's attorney, her grandfather, several others and about a grandson of the victim who had written a letter to "Voice Of The People" and talked about forgiveness. Anna explained to me on the phone that Italians don't picture Americans as being a very forgiving people, so she wanted to interview me. Of course I jumped through the open door. I had been waiting a long time for her to call; I just didn't know it until it happened.

Anna turned out to be a great person and we had a wonderful interview. We talked for hours. Their stories about Paula's case, including interviews with Paula, myself and others, were spread over two days in the Italian papers.

Then an Italian TV station called. They were doing a segment on Paula's case and wanted to know if I would come to Rome to be on it. Of course, I jumped through that open door. One of the reasons I wanted to go was that when Anna had finished the interview with me, she mentioned that over 40,000 people, mostly Italian school children, had signed petitions to have Paula taken off death row. I wanted to go and thank each one of them. When the American press found out that I was going to Italy, it became a media event.

The Gary Post Tribune ran the front page story: PELKE'S GRANDSON GOES TO ROME ON COOPER'S BEHALF. Three Chicago TV stations did interviews before I left.

During my time in Italy, I had constant calls from the American press. Every day the Gary Post, the Associated Press or someone would call wanting updated information on my trip, and it was a chance to talk about love, compassion and forgiveness. It was a chance to talk about Nana. It was a chance to talk about God and Jesus Christ. I loved every minute.

Judy and I were married on October 1, 1988, and we went to Italy for our honeymoon. Judy's mother was happy to accept our invitation for her to join us. Judy's mother had thought I was crazy for forgiving Paula, so inviting her along made me look a little better as her new son-in-law. It was a dream vacation for her. Judy and I had a wonderful honeymoon. I met many of the friends from my first visit to Rome and we all had a great time.

About nine months after we were married, I was at work, talking to Judy on the telephone, when she told me there was a beep on her end of the line. She put me on hold for a moment, then came back to say that someone from the Associated Press wanted to talk to me. The Associated Press had done a very nice story about my involvement with Paula. It was complete with pictures and it had run in newspapers throughout the country. When the reporter called me at work, he informed me that the Indiana Supreme Court had just overturned Paula's death sentence. The AP wanted a comment from me. The first thing I said was, "Praise the Lord!"

What a period of rejoicing I went through for a number of days. I was extremely happy that Paula was now off of death row, though it might be two months before all the paper work was completed and she could move into general population. The pressure of being on death row could now ease up for Paula, although she had learned to handle things very well. About five or six people had taken Paula under their wings and showed love and compassion to her. They all helped Paula plant the seed of hope within herself. She was responding to that love with love.

And Nana? I haven't pictured her in tears since the night on the crane ten years ago. When I picture her now she is smiling and happy and, I believe, proud of what I am doing.

Bill Pelke worked for over 20 years for Bethlehem Steel. In 1985, his grandmother was murdered by 4 teenaged girls, one of whom received a death sentence from the state of Indiana. Mr. Pelke became convinced that forgiveness was the answer to this family tragedy, and he began a correspondence with his grandmother's murderer, eventually working to overturn her death conviction. He is an active member of Murder Victims Families for Reconcilation.

FATHER MATTHEW REGAN

"Catholics and the Death Penalty"

The Jesuit periodical <u>America</u>, of 14 December 1996, has the former Provincial Superior of that order in the Netherlands, Father Jan Van Deenen, SJ, responding to this question: "As a visitor to the United States, what are your impressions of life here?" His answer: "Formerly, the enemy was Communism. Now it's immigrants and people of color. 'They are other than me, they are threats to my security and my ability to get ahead' is the feeling. Out of it comes the American reliance on prisons and on the death penalty."

I am not sure how long Father Van Deenen was in the United States when he made these remarks, but he very pithily digests thoughts I have had off and on for over twenty years. There is, indeed, a "trajectory"—a "continuum"—relative to fear of persons who are different, represented by the permanent underclass. This includes aliens, be they legal or illegal; people of another skin color; slum dwellers; teen-aged mothers, wed or unwed; addicts of any sort; the homeless; the retarded; and presumed killers (found guilty of anything from technical manslaughter through first degree murder).

In January 1989, the Roman Catholic bishops of California stated: "...capital punishment is not the best response we can make as a society to violent or even heinous crime...We dare to...raise this challenge because of our commitment to a consistent ethic of life by which we wish to give unambiguous witness to the sacredness of every human life from conception through natural death, and to proclaim the good news that no person is beyond the redemptive mercy of God."

To sentence someone to death is the obvious end-point of the continuum of trying to justify the slogan "out of sight—out of mind." Interviewed in the 9 November 1996 issue of <u>America</u>, Sister Helen Prejean, CSJ, author of <u>Dead Man Walking</u>, says, "Middle- and upper-middle-class white people...[who] live in the suburbs are for the death penalty. 'Keep those dangerous people in their place.' And they think the same about people in the inner city."

For a murderer to kill another person is for that person to unilaterally decide—at least implicitly—that the one killed has no value. For a state of our country or the federal government or any armed service thereof to legally and intentionally kill anyone, is for the representatives of whatever government or service to make the same judgment of worthlessness against the one killed. Any citizen of our nation agreeing with such a decision is also, implicitly, a killer.

The Roman Catholic bishops of New York State said in February 1994: "Capital punishment is a particularly egregious violation of our dignity as citizens because it is our government, acting on behalf of each of us... involved in the business of killing. Killing our brothers and sisters is a rejection of God's call to 'love one another as I have loved you.'

Death is never the answer...A state-sanctioned penalty of death makes the individual on whom it is inflicted a means to an end—a means of satisfying a desire for revenge. Human persons, because of their absolute and unconditional value, may never be used as a means."

The opposite of love is hate. There is an inexorable logic about the emotion undergirding any person who so denigrates another human being as to make that person so worthless the person should not live. The hate implied or expressed succeeds in ensuring that there will indeed be no possibility of change or transformation—in religious terms, of conversion or repentance—within the person killed, no possibility of a self-discovery which can be redemptive, both for the condemned person and for those in touch with him or her, and perhaps even further afield.

Given the horrendous increase in violence and the enormity of the results of this violence in our homes and schools and streets, the decade of the 1990s may be characterized as the "fear decade." On 30 November 1992, the Roman Catholic bishops of the State of Washington said: "Heinous crimes cause fear, anger, frustration and outrage. And justifiably so. We have reason to fear, however, that capital punishment can itself be the occasion for a public and state-sanctioned expression of vindictiveness and hatred which further brutalizes our society." In distinction from the so-called "gay nineties" of one hundred years ago, we now know, almost before incidents occur, the sordidness, frustration and desperation of the lives of the underclass of today's world. The "gay-ness" of the 1890s existed alongside remarkable slums, and a stupendous lack of opportunities and of justice. With rare exceptions, in the 1890's obliviousness of such conditions was normative because there was no immediacy of media consciousness via radio or TV or FAX or Internet, etc. Poverty and the powerlessness it represents cannot be avoided today, in spite of the so-called Welfare Reform Bill of September 1996, a Republican vehicle signed into law by a Democratic president. That watershed essentially posited that the scapegoating of the disadvantaged is needed to ensure that the freedom and opportunity and welcome symbolized by the Statue of Liberty not be carried too far!

Nat Hentoff, in the Hayward, California <u>Daily Review</u> of 5 January 1995, wrote: "Republican and Democratic candidates ran (in November 1994) as if expanding and hastening the death penalty would solve most of the nation's problems." Indeed, the surest way to be elected today, be this in California, New York State, Arkansas, or wherever, is to make sure that the ultimate in scapegoating—simple elimination from the face of the earth, killing because someone has been found guilty of having killed—be the order of the day.

Mr. Hentoff quotes the present governor of New York, George Pataki, a "good" Roman Catholic, as saying: "There's no question in my mind that the death penalty saves lives." Pataki's severely pro-death penalty platform defeated another "good" Roman Catholic, Mario Cuomo, who yearly, as governor, vetoed the legislature's vote for death penalty reinstatement. Hentoff describes Pataki's above stance as "the cherished myth of deterrence. Kill the killer and you'll stop those who would emulate him in their tracks."

I excuse in no way the killing of any person by another. Such an act is the most outrageous of human actions possible, if for no other reason than its finality, whatever one's belief in the "after-life" may be. One of the most enlightening and informative parts of the book <u>Dead Man Walking</u>, and of the movie of the same title, is the growing awareness on the part of Sister Prejean of the feelings of those who mourn people who have been killed. The need to minister to these as well as to the people found guilty of having killed would be an utter absurdity to gainsay. But to deny or restrict habeas corpus opportunities to death row inmates or others in prison can hardly be dignified as "ministry" to those who are saddened, very justifiably, by the deaths of loved ones. Specifically, I refer to the counter-terrorism bill passed by Congress and signed by the President in October 1996 which, as Anthony Lewis, of the <u>New York Times</u>, states: (guts) "the power of Federal courts to examine state criminal convictions on writs of habeas corpus, to make sure there was no violation of constitutional rights."

I guess, at a very basic, human, "gut" level, to be present at the "legal killing" of the one who has presumably killed one's daughter or son or spouse or parent or friend can bring some closure to the situation, at least for a brief moment. My own "gut" feeling, however, is that vengeance never really satisfies, simply because it writes off another human being whom the creator considered good—by electrocution or a deadly injection or by being hanged or shot or gassed. And beyond any gut feeling, at least for people calling themselves Christian, is the fact that Jesus Christ is reported to have said: "You have heard it said—you must love your friends and hate your enemies. But I say—love your enemies and do good to those who hate you."

And we know Jesus' utterance from the cross about his killers—"Father, forgive them—they do not know what they do." Do we realize that Jesus Christ represents the epitome of the injustice and vindictiveness and wastefulness that is capital punishment?

The Roman Catholic bishops of Kansas stated in January 1994: "The death penalty takes us down the wrong road of life. It fuels vengeance, diverts from forgiveness and greatly diminishes respect for all human life. We affirm strongly that the life of every person, regardless of the status or condition of that person, is in the hands of God. We affirm that each person created in the image...of God is of inestimable dignity and shares in the 'death penalty' of Jesus on Calvary." Bishop Daniel Reilly of Norwich, Connecticut, on 28 February 1990, said: "The challenging message of Jesus is that not only are the lives of the ones we love to be valued, but also the lives of our enemies. What stronger determination of the value of life could a society give than by sparing the lives of those who have taken life?"

Recently, we read about the ferocity of the vengeance "motif" as acted out in Afghanistan, and I think we profess at least a modicum of shock when we hear of the hand of a person being chopped off because of that hand's having stolen an apple in other parts of western Asia. But there can be a fascinating "logicality" to such sentences. Is there the same logicality to this...? Right after the "legal killing" (execution is, I think, a very, and almost satisfyingly sanitised word) of an alleged killer, relatives and/or friends say: "Now, finally, she or he (the original victim) can rest in peace!" Isn't this merely another way to express glee at vengeance having been carried out, glee or "rest" or "satisfaction"*for everyone but the original victim*—and the relatives and friends of, and ministers to, the one executed? But, as noted earlier, in this way governors, attornies general, senators, representatives, and even presidents are elected and re-elected!

In Our Sunday Visitor of 11 July 1993, Frank McNeirney, National Coordinator of Catholics Against Capital Punishment (CACP), wrote an article contrasting the execution in Virginia of Edward Fitzgerald, in the summer of 1992, with the sentence given a man called Alessandro Serenelli, who killed a 12 year old girl, Maria Goretti, in 1902. Maria forgave her murderer before she died on the day after his attack. She was declared a saint in 1950. Serenelli's sentence had been 30 years. When he was released three years early, his first act was to visit Maria Goretti's mother and beg her forgiveness. "Subsequently, he worked on behalf of Maria's canonisation, and spent the remaining four decades of his life as a laborer in a Capuchin monastery in Italy...He died in 1970...at age...88. For those who believe in the concepts of repentance and redemption, the story of Serenelli is a powerful argument against the use of the death penalty." McNeirney goes on: "When Eddie Fitzgerald was executed...we as a society...said two things: One, that some people are beyond God's redemptive powers; and two, that we, not God, are the best judges of whether, and how, such individuals will make reparation for their sins. Each of these two statements is a terrible form of blasphemy in the minds of Catholics, other Christians and members of many other religious faiths. Yet our society is guilty of it each time we carry out an execution."

Since the autumn of 1994, I have regularly visited a man on Death Row at San Quentin State Prison in California. We are now close friends. I have become convinced that he is entirely innocent of any of the crimes with which he was charged and found guilty. His name is N. I. Sequoyah. His background as a Native American is Cherokee. As far as I can determine, he is, in the purest sense of the term, a political prisoner. Growing up in Tahlequah, Oklahoma, the city which became the headquarters of the Cherokee Nation after these Native Americans were forced by President Andrew Jackson to travel from North Carolina and Georgia along what became known as the "Trail of Tears" in the 1830s, Sequoyah experienced not only the possibility—but the actuality—of prejudice. After having served honorably as a member of the United States Navy for ten years, he then continued as a non-violent activist, working for equal opportunities for all indigenous peoples. He even developed into a well-known and remarkably fluent Esperantist, having been attracted by the proven ability of the international Esperanto movement to foster unity and peace between and among nationalities and races by providing a neutral common bridge language. Consequent upon these activities of Sequoyah, he became suspect to the extent that, on international travels, he was frequently harassed at country border points at the behest of Intelligence interests of the United States. In 1984 and 1985, Sequoyah founded, in Switzerland, UNAP (United Nations of Autonomous Peoples). When he returned to the United States, Sequoyah was arrested in what was, apparently, a classic Cointelpro (Counter Intelligence Program) operation. He was saddled with many unsolved crimes. International agencies, working for justice for political prisoners, have taken up Sequoyah's cause. These include the Swiss section of Amnesty International and INCOMINDIOS (a Swiss-German acronym for the International Committee for the Indians of the Americas). INCOMINDIOS has proclaimed Sequoyah's innocence and its support of him as a political prisoner. Such a proclamation has been made by the organization for only two Native Americans—Leonard Peltier and N. I. Sequoyah.

The way N. I. Sequoyah and I got in touch is that I was sent a name, at my own request, by Death Row Support Project of Liberty Mills, Indiana, because I thought being a correspondent, a "pen-pal," with someone in a death row would be one tiny action showing, if only to myself, that I was sincere in my conviction that killing is wrong—*period*! It is fortuitous that the death row name given me turned out to be a person whose legal killing would be a pristine injustice, due to Sequoyah's innocence.

I am acquainted with other Death Row inmates at San Quentin, about whose literal guilt or innocence I cannot make a judgement. The fact is that their being killed, as if this were the only way to "protect" society against any further depredations they might try, is clearly contrary to any true assessment of the basic spirit of Christianity. This has been borne out progressively, at least by the leadership in the Christian communion to which I belong—the Roman Catholic—in recent years.

However, one of the immediate problems confronting anyone who attempts to cite a movement towards more compassion on issues of social justice on the part of Roman Catholic church leadership—emanating from Rome itself (the Vatican) or from the United States Conference of Bishops or from bishops of individual dioceses—is that there has been a constant and quite consistent erosion of confidence in and, indeed, respect for, ecclesiastical authority in the Roman Catholic communion, during the past thirty or so years. The reasons for this are, at one level, quite complicated—at another, quite simple. Because a discussion of the former would deflect from the immediate purpose of this paper and the volume in which it is included, suffice it to say that certain decisions and emphases in the teaching of church authorities have come to be treated as ultimately irrelevant in the lives of most church members. This is notably so in the approach to the morality and ethics of sexual behavior generally. Since this particular area is so all-encompassing and immediate in the lives of most church members, there is, apparently, a transfer of the judgement of irrelevance or non-application to other areas, on which a bishop or a group of bishops or the papacy may speak with great articulateness and conviction, but which do not or may not impinge directly on the lives of the Roman Catholic "in the pew." And, of course, there are, partially for the reasons outlined above, many fewer Roman Catholics in the pews these days to even hear, or become aware of, official church stances in various "non-immediate" areas, assuming that these stances are given any emphasis at all "from the pulpit." Abigail McCarthy wrote in the 31 January 1997 magazine <u>Commonweal</u>: "The danger is that the laissez-faire attitude toward sexual teaching may be extended to social teaching. Opposition to capital punishment and a concern for and an obligation to help the poor are, for the majority, no longer considered essential to being a good Catholic."

In the 9 November 1996 <u>America</u> interview cited above, Sister Helen Prejean says: "It's true that the bishops (of the United States) have issued strong statements...But I haven't seen much moral energy coming from them to educate the people in the pews, and priests tend to be afraid of preaching about it (the death penalty). The <u>Times-Picayune</u> of New Orleans interviewed...church leaders about how they handle controversial subjects. Almost all of them said they were personally against the death penalty, but when asked if they would preach about it, they said, 'Not on your life!' They were afraid it would divide their parish communities and hurt the collections...[but] anyone close to the poor and oppressed has a passion for this issue."

Everyone knows about the Crusades and the Inquisition and "autos-de-fe," or can recall at least briefly adverting to these historic instances of Christian and/or Roman Catholic engagement in the occupation of gratuitous killing. One can only wish that such periods in the history of the church of Jesus Christ had not occurred—but they have. However, despite stands taken by some current "Christian" movements of a fundamentalistic nature in our own country, which have become very politically active, and instances such as unbelievably appalling prison conditions in so-called Roman Catholic countries such as Peru, at least Roman Catholic and other "mainline" Christian communions have become closer to the "line" of Jesus Christ in recent decades.

In the Catechism of the Catholic Church, published by the Vatican in 1994, Sections 2258 through 2266 speak specifically of subjects relating to the death penalty.

"2262—In the Sermon on the Mount, the Lord recalls the commandment, 'you shall not kill,' (Mt 5, 21), and adds to it the proscription about anger, hatred, and vengeance. Going further, Christ asks his disciples to turn the other cheek, to love their enemies (Cf Mt 5, 22-39; 5, 44). He did not defend himself and told Peter to leave his sword in its sheath. (Cf Mt 26, 52)."

"2263—The legitimate defense of persons and societies is not an exception to the prohibition against the murder of the innocent that constitutes intentional killing."...[but]..."2266—Preserving the common good of society requires rendering an aggressor unable to inflict harm. For this reason the traditional teaching of the Church has acknowledged the right and duty of legitimate public authority to punish malefactors by means of penalties commensurate with the gravity of the crime, not excluding, *in cases of extreme gravity* (my emphasis), the death penalty...If bloodless means are sufficient to defend the human lives against an aggressor and to protect public order and the safety of persons, public authority should limit itself to such means."

(Interestingly enough, I am, mainly through correspondence, in close touch with another man on San Quentin's Death Row, principally because of an extraordinarily erudite and incisive letter written by him to The London Tablet in a November 1994 issue. His letter critiqued the above Catechism of the Catholic Church for its stance on the death penalty. This particular gentleman, Steven King Ainsworth, is also the reason I am included in this volume, as he, by letter, introduced me to Julie Zimmerman, co-editor of this book and head of Biddle Publishing. He also writes herein and has contributed some moving illustrations to the volume.)

In March 1995, Pope John Paul II issued his encyclical <u>Evangelium Vitae—The Gospel of Life</u>, which took a relatively giant step towards firming up the Roman Catholic Communion's official opposition to the death penalty. Especially relevant are Sections 53 through 57 of Chapter III, entitled <u>You Shall Not Kill</u>. Having reviewed carefully the <u>Catechism of the Catholic Church</u>'s arguments for life, the Pope, in my opinion, nuances them more strongly.

"55—To kill a human being...is a particularly serious sin...Yet there are situations...which...involve a genuine paradox, for example...a true right to self-defense...Unfortunately it happens that the need to render the aggressor incapable of causing harm sometimes involves taking his (sic) life..."

"56—This is the context in which to place the problem of the death penalty. On this matter there is a growing tendency, both in the Church and in civil society, to demand that it be applied in a very limited way or even that it be abolished completely..."

Regrettably, except in the case of offical statements of the Roman Catholic bishops and of other "mainline" Christian church authorities, this "growing tendency" is non-existent in our country. Indeed, the opposite has occurred and continues to occur, especially in the rhetoric of politicians from the White House to the most modest Sheriff's office, in order to be elected or to stay in office. Furthermore, in my experience, the majority of the Roman Catholic laity either have no interest in the death penalty as an issue or are, indeed, in favor of its expanded practice—for purposes of "safety" and because "they (people convicted as killers) don't deserve to live." Again, how different from Jesus' forgiveness of those practicing the death penalty in his own case! In late 1996, Louisville, Kentucky Archbishop Thomas Kelly, OP, said, "No human life, no matter how wretched or how miserable, is without worth."

Complaining that prosecutors in New York City did not "go for" the death penalty in three cases during the latter part of 1996, the <u>New York Daily News</u> said in an editorial quoted in "The Talk of the Town" section of the <u>New Yorker</u> magazine of 25 November, 1996: "What's a guy gotta do to get executed in this town?" The <u>New Yorker</u> goes on: "The prosecutor's reluctance to bring capital charges...probably has as much to do with tactical considerations as with moral ones...A jury might find that 'mitigating factors' outweighed the 'aggravating factors'...Brooklyn's Charles Hynes, District Attorney, says, 'I doubt very much if I'll still be in public life when the first execution in New York State is carried out. *Perhaps the death penalty had to be inacted in order to become irrelevant.' "*(my emphasis)

How good it would be if the majority of Roman Catholics might be able to express themselves as having had an experience similar to Bishop Tod Brown, of Boise, Idaho, who wrote in an article in <u>The Idaho Register</u> on 4 March 1994: "Many years ago...I was an adamant proponent of legalized executions for persons convicted of first degree murder and other capital crimes. My position on capital punishment changed slowly...during the late 60s and early 70s...the argument of respect for God's gift of human life at all stages, from conception to natural death, provided no exception for the execution of convicted capital offenders. The popular argument that the death penalty provided an effective deterrent was not verifiable."

Section 56 of the <u>Gospel of Life</u> goes on: "Public authority must redress the violation of personal and social rights by imposing on the offender an adequate punishment for the crime...*The nature and extent of the punishment must* be carefully evaluated and decided upon, and ought not to go to the extreme of executing the offender except in cases of absolute necessity: in other words, when it would not be possible otherwise to defend society. *Today however, as a result of steady improvements in the organization of the penal system, such cases are very rare, if not practically non-existent.*" (my emphasis) In view of this statement, Cardinal Joseph Ratzinger, the Prefect of the Vatican's Congregation for the Doctrine of the Faith, has stated that in a new edition of the <u>Catechism of the Catholic Church</u>, comments on the death penalty will have to be revised. The big question in my own mind is this: How many Roman Catholics know about, or are at all interested in, what either the <u>Catechism</u> or the Pope says on this life and death subject?

The Pope had also written previously"...Before the moral norm which prohibits the direct taking of the life of an innocent human being there are not privileges or exceptions for anyone. It makes no difference whether one is the master of the world or the 'poorest of the poor' on the face of the earth. Before the demands of morality we are all absolutely equal." (John Paul II, Encyclical letter <u>Veritas Splendor</u> (6 August 1993, 96).

I believe that the connection or continuum between the direct and indirect taking of lives cannot be avoided in reading or reflecting on a statement such as the last two sentences. When are we going to be willing to attack the endemic problems in our own society which result in so many being classified "the poorest of the poor," and not merely impersonally attempt to balance the Federal budget (and now state, county and local city, town and village government budgets) on the backs of these poor, while trying to lower corporate taxes, capital gains taxes, etc? When are we going to stop building more prisons for the mere warehousing of unwanted members of our society, without regard to the intense and necessary rehabilitation of the imprisoned individuals? This mere treating of symptoms instead

of getting to the roots and causes of poverty and indigence and a large growing underclass, which regrettably breed most violent crime, is analogous to
giving aspirin for a persistent headache and not bothering to find out if there
is a tumor growing in the brain and doing something about it.

When are we going to be willing to put aside the present guiding
spirit of international relations—"trade not aid"—and find ways to attack
the abysmal conditions in which the majority of people live in the so-called
developing Third World, without merely saddling these countries with impossible debt structures which, essentially, only bring profits to so-called
First World nations and multi-national corporations?

Since whatever one answers to all these questions refers to life, the
following statement by John Roach, until recently archbishop of St Paul-
Minneapolis, in The Catholic Bulletin of 6 February 1992, has a deep meaning: "We have a very consistent commitment as church to defending the
sanctity of human life. We struggle mightily against abortion; we have a
commitment and concern for the poor; we deplore racial and sexual discrimination and the self-destructive use of drugs. Our position against the
use of the death penalty falls into that continuum. We believe that an issue
such as capital punishment is not just a question of public policy, but is at its
very core a moral issue, and therefore a religious issue, and we must speak
to it. The death penalty adds to the cycle of violence rather than diminishing
it. Killing just isn't the solution to killing."

Ending these reflections, I can do no better than to make my own this
statement of Bishop Walter Sullivan and Auxiliary Bishop David Foley of
the Richmond, Virginia diocese, and of seventeen other religious leaders in
the state, issued in January 1993: "The preeminent moral argument against
the death penalty is that...state-sanctioned killing weakens respect for human life. As a society, our attempts to encourage a respect for human life
will not be credible until we repudiate the death penalty."

Matthew R.D. Regan, a priest of the Archdiocese of Castries, Saint Lucia in the West Indies,
is a priest in residence at Saint Leander's Parish, San Leandro, California. Father Regan is
a full-time preacher on behalf of Food For the Poor, an ecumenical, non-profit organization headquartered in Florida, which aids the desperately poor in the Caribbean area and
Central America. He is a weekly visitor to Death Row at San Quentin State Prison.

Catechism of the Catholic Church, Liguori Publications Liguori, Missouri,
        63057, 1994.
The Gospel of Life (Evangelium Vitae—by Pope John Paul II, Random House
        (Times books) New York 1995.
All the quotations from bishops are from various issues of the Newsletter of
        Catholics Against Capital Punishment, Arlington, Virginia.

ADRIA LIBOLT

"Capital Punishment: Sacred Considerations"

You brought out feelings in me I didn't know a human being could have...
how to hate, that I could kill you little by little, one piece at a time...
I hope the Lord can forgive me for how I feel about you...P.S. May you burn in hell.
> Sandra Miller to William Bonin, who murdered her 15-year old
> son, Rusty Rugh, after beating and sexually assaulting him.
> Bonin was executed on February 23, 1995

Religious attitudes toward capital punishment are complex and deeply shaped by our personal experience. Sandra Miller, mother of a victim of a brutal murder, wants the Lord's forgiveness (or indulgence) for her desire for vengeance and, since she is powerless to carry out that vengeance, the Lord's help on the other side—("May you burn in hell"). Sister Prejean, the author of <u>Dead Man Walking</u>, represents a different set of experiences. She, an opponent of capital punishment, has had her views shaped in part by her experience in providing spiritual counsel to a convicted murderer, Patrick Sonnier, shortly before he was executed. For her the crucial question is the redemption of the murderer.

The Christian tradition, which I represent, is broad with respect to such issues as capital punishment, embracing both passionate advocates of the practice and equally passionate opponents. Often, personal experience, prejudice, and social background determine the position a person takes. Religious reflection is secondary, used to justify whatever position the person has already adopted. Or, at least, so it seems.

But a tradition is like a gently flowing river. Each of us, swimmers in the stream, seems free to make up our own mind and swim in our own direction, and yet, when we look around, we see that we have moved downstream, swept by the slow but powerful current. My interest in this essay is not the opinion of individual Christians or even the mass of them, but the direction of the stream. What does the Christian, Biblical tradition have to say about capital punishment?

The Bible is a book both of God and of the community. The community has a certain historical setting and historical attitudes toward such matters as punishment and, in particular, capital punishment. To take a single example, the Biblical regulatory principle, "an eye for an eye, a tooth for a tooth," is not originally a call for vengeance but a limitation of vengeance to the harm done. In a society without a formal system of justice, in which one murder called for two, one knocked-out tooth for a mouthful, such a principle brought some semblance of lawfulness to the relationship between crime and punishment. The bulk of Biblical regulation follows this pattern: adopting the general standards of punishment of the time and place, it regulates these standards and provides for exceptions and mitigating circumstances. The Bible frequently invokes capital punishment for crimes for which none of us would invoke it (insulting parents, for example), but at the same time, capital punishment is more carefully regulated than it otherwise might have been.

I will call this set of community regulations and rulings the "margin" of Biblical tradition. Some people have made these (or some of these) rules the center of the tradition, suggesting that Biblical tradition *requires* capital punishment, but on a straightforward reading of the Bible and Christian tradition, this is hard to do. Almost no one would adopt all the rules of the Bible for application to contemporary society. These would require putting people to death for such things as adultery, blasphemy, and various sacerdotal sins. Almost every reader of the Biblical tradition understands that some of these practices belong to the margins of the tradition and to the past, not to the vital center of the tradition as it comes to us in the present.

Through the center of this welter of time-bound community regulations and decisions runs a deep and subversive stream, which most Christians readily identify as the center of the faith—the voice of God in the Bible and the tradition. This stream tends to undermine the community regulations and practices, to call them into question. The remainder of my essay is a reflection on this stream, and in particular, on three themes within it—creation, incarnation, and crucifixion—and their relationships with capital punishment.

There are two sides to the Biblical story of creation: the complexity of the human character and the gracious but troubling restraint of God. The Biblical creation story presents human beings as "animals full of light," created in the image of God, namers and keepers of the rest of creation, filled with the powers of creativity, responsibility, and choice. It also presents the other side, the story of the Fall of the human race issuing in the murder of Abel by Cain. Giftedness and destructiveness go side by side—alleged Unabomber Theodore Kacyznski, apparently equally gifted in mathematics and the making of bombs. This is the story of the human race.

Keeping both parts in focus is hard, hard to remember the darkness within "the good people," even the adorable child on your knee, and light within "the bad people," even the man on death row. A Christian ethicist has said that the fundamental Biblical perspective is that there are no good people. Nor are there any unredeemable bad people. As a prison official, I observe almost daily the surprising goodness of prisoners, who have—one must not forget—committed horrendous crimes, and the equally surprising venality of prison employees—who have not committed such crimes. Prison is a human system of sorting: some people are behind bars and some in front of them. The Bible reminds us that before God we are the same: "for all have sinned and fallen short of the glory of God."[1] Every person is evil; every person is created in the image of God. Sort we must, for justice and the safety of society requires it, but we must not forget in our sorting the holiness of the human person.

This holiness is captured in the Biblical idea of redemption: what God has created God not only can but wishes to recreate. God has brought into the world forgiveness and the power to change. The possibility of redemption makes us pause before casting anyone into the dustbin of history, before taking that final step of taking someone's life. Who will be touched by the power of God? The fact that prisoners often commit new crimes makes people cynical about the idea of change, and yet those of us who have been working with prisoners know that we sometimes observe real change. We receive word from some prisoner, often one we least expect to have been touched by anything, that he or she has found a new way of life. We watch prisoners changing other prisoners. These experiences humble us, remind us of the "light" within persons whom many have relegated to the status of animals. The possibility of redemption does not make capital punishment morally impossible, but it gives us pause.

One of the problems in our secularized society is that we have ceased to believe in the power of God. Our underestimating the power of God is a subject many Christian writers have explored. In The Habit of Being, Flannery O'Connor writes that one of the effects of modern liberal Protestantism has been gradually to turn religion into poetry and therapy "...and gradually to come to believe that God has no power, that he cannot reveal himself to us, and that religion is our own sweet invention ... " Annie Dillard also writes about our failure to believe in the power of God. In Teaching a Stone to Talk, she asks, "Does anyone have the foggiest idea what sort of power we so blithely invoke or, as I suspect, does no one believe a word of it?...the sleeping god may wake someday and take offense, or the waking god may draw us out to where we can never return." The subversive center of Christian tradition stands in awe before the re-creative and redemptive power of God in the world. It makes us pause before we take the power of God in our own hands in capital punishment.

This power of God is the power of love—not the power of the state which is finally the power of violence, but that power which comes quietly, surreptitiously. The central subversive stream of Biblical tradition believes that the most powerful force in the universe is not the force which drives us apart but the force that brings us back together. Thus, at the heart of the tradition is incarnation: the birth of a child in a stable among the poor. As Elijah learned in the cave of the mountain, God comes not on the wind or the fire or the earthquake but in the still, small voice,[2] or the cry of a child.

There is a deep and fundamental suspicion in the Bible about the power of the state. While the need for the state is recognized, the Bible rarely misses a chance to point out that states misuse the power at their disposal and that violence seldom settles much. The place where the Christian approach to violence and coercion is worked out is in the teaching of Jesus, particularly in Matthew's summary of Jesus' teaching, which we now call "The Sermon on the Mount."[3] In this sermon, Jesus takes on the traditions of his time, including an eye for an eye, a tooth for a tooth: "You have heard it said, 'An eye for an eye and a tooth for a tooth,' but I say to you, 'Do not resist an evil person. If someone strikes you on the one cheek, turn to him the other also.'" This is not intended as a formal principle of conduct but a creative suggestion for how to deal with the violence endemic in the society of that day, in which the Roman empire occupied the Jewish nation. Do what is least expected. Do what interrupts the cycle of violence.

Jesus sought to shatter the hierarchical thinking that makes one person better than another: "So the last will be first, and the first last."[4] To the religious leaders who brought Jesus a woman caught in adultery, a capital offense in the old law, Jesus said, "If any of you is without sin, let him be the first to throw a stone at her."[5] The leaders slunk away without so much as picking up a pebble. He encourages his followers to "love your enemies and pray for those who persecute you."[6] Central to the teaching of Jesus is the idea that official violence is often directed toward the losers in society, not toward the goal of controlling private violence.

The need for control is patent. Governments do need to restrain evil and to punish wrongdoing This is the function of corrections departments. We are asked to take away the freedom of prisoners for the sake of society and for the sake of punishment. Incarceration does these things. It restrains evil. Even where the Bible upholds the state,[7] it is this restraining function that is central. Still, another idea about the state keeps arising: the idea that the state is the instrument of vengeance, that it is the duty of state to impose on people their just desserts. It is this idea which is dangerous, for it is always carried out by persons whose view of what the "just desserts" of others' actions are may be less than pure. Capital punishment as practiced in our society falls disproportionately on minorities, the poor, and those without the resources to make an adequate defense. Jesus encourages us to be suspicious of official acts of violence done in the name of justice.

Incarnation, then, has two aspects for Christians reflecting on moral matters like capital punishment. The first is that God seems to choose to reside among those whom society has marginalized. The birth of the king in Bethlehem calls into question the legitimacy and the practices of the king in Rome. Secondly, this humble-born king, by his own life and teachings, reinforces what the incarnation itself proposes: that the life of God is a life which reaches out to those abandoned by society. Both lead us down the corridor toward the occupants of death row.

Finally, there is the matter that Jesus himself was executed as a criminal. The cross, the central Christian symbol, is an icon of an execution device. Wearing a cross around one's neck or placing one at the front of the sanctuary was the equivalent for that time of what hanging an icon of an electric chair around one's neck or placing a noose at the front of the community worship space would represent in our time. By themselves these are defiant acts. But they speak to something deeper, something totemic about capital punishment. This may explain the ritualistic aspects of our practice of capital punishment. It is carried out according to the strictest rules and traditions. Specified witnesses are present. The prisoner is fed a last meal of his or her own choice. The prisoner is given a shower. A Christian cannot help but think of the Lord's Supper and baptism. Often a doctor presides. These ceremonies suggest that capital punishment itself has religious meaning.

These rituals of capital punishment lead to manifest absurdities. Prisoners who would have died by other causes are prevented from doing so. When a director of a certain corrections department was asked why convicted killer Robert Brecheen, who had overdosed on sedatives just hours before his execution, was revived, he said, "We're bound by the law, the same law he violated." Part of the problem is that we are all bound by the law. We are trapped by the usual way of doing things.

A little understood aspect of the crucifixion of Jesus relates to the way that we get ourselves bound up in our thinking, trapped by the law. The time of the crucifixion of Jesus was the time of the slaughter of animals for sacrifice. When he says, at the end of his life, "It is finished," he declares himself as the last sacrifice. No longer would the death of animals have religious significance. As Isaiah the prophet said, speaking for God, "This is the one I esteem: he who is humble and contrite in spirit, and trembles at my word. But whoever sacrifices a bull is like one who kills a man, and whoever offers a lamb, like the one who breaks a dog's neck."[8] The connection between the death of animals and God's favor had once seemed inexorable; now it was broken. Does the cross, in the same way, break the connection between punishment for murder and execution?

Murder is a "heart" problem. It does not occur because of bad up-bringing, poverty, or lack of education, though contributing factors to crime cannot be ignored as the high rate of poor, minorities, and retarded on death row show. Nor will execution fix it. Subtracting one life for another will never provide the balance for which we are looking. We are not talking math. Lives are not commodities. In advocating the death penalty, Governor George E. Pataki claims that the law is balanced to safeguard defendants' rights while ensuring that New York has a credible and enforceable death penalty. He also cites the "majority of voters" who demanded the death penalty as justification for it. Donald Cabana, in an article by Steven Hawkins, "Death at Midnight...Hope at Sunrise," refutes this idea of "balance" from his experience as a warden who gave the order to execute men at the Mississippi State Penitentiary in Parchman with this comment: "I questioned how the sordid business of execution was supposed to be the great equalizer."

Life-long confinement is itself difficult. John Edgar Wideman writes, "Prison time must be hard time, a metaphorical death, a sustained, twilight condition of death-in-life...Yet the little death of a prison sentence doesn't quite kill the prisoner, because prisons, in spite of their ability to make the inmate's life unbearable, can't kill time...Life goes on and since it does, miracles occur." It is this last, this waiting on miracles, this choosing life even when someone else has chosen death, that represents the best of my tradition.

On August 31, 1995, Barry Lee Fairchild, retarded and perhaps co-erced into confession, was executed. Hors d'oeuvres were being served in the warden's office. Conversations among staff went on as if nothing were happening. We so easily lose sensitivity to the sacredness of life. The life, the teaching, and the death of Jesus call us to reconsider what we are doing, to think about our actions. Marie Deans, founder of Murder Victims' Families for Reconciliation, explains her opposition to the death penalty this way. "I have the need to understand why we are so good at passing on violence and so bad at passing on love." Jesus, as he was being executed, tried to inter-rupt that very cycle of violence, saying, "Father forgive them, for they know not what they do."[9]

In the end, capital punishment may be Biblical, but only in the mar-ginal sense. The central subversive stream of the Christian faith calls us to choose life whenever and however we can.

My views are not necessarily the views of the Michigan Department of Corrections.

Adria Libolt attended the University of Michigan and Calvin College, where she studied religion and developed a rich knowledge of the scriptures. She is a member of the River

Terrace Christian Reformed Church where her husband, a Biblical scholar, is pastor. Ms. Libolt is Deputy Warden in the Michigan Department of Corrections.

Footnotes:

1. Romans 3:23
2. II Kings 19
3. Matthew 5-7
4. Matthew 20:16
5. John 8:7
6. Matthew 5:44
7. e.g., Romans 13
8. Isaiah 66:2-3
9. Luke 23:34

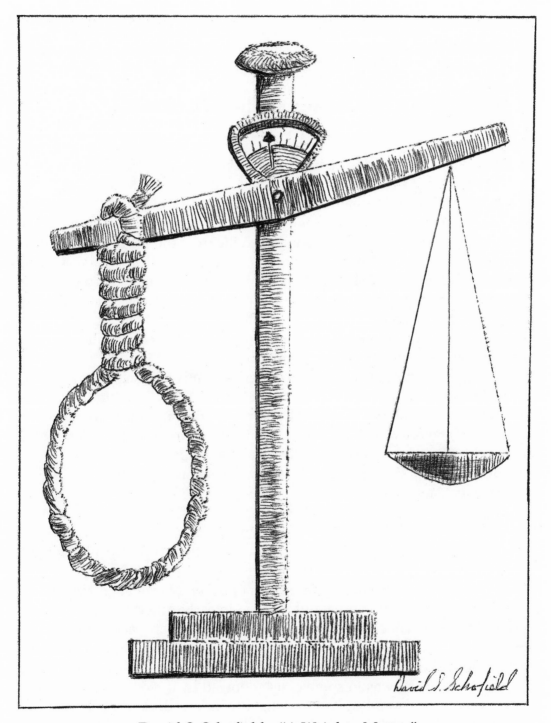

David S. Schofield - "A Weighty Matter"

EUGENE G. WANGER

"The Evidence Against the Death Penalty"

In 1787, when the American patriot Dr. Benjamin Rush of Philadelphia began the movement to abolish the death penalty in our country, there was very little in the way of what we would call "scientific evidence" bearing on the subject. Instead, Rush and his early followers relied mostly on a clear faith in the efficacy of human reason stemming from the 18th Century European Enlightenment (including the arguments advanced by the Italian Cesare Beccaria in his famous 1764 essay "On Crimes and Punishments"); on a strong belief in the hopeful message of the Gospels (Rush himself was a staunch Christian); and upon a widely-shared feeling born of the American Revolution that, since harsh and bloody laws marked monarchies, mild and benevolent ones should characterize republics.

It was not that Rush lacked an understanding of the scientific method. He had earned his medical degree at the University of Edinburgh in Scotland (which was probably the finest University in the English-speaking world at that time) before returning to sign the Declaration of Independence and serve in the Revolution. The problem was rather that then (and for many decades afterwards) there was almost nothing available in the way of reliable criminal statistics.

Deterrence

The first evidentiary matter to attract the attention of Rush's contemporaries was the question of what effect the repeal of capital punishment—which was then a punishment for scores of different crimes in Europe, as many as 200 in England and about a dozen in early America—would have on the commission of crimes. The official reports from abroad indicated that the repeal or restriction of the death penalty by those few European monarchs who had done so had not led to an increase in murder and mayhem but, to the contrary, was in some cases followed by a reduction. The anecdotal experience also failed to show that executions discouraged crime, as in England where picking pockets was a hanging offense—and where the

London pickpockets most successfully plied their trade at public executions when everyone else "was looking up." Moreover, English juries often refused to convict the guilty where the penalty might be death; and London's bankers at one point had to petition Parliament to repeal that penalty for forgery so that the crime could be successfully prosecuted. If capital punishment could not visibly deter petty theft and other crimes where the principal motive was simple greed, these abolitionists asked, how could it deter a crime like murder where the passions were so deeply involved?

When Michigan abolished the death penalty for murder and lesser crimes in 1846 (the first government in the English-speaking world to do so), and a few other states followed, their officials frequently were asked if this action had caused the murder rate to go up. Their responses, as shown by the literature of the time, were uniformly negative. The response to this evidence from those who favored the death penalty, as shown by their writings in the 19th Century, was to almost universally ignore it. Mankind was governed by fear, they believed, and it feared nothing so much as it feared death. How then could capital punishment fail to be a deterrent?

As America advanced into the 20th Century, more complete and accurate crime statistics were collected and published which made possible further comparisons bearing on the deterrent effect of capital punishment. As the data accumulated, these comparisons were set out in four groundbreaking and influential books: Raymond Bye's doctoral thesis, <u>Capital Punishment in the United States</u> (1919), Warden Lewis Lawes's largely statistical <u>Man's Judgement of Death</u> (1924), Englishman Roy Calvert's eloquent <u>Capital Punishment in the Twentieth Century</u> (1927), and Criminologist Thorsten Sellin's powerful monograph for the American Law Institute, <u>The Death Penalty</u> (1959). Sellin's work, being based on more recent and complete data, is still of great interest today.

These works, along with numerous later scholarly studies, all clearly failed to show that people—whether they are policemen, prison guards or just ordinary citizens—are any safer from being victims of homicide where they have the death penalty. The abolition of that penalty in a state does not cause the homicide rate to go up, nor does its restoration or a higher frequency of executions in a state cause the homicide rate to go down. And in those localities where executions are carried out, there are no fewer killings near the times of well-publicized executions when any deterrent effect should be greatest. Sometimes there are more. In short, there is no correlation between the ups and downs of the homicide rate on the one hand, and the presence or absence of the death penalty on the other. It's like an automobile. If your car runs at the same speed regardless of whether the brakes are on or off, that's pretty strong evidence that the brakes are not working. The evidence was massive, and remarkable for its consistency of agreement.

Probably no single subject in criminology had been studied more. The best deterrent, criminologists agreed, was the certainty and swiftness of conviction and punishment, not the draconian severity of the punishment itself.

A shadow was briefly cast on all this social science research in the early 1970s when a practitioner of the abstruse science of econometrics, Professor Isaac Ehrlich, announced that his calculations indicated that every execution "may" lead to several less homicides. Econometrics, unlike more traditional social science analysis, tries to account for many factual variables at a time, instead of just one or two, and requires creating long mathematical formulas of many elements which often have to be based on a good number of arbitrary assumptions. These many elements are all strung together and a very small mistake in one element can produce very large changes in other elements and in the end result. Ehrlich's study, and papers by a few of his disciples, being contrary to all previous research, riveted the attention of the academic community. The National Academy of Sciences commissioned a special study headed by one of the world's leading econometricians, Nobel Laureate and President of the American Economics Association, Professor Laurence Klein, which after careful analysis thoroughly discredited Ehrlich's result. Other scholarly studies agreed. In fairness it should be added that Ehrlich was not a promoter of the death penalty and that his work had been vigorously exploited and exaggerated by many who were promoting it far beyond anything that he had apparently anticipated.

Innocence

Not one unit of government in America keeps a list of its mistakes. It is human nature to deny them, cover them up, or push them into the background as soon as possible. In a few short years the public forgets and the surviving players can breathe more easily. Exceptions exist, but they are few. So it is not surprising that although many references to the execution of the innocent have been made since the beginning of the abolition movement, the surviving evidence of the individual cases has become scattered and hard to find.

As a result of prodigious research efforts, Professor Hugo Bedau in his book The Death Penalty in America (1964) and in his Stanford Law Review article written with Professor Michael Radelet, Miscarriages of Justice in Potentially Capital Cases (1987), collected 350 examples of mistaken conviction occurring in America since 1900. The decade with the second highest number was the 1970s. All 350 were convicted of the capital or potentially capital crime of murder or rape. Well over half were convicted of first-degree murder. But in all 350 cases it was later discovered either that no crime had been committed (for example, seven of the murder victims turned up alive!) or that the person convicted of the crime was neither physically nor

legally involved in it at all. In 88% of these 350 cases, the State
rected the error; but in only about 10% did the authors find tha
was discovered by state officials! Usually it was a random stroke o
the evidence of innocence was found. But 40% of them had been s
to death and 23 had been executed. Later the authors, together wi... writer
Constance Putnam, uncovered and reported 66 more such cases in In Spite
of Innocence (1992), and today hardly a month seems to go by without
another one being reported by the nation's press. How does this happen?
Mostly it is perjured testimony or mistaken eyewitness identification. And
unhappily it all too often involves inefficiency or corruption in our American legal system, where a very small number of bad actors can do a lot of
harm. When you understand how easily these errors can happen and how
hard it is to uncover them later, it is obvious that there are far more of these
tragic cases than we will ever know.

Cost

Many people are astonished when they first hear that the death penalty system costs far more than the life imprisonment system. After all, they
say, think of the mouths we won't have to feed. A lot of them seem to feel
about life imprisonment for murder like many people felt about the Viet-
nam War. They don't want their tax dollars to help pay for it. But the truth is
about all you can be sure to really save by executing someone is the mar-
ginal cost of his or her food and laundry; for the persons executed are such
a small part of the whole prison that their absence has no effect on prison
programs or staffing or maintenance or even—politics being what they are-
-on prison building programs.

By taking out a few inmates you can never save their average costs,
determined by dividing total prison costs by the total prison population;
and anyone who has ever run a large organization knows this. America now
has a death row population of 3,153, which is only 0.27% of our total prison
population of 1,164,356. We now execute about 50 of them a year and the
number's rising. Even if we executed 500 a year for 30 years that would only
add up to 1.29% of the total prison population, assuming it stays about the
same. (If it goes up the percentage would be even smaller.) It would be a
very rare case indeed where we could save more than the marginal cost
with numbers anything like that.

Even if we could save the full average cost of a murderer's life imprisonment by executing him, the evidence shows that the costs of maintaining the state's capital punishment system are far greater. The trials are
far longer, the investigations far more involved, the appeals far more complex and the death row costs heavy. Usually the taxpayers must pay for the
defense as well as for the prosecution, because the defendant is indigent. A

Juke University study, <u>The Costs of Processing Murder Cases in North Carolina</u> (1993) estimated that these extra death penalty expenses were costing that state over $2 million per execution. Earlier studies indicated that these extra costs totalled $90 million in California and would total $118 million in New York annually. Texas taxpayers pay an average of $2.3 million per death penalty case, which is about three times the cost of life imprisonment for 40 years there. In Florida the ratio is six times. Without capital punishment, all this money could be used to lower taxes or to fund more effective ways to fight and prevent crime or for some other useful purpose.

It also surprises many people a lot to learn that first-degree murderers, as a whole, are the best behaved group of inmates in prison. The truth, contrary to the political hype, is that those with really tough prison behavior problems are a small percentage. The others, including many who could have been executed, often hold prison jobs in which they save the state considerable money and (where state law provides for it) must pay restitution money from their prison earnings to their victims' families. These cost savings and restitution benefits are cancelled when the culprit is executed.

<u>Fairness</u>

Until perhaps fifty years ago, we Americans had a powerfully strong belief in the value of "fair play." While cultural changes have since rather eroded that belief, there are still many Americans who feel that when big benefits or big burdens are being handed out by the government, it should be done as fairly as possible. The death penalty is the largest burden anyone could receive, and it doesn't even begin to pass the fairness test.

Suppose your prosecutor charges you with murder and wants you executed. The first thing you'd want is a good lawyer to investigate and present your claim of innocence in the best possible light; and even more important if you are found guilty, to show that your guilt is not so black that you should die.

If you've plenty of money...Hey! No Problem! The people who get to death row are all (with rare exceptions) dirt poor, so you almost certainly won't qualify. In fact, Warden Clinton Duffy of San Quentin, who presided over 90 executions, called capital punishment "the privilege of the poor." You'll have to pay a fortune in legal fees, but that money won't be wasted.

However, if you're poor, the recent evidence shows you're in deep trouble. The odds are good that (depending on where you live) the judge will assign a grossly underpaid and inexperienced private lawyer to represent you, who may or may not be the best that the judge can find; or you will be assigned to an overworked public defender whose caseload is so huge that he or she can't possibly spare the time to represent you adequately. And very likely neither lawyer will be given enough money for the factual investigation you're desperately going to need.

We are talking about major incompetence here: lawyers who have never tried a criminal case, who don't look up the law, who do nothing to prepare, who never interview the key witnesses, who are asleep or drunk or even absent during part of the trial. Often they are selected through the local political patronage system; and sometimes their principal role seems to be just to speed the trial along. An investigation in Kentucky showed that one-quarter of those under sentence of death there had been represented at trial by lawyers who had since been disbarred or had resigned rather than face disbarment.

If this sounds like a crisis situation, it is. The American Bar Association has been blowing the whistle for years, but almost no one has been listening. Meanwhile the Congress has just drastically cut back the funding for lawyers for indigent death row defendants and the Supreme Court, in a series of cases, and with Congress's help, has been severely cutting back your right to appeal. Once your lawyer makes mistakes in your case, there is often no way to get the errors corrected; and now there are even fewer ways to try. Of course, you can pay for this with your life.

The second thing you're going to want is an impartial jury. One that will decide the case fairly or (let's be frank) that will maybe lean just a little bit in your favor. One that, even if they find you guilty, might just let you live. You're in real trouble here too, because the law requires that in death penalty cases juries have to be "death qualified." That means that no one who is really against capital punishment (and a lot of Americans are) can serve on the jury, which you can understand because without that we'd almost never get anybody executed. The difficulty is that the social science research shows these "death qualified" juries generally are not impartial. They are conviction prone, and much more likely than average to agree with the prosecutor and think that you wouldn't be there in the first place unless you were guilty as charged. There is probably no good way around this. It is a price of unfairness we must pay if we're going to have the death penalty. How do you think you'd like it in your trial?

Third, you will want a judge who really knows the law and will give you all the rights you are entitled to when being tried for your life. It is the glory of our system that even the worst felons are nevertheless entitled to be convicted only in strict accordance with the law. But death penalty law is a specialty. It is very complex and the evidence seems to be that America's state judges, on average, are not very good at it. The president of the American Bar Association has reported that serious constitutional error was found in one-third to one-half of all the state death penalty cases by the federal courts; and since virtually every state death sentence is appealed to federal court, that is a sobering figure. Scholars later reported that death row inmates secured federal court relief in about 47% of their habeas corpus cases between 1976 and 1991. We must hope that this does not really represent an average lack of legal ability in the state courts; but it is clear that there are a lot of state judges who are not applying the law correctly. It's been suggested that instead of following the law, some of these judges are following the election returns, as many voters want executions. Since you won't have any say in who your judge will be...Here's Luck!

Fourth, you'll want to be sure that the race of the parties involved won't affect the result of your trial. I know it's annoying to be reminded of race all the time. And if you (like most of us) are white, you're home free anyway...Right? Well, not exactly.

Professor David Baldus in Equal Justice and the Death Penalty (1990), the most thorough study of the subject ever done, discovered that in Georgia white murder defendants in the city are more likely to be sentenced to death than black murderers are. It's an outrage, but people there seem to be getting the death penalty because they are white! On the other hand, in the rural areas of the state blacks are more likely than whites to be sent to death row, Baldus found. That's monstrous, considering the other race problems blacks have.

Happily, when Baldus put all these figures together for his state-wide study, they cancelled each other out, so that for Georgia as a whole such discrimination doesn't appear in the end result. It reminds one of what the old lawyer said at his retirement party: "When I was young I lost many cases I should have won. When I was old I won many cases I should have lost. And so, in the end, justice was done." If you're a white being tried in the city or a black being tried in the Georgia countryside, perhaps you'll take comfort from that.

When Baldus looked at recent but less detailed studies in some other states, he was unable to determine that discrimination based on the defendant's race existed there, although all the experienced death penalty defense lawyers he talked to were sure that it did. So while it's just possible that this discrimination is unique to Georgia, don't bet on it. You'll have to take your chances. However, the major finding of Baldus's study was not about the race of the defendants. It was about the race of the murder victims. He discovered that, regardless of whether you are a white or a black murderer, in most cases you are much more likely to be sentenced to death if your victim is white—on average, more than four times as likely! Studies from other states strongly agree. In other words, in America death sentences are being handed out on the basis of a factor (the victim's race) which has no bearing on the heinousness of the murder or the moral guilt of the offender. People who are killing whites are getting sentenced to death, and people who are killing blacks are not.

To those Americans who were under the illusion that American law or practice was limiting the death penalty to only the most heinous crimes, this finding was a real eye-opener. It was further confirmation of the highly arbitrary and capricious way in which that penalty is actually inflicted. We read and hear a lot about the sensationally horrible murderers in a state who get the death penalty; but are often completely uninformed about the equally culpable ones there who do not get it and the substantially less culpable ones who do, notwithstanding formal guidelines in all the death penalty states designed to prevent that result.

Warren McCleskey had a particular reason for not liking all this. He was a black man on Georgia's death row for murdering a white person, and he asked the United States Supreme Court for relief on the basis of the Baldus study. While the Court was very nice to Dr. Baldus, it didn't give Mr. McCleskey any help. Even though the study shows a big pattern of race discrimination in death sentencing in your state, the Court said, it doesn't clearly prove that this race discrimination actually happened in your case, so you should take this matter up with the Legislature. (Yes, the Supreme Court actually said that.) Mr. McCleskey, having no swat with the Legislature, is no longer with us. The Supreme Court is full of surprises because, as all serious Court-watchers know, if McCleskey had been complaining that such a clear pattern of racial discrimination was interfering with his employment rights, for example, he could have pointed to a number of cases where the Court had allowed relief. But the social science evidence that would have been sufficient to save McCleskey's job was not considered sufficient to save his life. Like they say, "Death is different."

Indeed death is "different;" and in the four areas described above, that difference is presently accompanied by seemingly insurmountable barriers to the fair administration of capital punishment. If that penalty stays on the books we can all sincerely hope that those barriers may someday be conquered. But nobody has figured out how to do it, so those good intentions won't do anything for you in your death penalty trial today. That trial is likely to be Hell; and the road to Hell is paved with good intentions.

While admitting these grievous faults should be corrected, some death penalty proponents ask why we should be unduly concerned about how we treat these vicious and depraved killers. This begs the question, for of course we don't know who the vicious and depraved killers—those who presumably deserve to die—are unless they have been accurately and fairly selected. And they forget that these faults must also be borne by those defendants who are acquitted.

Protection

A friend from out west has asked me if Randy Greenawalt, on death row there, shouldn't be "eliminated" just for the safety of the rest of us...no other reason. A clipping he sends from the The Denver Post of January 20, 1997, shows that Greenawalt is a vicious and depraved killer, who being in prison for life for murder, escaped and brutally helped murder six more on a crime spree. This is a very hard case. It is also a rare one; and, paradoxically, its very rarity seems to lead people to be even more upset about it.

The facts of the case are so horrible it's hard to remember that we can't have the death penalty just for Greenawalt. The state has to draw guidelines; and experience shows that whatever guidelines are drawn for imposing death will almost surely be used by prosecutors and juries to cover a wider variety of cases than was intended, and with all the probabilities for error and unfairness described above. In fact, in the sensational cases there is more risk of error.

But, as suggested by my western friend, one could draw this very strict guideline: "People serving life for first-degree murder, if they escape and commit first-degree murder again, will be executed." Let's see how the two parts of this guideline would have applied to Greenawalt. He was in prison for life for murder, all right. According to The Denver Post he was in "medium security" which "offered an informal picnic setting" where his escape accomplices "had little trouble smuggling in an ice chest packed with revolvers and sawed-off shotguns." In other words, a state's incredibly lax prison administration cost six innocent persons their lives. In a properly run prison, it wouldn't have happened. To let such mistakes determine our policy on the death penalty is plainly to let the tail wag the dog.

Would that threat of execution for future killings deter someone like Greenawalt? Well it didn't deter him, did it? The evidence discussed above fails to show that the public is any safer where they have executions. Other evidence shows that some persons, usually weak minded and under stress (like many in prison), commit murder so that the State will execute them, as a means of suicide; and there are clinically documented cases of this.

Greenawalt also fits the second part of our guideline because he murdered again. Must he be executed to protect the public from him now? If he were allowed to live, you may be sure that this time the state's prison system (like other well-run penal systems) would keep him locked up tight until he dies...and that (as shown above) would be cheaper than executing him. There are no absolute safety guarantees in this life. But capital punishment for the Greenawalts of the world doesn't increase the odds for law-abiding citizens, it just costs them more money.

It should be emphasized that the above description of Randy Greenawalt is based solely upon my friend's newspaper clipping; and that additional facts, as developed in a recent evidentiary hearing, show him in a more sympathetic light. However, to go into these facts here would obscure the point that my friend was so vividly trying to make.

America's Isolation

Every Western industrial nation except the United States has stopped executing criminals. Most of them have formally abolished the death penalty; and the few who keep it on the books never use it. America stands alone among its traditional peers in having capital punishment today. The evidence of this has only been brought together in recent years...since Amnesty International was awarded the Nobel Prize. The ancient nations of Europe, from whence many of our ancestors came, have repealed it. It no longer exists in Britain, Holland, France, Scandinavia, Spain, Italy or Germany. It has been repealed in Canada and Australia and most of the countries in South America. It was abolished even in South Africa, which until recently was among the world's leading executioners. So it is not surprising that many people from abroad regard America's retention of the penalty as the indication of an innate American savagery that we refuse to address.

Some of them even come over to the United States to view our capital punishment operation, and a number of them are immensely helpful workers in our woefully understaffed criminal justice system. But one can't help but see that they tend to regard us rather like monkeys in a zoo. It doesn't seem to help much to tell them that we have problems of our own and that people everywhere tend to resort to barbarism under stress. Yes, they say, but if you grew up where every single family during the last 80 years has had some of its members brutally killed for what (from the killers' point of view) were "very good reasons," you wouldn't feel that way. We've seen you up close and there are millions of you who just love to sit in your soft chairs and hear, without any risk, about somebody being "fried." It seems almost as hard to convince them that they are wrong as it is to convince many Americans who believe in the death penalty of their mistake. But one thing is incontestably clear from the evidence: The world's main executing nations are Iraq, Iran, Nigeria, communist China and Somalia. And America seems to be among the top ten. How does it feel to be among select company like that?

Long experience teaches me that when first exposed to the evidence about the death penalty many people say, "Things can't possibly be this bad; not in America! Isn't this person misinformed or exaggerating?" I'm afraid the answer is that things are this bad...and sometimes worse. The evidence discussed above, and set out in the references below, show capital punishment to be nothing but hollow vengeance at high public cost.

Eugene Wanger, a member of the Michigan bar, was a delegate to the MI Constitutional

Eugene G. Wanger

Convention of 1961-2 where he authored the state's constitutional prohibition of capital punishment. He has been co-chairman of the MI Committee Against Capital Punishment, was co-founder of the MI Coalition Against the Death Penalty, and past national board member of the National Coalition to Abolish the Death Penalty. Mr. Wanger is a graduate of Amherst College and the University of Michigan Law School. His library on capital punishment is perhaps the largest in America in private hands.

References:

Cesare Beccaria, On Crimes and Punishments (1764) is available in several editions; the Paolucci (Library of Liberal Arts 1963) and Young (Hackett 1986) translations have valuable introductions.

Benjamin Rush, Essays Literary, Moral and Philosophical (1806); the Meranze edi tion (Union College 1988) contains a valuable introduction; see also

Philip English Mackey, Voices Against Death (Burt Franklin1976) for expressions by Rush & his early successors.

Eugene G. Wanger, Historical Reflections on Michigan's Abolition of the Death Penalty (Thomas M. Cooley Law Review [Journal] 1997).

Raymond T. Bye, Capital Punishment in the United States (Yearly Meeting of Friends 1919).

Lewis E. Lawes, Man's Judgment of Death (Putnam's 1924), reprinted by Patterson Smith 1969; later famous for popular writings on prison reform.

E. Roy Calvert, Capital Punishment in the Twentieth Century (Putnam's 1927); last edition reprinted by Patterson Smith with a valuable introduction 1973; perhaps most eloquent.

Thorsten Sellin, The Death Penalty (American Law Institute 1959); see also his Capital Punishment (Harper & Row 1967) & The Penalty of Death (Sage 1980); until his death perhaps America's greatest criminologist.

Hugo Adam Bedau, The Death Penalty in America (the Anchor 1964, Aldine 1967 & Oxford 1982 editions differ substantially); a 4th Edition of this superb reference will soon be issued by Oxford.

William J. Bowers, Legal Homicide (Northeastern 1984); studies of deterrence, brutalization, discrimination; lists American state executions.

Stephen Nathanson, An Eye for an Eye (Rowman & Littlefield 1987); strong philosophical & deterrence analysis.

Kenneth C. Hass & James A. Inciardi, Challenging Capital Punishment (Sage 1988); studies of deterrence, error, brutalization, fairness.

William Bailey & Ruth Peterson, Murder and Capital Punishment in the Evolving Context of the Post-Furman Era (Social Forces [Journal] 1988); reviews deterrence studies.

Roger Hood, The Death Penalty (2nd Edition Oxford 1996); world view, deterrence.

Welsh S. White, The Death Penalty in the Nineties (Michigan 1991); fairness, discrimina- tion.

Charles L. Black, Jr., <u>Capital Punishment: The Inevitability of Caprice and Mistake</u> (2nd Edition Norton 1981); seminal legal analysis.

Hugo Adam Bedau & Michael L. Radelet, <u>Miscarriages of Justice in Potentially Capital Cases</u> (Stanford Law Review [Journal] 1987).

Michael L. Radelet, Hugo Adam Bedau & Constance E. Putnam, <u>In Spite of Innocence</u> (Northeastern 1992).

U. S. House Judiciary Subcommittee Staff Report, <u>Innocence and the Death Penalty: Assessing the Danger of Mistaken Executions</u> (Death Penalty Information Center 1993); adds even more cases.

NAACP Legal Defense and Educational Fund, Inc., <u>Death Row, U.S.A.</u> ([Journal] Summer 1996); a quarterly long the best source of American death row statistics.

Darrell K. Gilliard, et al, <u>Prison and Jail Inmates</u> (U.S. Bureau of Justice Statistics Bulletin 1995); a standard source of American prisoner statistics, updated periodically.

Philip J. Cook & Donna B. Slawson, <u>The Costs of Processing Murder Cases in North Carolina</u> (Duke University 1993); the most complete & professional of many cost studies showing that capital punishment is more expensive than life imprisonment.

Richard C. Dieter, <u>Millions Misspent: What Politicians Don't Say About the High Costs of the Death Penalty</u> (Death Penalty Information Center 1992); valuable reference.

Ronald J. Tabak, et al, <u>Is There Any Habeas Left in This Corpus</u> (Loyola University Chicago Law Journal [Journal] 1996); valuable on fairness, error.

Richard C. Dieter, <u>With Justice for Few: The Growing Crisis in Death Penalty Representation</u> (Death Penalty Information Center 1995); valuable reference.

David C. Baldus, et al, <u>Equal Justice and the Death Penalty</u> (Northeastern 1990). Amnesty International, <u>When the State Kills...</u> (Amnesty International USA 1989); world view.

Amnesty International, <u>Amnesty International Report 1995</u> (Amnesty International USA 1995) updates world view.

Domingo - "Prayer for my People"

EQUAL JUSTICE FOR ALL

Charmaine White Face - "Native Americans and the American Justice System"

Abdullah T. Hameen - "The Road from Innocence to Death"

Shakeerah Hameen - "Living With Death"

Jessica Scannell's Class, The Fortune Society - "The Death Penalty"
Noel Bruno
Benjamin Jimenez
Robert Lopez
Tony Vaello

Pamela Crawford - "My Brother, Ed Horsley"

CHARMAINE WHITE FACE

"Native Americans and the American Justice System"

I was recently asked by a white child of seven, if I was an Indian, why didn't I wear a dress with the fringes on the arm and my hair in braids. She has known me for five years and has never seen me wear anything other than ordinary clothes and my hair in an ordinary style. It was the racist stereotypes that placed me in the context of the 1800s that appalled me. This child lives in a state where there are major reservations and many Native American people, where the state's Attorney General was a Native American and ran for high political office. This child attends Chief Joseph School. Yet, she has been taught the racist stereotypes that are still placed on Native American people after more than 200 years of contact.

How does this relate to the death penalty? Because it is these same kinds of stereotypes of Native American people as brutish, ignorant savages that, I think, influence not just judges, police officers, juries, and witnesses to crimes involving Native American people, but the entire American Justice system, the Congress and the Supreme Court, in their laws and treatment of Native American people in all crimes. What else can explain the high percentage of Native Americans on death row, 49, or 1.55% of the total 3,153, according to the Bureau of Criminal Justice Statistics as of July 31, 1996? What does this say when compared to the infinitely small number of Native American people in the entire United States population? Native Americans, according to US Census Bureau information, total 2,210,000 or only 0.008% of the total US population of 248,718,291. To have 1.55% of the total number of inmates on death row be of Native American descent is proportionately 19 times more than the number of Native Americans in the US population. Something is definitely wrong! Could this be only the result of racist stereotypes of the smallest race of people in the world? There are other factors to consider and these factors are also based on the race of Native American people.

Native Americans are the only race in the United States who have a section within the USCS that deals specifically with a certain group of people.

Called the Major Crimes Act, the law itself came into being in violation of the federal government's own laws and, of course, treaties. Prior to 1885, crimes committed by a Native American person against another Native American person were left to tribal custom and law. But in 1884 a Sioux man who was working with the United States government was killed by another Sioux leader for the first's traitorous acts to the Sioux people. The federal government was outraged that one of their collaborators was killed, and the original Major Crimes Act was passed. This Act undermined all tribal customs and laws that policed the actions of Native American people, and further undermined the power of tribal leaders. It was a political move rather than an attempt to provide a more just system. This Act is still in effect today. How many of the 49 Native Americans on death row were also subject to the Major Crimes Act, since only two of the victims were white?

Cathryn-Jo Rosen stated the muddying of legal waters when related to Native American people more succinctly when she said, "...an Indian is often confronted with different burdens of proof or different punishments than a non-Indian committing the same crimes but prosecuted under different jurisdictional statutes."[1] In other words, Native Americans do not necessarily have the same rights and privileges as other citizens of these United States because of the confused legal system created by the federal government.

Another complication, again in direct relationship to the Native American people as a race, is the genetic predilection for alcoholism. In the past, studies demonstrated that the vast majority of crimes committed by Native American people were committed while under the influence of alcohol. Now, statistics only give the major crime and do not include this very pertinent information. How can rehabilitation for a crime not address the physiological state of the criminal at the time the crime was committed?

Alcoholism has long been considered a disease, but the organic, genetic susceptibility of Native American people is only recently being made public. Today I read of another Native American man convicted of murder for killing someone over a can of hair spray for the alcohol content. Alcoholism and drug abuse are symptoms of poverty and oppression. Native Americans have experienced generations of both, but the additional physical, genetic predisposition also needs to be considered, studied, and addressed. According to statistics from the US Bureau of Justice's Sourcebook, the number of deaths and death rates for alcohol-induced causes by minorities is twice that of whites.[2] With the number of Native American men on death row at such a high percentage in relation to the Native American population, I wonder how many of their crimes were alcohol related?

As I write these kinds of statistics, and as I know the small percentage that we are as a total population, and the even smaller percentage of tribal people that know, or have been exposed to our old traditions and culture, I am reminded that some cynics would say that I was a fool to try to even write about the problems we face, as we are going to be extinct in the not too distant future anyway. But I think about the wisdom that our peoples had. I must say "peoples," as there are still hundreds of Native American nations living today despite the monumental attempts to destroy us. I look around the world and particularly the United States, and I think maybe a tiny piece of that wisdom could possibly help someone, or some nation, to become a little bit more humanized, a little bit more civilized. To be civilized does not mean to be technologized.

One of the greatest disservices the Europeans who came to the Americas did was to themselves. Their ethnocentric, racist attitudes judged Native American people to be nothing more than savages with limited social structures, because of a difference in understanding about technology. Only now, with the total destruction of the environment, are environmentalists and others looking to the philosophy and practice of Native Americans about how to live on this Earth. Could it be possible that there were other social practices that Americans and the world might learn? But will the stereotypes of two to three hundred years stop even that? Will we, Native Americans, become extinct because of the racist, paternalistic practices of the United States government before what few gems of wisdom are still left will be able to be uttered?

The framers of the American Constitution were amazed at the system of government offered in the Great Law of Peace of the Iroquois, and copied part of that Law in forming the foundations for the Constitution of the United States. But they were impatient and failed to look further than what they had already experienced with systems of government, so they only picked up a piece. The world marvels at what they did with the small piece of the Great Law that they did learn. Their tiny morsel of knowledge created a government that within a relatively short period of time is the dominant force in the world. I keep wondering what would have happened if the founding fathers of the American government had been more patient and tried to learn all of the pieces.

There were definite laws within every Native American nation covering every aspect of social interaction. But punishment as it is, and was, understood in the Euro-American world was alien. The act of striking a child to teach that child something was abhorrent and unheard of in the Native American world. Children had just come from the other spirit world. They were still innocent and pure. There were no orphans. Children belonged to all the people, not just their biological parents. Widows with children were cared for, not as burdens, but as part of families. The leaders were those who gave whatever they had to those who were most in need. The elderly also were cherished for their closeness to the next world and their wisdom of this world. Rape, incest, suicide were anathema.

There was murder. The act of killing another two-legged, or human being, had repercussions during the murderer's entire life, including the prohibition from certain religious ceremonies. The reasons for murder were different than today and were different because of different values and social structures. The circumstances surrounding the taking of another human life were taken into consideration—not by a judge and jury but by the family. There was no punishment for murder according to European and American standards. There was retribution to the victim's family and the community. The murderer was held responsible for the absence of the victim's life. The murderer was held accountable for what that absence did to the entire community.

How much thought would someone have before killing another person if the perpetrator knew the victim's family would decide his fate? How much thought would the murderer take if he knew that he would have to provide whatever service the victim provided? What if the victim was a woman with small children? How could the murderer provide the mothering necessary to those children and the grandchildren and the great-grandchildren for the rest of their lives? That would be the kind of restitution that was required in the Native American societies, societies that were held in disdain by Americans.

Indeed, during the Congressional debates on the passage of the Major Crimes Act, Representative Cutcheon said, "It is an infamy upon our civilization, a disgrace to this nation, that there should be anywhere within its boundaries a body of people who can with absolute impunity commit the crime of murder there being no tribunal before which they can be brought for punishment."[3] Did Representative Cutcheon know what the tribal remedies were for murder? I doubt it. The wiser, more humane system of justice that was the guiding hand of Native American social systems was undermined for political purposes with an underlying goal of the acquisition of land and wealth.

The idea of a society that murders murderers is illogical. It perpetuates murder. According to information sent from the South Dakota Department of Corrections, "Murder rates are almost twice as high in states with a death penalty as in states without." What if the murderer was denied the escape of the death penalty and was given a life term of providing for the family of his victim instead? Not only would he have to continue to live with his past demons, but now added is the additional responsibility that he places on himself of the ghost of his victim and being confronted with that ghost in the form of providing for the victim's family for the rest of his life.

Cultural genocide is more than just changing the way someone wears their hair, or changing their clothing from buckskin to cloth. From the viewpoint of Native American people, cultural genocide was also the destruction of a more humane way of living. No, the remedy of requiring murderers to be responsible for their actions and living up to those responsibilities for the rest of their lives could not be accomplished with the signing of a law. The entire societal system of Native Americans that said children were treasured, and the responsibility of each individual person was for the good of the whole, are concepts that would need to be instilled in every man, woman, and child. But the alternative is what we have today where we, the victims, pay for the death of those who rob us of the lives of possibly other very productive people.

As I think of technology, and the advancement of this technological world in the United States for the last 200 years, it always amazes me that the United States offers such a limited view of the world, a view based only on technology, material wealth, and greed. When will the United States start offering other views, other medicine, to address society's ills, other views that were tried and improved by cultures much older than 200 years? But then the stereotypes that require that I am not an Indian unless I wear buckskin and braid my hair would also have to be dropped. The stereotypes that contribute to the legal murder and incarceration of many Native American men would have to be looked at. The United States might have to admit that there might be another way other than the ethnocentric view that says the way of the United States is the only way for societies to live.

Until the time comes when the United States starts taking a critical look at itself, and starts admitting that they are a very young culture that might learn something from some other, older culture, American Justice for Native Americans will continue to be entrenched in the 18th and 19th Centuries. I keep wondering if there will be any of us, Native American people, left by the time the attitude has changed.

Charmaine White Face is an enrolled member of the Oglala Lakota (Sioux) Tribe from the Pine Ridge Reservation located in southwestern South Dakota. She is married and resides in Rapid City. Ms. White Face is a free lance writer and teaches part-time at a local college.

Footnotes

1. Cathryn-Jo Rosen, "The Allocation of Criminal Jurisdiction in Indian Country— Federal, State and Tribal Relationships." University of California, Davis, Law Review 109 (1975).
2. Sourcebook, US Bureau of Justice Statistics, Correctional Populations in the United States, Table No. 140. (1994).
3. U.C.D.L. Rev. 114 (1975).

ABDULLAH T. HAMEEN

"The Road From Innocence to Death"

From the point of my very conception down through the gateway from my mother's womb, I have made my journey, and where has this journey landed me? Is it a state of continuous growth and development, or is it a state of pain, turmoil, destruction and bloodshed?

> *He who has made everything which he has created most Good: He began the creation of man with (nothing more than) clay, and made his progeny from a quintessence of the nature of a fluid despised: but He fashioned him in due proportion, and breathed into him something of His spirit, and He gave you (the facilities of) hearing and sight and feeling (and understanding): Little thanks do you give!* Holy Qur'an 32:7-9

I was born September 7, 1963 to Cornelius Edward Ferguson Sr. and Lydia M. Watts at Old Chester Hospital in Chester, Pennsylvania, their second, but first male, child.

As I reached the gateway of life, the following events were unfolding in a world in which I was yet to become a functioning participant: the last prisoners were being removed from Alcatraz and no longer would it be used as a prison; the Soviet Union sent the first woman into outer space; Martin Luther King Jr. delivered his famous "I Have a Dream" speech at a peaceful demonstration in Washington, DC; President John F. Kennedy was shot dead in Dallas, Texas by Lee Harvey Oswald, who was himself killed by Jack Ruby; and, to top it all off, the median income for a family was $6,249—oh hell no, not for my family or any other in the black community. That was the median for white America.

As a child growing up in the Fairground projects in Chester, Pennsylvania, with my mother on welfare and my father working but absent, I faced a very unstable childhood. This was due in part to my mother and father's inability to adjust and cope with the precepts of life dictated by white America. It was in this vein that my first brush with racism and injustice occurred. It was on a warm spring evening and, once again, we were left home alone to fend for ourselves. We had grown accustomed to this circumstance, but this time someone called the cops who notified child services. I watched how callously my mother was being treated by the two white officers. As my mother and great-grandmother wrestled with the police and child services people, telling them they could not take us, out of anger and fear I lashed out, saying, "You honkeys leave my mother alone!" The police threatened to lock them up; subsequently my great-grandmother took the two girls with her, and the four boys were placed in the custody of Child Care Service. As I sat thinking and wondering where these strange people would take me and my brothers, and what they would do to us, I kept thinking about the words of my great-grandmother before we were separated. "Don't be scared, I will bring all of you back home." That is all I kept hearing again and again.

It was this incident which served as the stimulus for my hatred of white America, although, at the time I didn't see nor understand the significance this event would play in my future. I could not trust white people or the black family with whom I lived until I turned fifteen years old. Being taken from his parents and those whom he had grown accustomed to being with has very far reaching affects on a child's well being.

It was at this stage of my young life that I became rebellious and uncontrollable. I became very reclusive and deceptive; no longer was I that bright-eyed advancing student. The stage for failure had been set, and I was assuming my role wholeheartedly. By doing so, I refused to accept my new parents as people capable of loving me. I began to create problems at home and school, all in hopes of being returned to my parents, sisters and brothers.

My hatred was enhanced during each of our family visits at the Child Care Center in Chester. At these visits we would be driven from Philadelphia to Chester where my younger two brothers, who were in foster care in Chester, would meet us and our mother for a monthly visit under the supervision of a white female case worker. I remember how insensitive they were toward my mother. Surely they could see her sitting there, fighting back the pain and tears at having to face the results of her inexperience in raising children as third class citizens with limited rights in a supposedly free society—a society not only divided by color but also by class.

Are you of that segment of society that believes she should have done better, or that we could have gotten more out of life? If so, I ask you to try and understand the racial bias and unfairness which affected this country's former slaves whose ancestors are still captive to unempowerment and lack of education. If white America can see and understand that other ethnic groups are truly no different in their human form of creation and existence, then maybe it will be possible to stop blaming the victims of oppression for their failures and inadequacies. White America is too quick to say that the opportunity to succeed is equally open to all, and that the black populace is free to achieve—all they have to do is apply themselves.

When I was a young man striving to reach manhood, I understood little of racism or classism. Yet, I participated in its perpetuation on a daily basis as I learned and spurted out racial slurs to the whites, Hispanics, and other black children in the neighborhood. Why was this child in such a frame of mind, and what produced this unhealthy existence? Was it his parents, teachers, preacher or the other children that created this young corrupt mind? The answer would have to be a resounding yes, because it was through each of these sources that he gained his lessons of life. At the same time we must not let off the hook those who miseducated and withheld the proper resources and stripped the minorities of their basic free will and human right to succeed.

In such an environment, can it be said that my childhood was truly innocent, and was I equipped with the proper tools and skills that my white counterparts had acquired at this same stage of their development? Innocence and freedom grow out of, not the negative stains of guilt and evil, but the ability to think, rationalize and act openly without fear of repercussion and without being singled out as a smart-ass, trouble maker, or being labeled as one who can't follow instructions or who is hostile towards authority figures. Poverty produces unpredictable behavior, thought patterns, and life styles at every level and stage of growth and development. It does not matter where it strikes. It's guaranteed to affect everyone and everything it touches.

Although other black youth in similar situations do go on to succeed, you can't know how a particular child will respond to a given situation, just as you can't know which affluent youth will fail. We can say with some degree of certainty that they won't all respond in the same manner. So with that in mind, let's venture a little further down the road toward death's door.

I grew into manhood, according to my interpretation of manhood (the ability to be sexually active and maintain physical strength over others) within my closed environment, unwilling to be exposed as the uninformed and uneducated, scared and low self-esteem boy I was. In my continuous effort to overcome a female dominated household, I had to undergo a self induced transformation. It was during this transformation that I began to build a reputation that would propel me past all in my immediate surroundings.

I had developed a style of walking, talking and subtlety that I knew would infuriate those who considered themselves better or equal to me. Oh, how it worked—it worked especially well when a threat of violence was uttered. I would inquire if the person truly wanted to engage in such activity by asking, "Are you sure you want to mess with me?" I thereby set the stage for what I termed "the prevailing victim syndrome," where I would become the person defending myself from a brutal attack or insult. I must admit that it only worked with children and very few adults. No matter which way it went, in the eyes of the authority figure I was always to blame, and it was that factor which pushed me over the edge.

In school I furthered my reputation and notoriety through playing soccer and making the varsity team in junior high and high school, on top of my boxing and street-fighting skills, as well as an ability to acquire female friends without the ability to relate to them outside of the bedroom or the dance floor. All this was necessary in order for me to be able to relate to my peers. No matter how popular I had become, even in the midst of my friends I felt alone and lonely.

I was kicked out of high school in my second year of ninth grade, and kicked out of Job Corps with a police escort to the next town. After my return to Chester, I met my son's mother. When she became pregnant, she made me aware that I needed to change my life of selling, using drugs and hanging out. I lasted in this fresh start for four months. I had enrolled in O.I.C. to obtain my G.E.D., and from a group of over three hundred youth city wide, I was chosen to sit on a youth committee which addressed the problems which youth face in their daily lives and the programs which are needed to help them.

Right when I thought I had finally gotten a grip on my life, and was willing to confront my inner ghosts, I found myself in prison for first degree murder. Here's what happened: Wanting to continue being known for being a friend to a friend, I had ended up back in one of my old hangouts to make one more run to New York City to pick up 500 bundles of heroin with a friend who trusted me to get the job done. The murder occurred as I awaited his arrival. The bar was full with both family and friends. My mind was focused on getting this job over and earning another quick thousand dollars. A woman kept grabbing my buttock and making obscene gestures. I told her I wasn't for it, and she became loud and abusive. So when she reached over again, I grabbed her arm and yanked her off the bar stool, at which time her husband made a threatening comment. We had words which led to a fight and he ended up on the floor. As I was about to exit the bar, someone yelled, "He has a gun!" As I turned, I was handed a gun by a friend and I fired one shot, hitting him in the chest. I was arrested two days later.

Awaiting trial in the county jail, while sick with the flu, I was snatched out of bed and locked in solitary confinement, pending the disposition of a white boy's medical status. Someone had beaten this dude pretty bad, and the other white boys were made to say that I had done it. It was at this point that the old self was fully reawakened along with my hatred towards white America. So I became that young black man who rebelled against prison administration and labeled them all racist devils.

When I went to trial at age seventeen on this murder charge, I was tried as an adult and offered a twenty to life plea, followed by a ten to twenty year sentence. But when I decided to have a trial before only the judge, my judge was switched and a black judge sentenced me to three and a half to ten years. If I had gone to trial before a white judge and a white jury, I am sure I would have been in prison for life, another sacrifice of the judicial system as a warning to other black youth in Chester.

Although my encounters with racism were subtle at this point, I firmly understood that the "average" black male never receives justice in American streets, courts, the job market or living conditions, even though he has to compete for the same necessities.

While I spent my time in prison trying to improve myself through gaining an education (G.E.D.) and reading numerous books on the black experience in every corner of the globe, I knew that I was not fully cured of the illness which affected my thinking and actions. I spent a year in the hole for being unable to adjust to white men in a position of authority who disrespected me as a man.

As other black youth in America, my anger and rage were usually carried out in the form of black on black crime. In my twenties, frustrated and angered that I could not change my status in life and that I was looked at as less than human, I became my worst enemy, and it was this fact that landed me on death row.

One would ask where is the racism in my case? When I took the life of my victim, during an argument which got out of control, he was another black male. The fact that there is inequality in how the death penalty is applied in Delaware allows one to see how unjust the legal system really is, so let's take a look at its effect on my case.

While I was on trial, there were two other individuals on trial for First Degree Murder. There was Jerry, a young Hispanic, whose case resembled mine in almost every aspect, but he was not sentenced to death; he received life plus six years. With the help of a very energetic black public defender, Jerry was eventually released, on the very same grounds which I raised on appeal. Then there was Kevin, the young Italian, whose case was proven to be premeditated murder, but the State did not seek the death penalty; he received two life sentences plus thirty years.

Neither of them were gone after like I was by the attorney general, which suggests the abuse of authority when you look at my case in comparison to the above cases regarding location of wound, severity of wound, under-lying motive and the circumstances surrounding the crime. When you have a court system that is no longer based upon ethical principles, the true facts of a case on trial carry no weight if they will lead to an acquittal or lesser degree of murder. Higher courts both at the State and Federal levels of the appeal process cover and smooth over the errors and injustice of the lower courts.

In Delaware there is an Ex Post Facto issue, stemming from a new death penalty statute. This new statute was the result of racial fury and re-venge against four black men who killed two armed guards; what was to be a sure death sentence case turned out to be a sentence for life. As a result of this case, the legislators, attorney general, even some attorneys, called for stricter guidelines since New Castle County (with Delaware's largest black population) juries were reluctant to return a death sentence. A new statute was created to give the judge the final say, thereby making it easier to win a death sentence for the average black defendant whose life is full of mitigat-ing circumstances based on the need to survive in America's inner cities.

As long as discretion in the criminal justice system is used, as it has always been used, to single out the poor, the friendless, the uneducated, racial minorities and the under-represented, then discretion becomes injus-tice.

Delaware has recently exposed itself for all to see. When two all-American white college students killed their own flesh and blood and then discarded it as a piece of trash, the whole Delaware Criminal Justice System catered to them (a younger version of themselves), and provided them with a vehicle to get around being tried as capital defendants. That is the power of discretion—to be able to mitigate the circumstances and harshness of the overall penalty by narrowing it to a lesser degree. As sad as their case is, it was needed in order to really awaken the movement against capital punish-ment here in the First State.

So when I woke up on that 7th day of December, 1992, I already knew what was awaiting me, what my fate would be. It was only a matter of read-ing it into the record in open court. I remember walking into the court room that morning, trying to spot my family and friends, which to my surprise was not too difficult. I remember becoming alarmed by seeing so many white school children in the court room; it made my mind flash to a scene in the documentary "Roots," *where the white folk would gather with their children to watch how the condemned black man would respond to hearing that death was upon him.* My first words to my public defender were to ask for the children to be removed from the court room, but he responded that it was their constitu-tional right to be present at a public hearing. Ask every white person in the prison system how many of them had an all black group or class sit in at any stage of their proceedings!

They say I am a prime candidate for death row. Because the murder was heinous, gruesome, or committed upon an upstanding citizen? No! It is the fact that I am educationally, economically, socially unequipped, and a poor black male with no visible support. I had done time on a previous murder conviction in my home state, and they felt I should never have been released, so they took up the cause of the past by giving me the death penalty. To focus upon the case at hand would have removed me far from the clutches of death—a single gunshot wound with entry in the lower hip area, ricocheting off the rib cage in an upward motion, causing internal damage resulting in death. This is a far cry from the cases which have been tried as capital cases in Delaware.

When I said I was innocent, it was not innocence of the crime which I proclaimed, but innocent of the charges which I faced. I was black, fighting for my life with a jury of ten whites, one black, and one Spanish, with two white prosecutors, two white public defenders and a white judge. Even my own attorneys were convinced I was guilty as charged!

As I walk through this man-made valley of death, I watch the effects which my situation has produced upon my family. It is both frightening and painful. Being from a family that is not tightly knit, and being the one who has always tried to be that binding force between my mother's side of the family and my father's created within me a love that refused to allow my family to be hurt by outside forces. But to realize that their hurt was coming from my situation was crushing. No longer could I be there to protect them and be able to help them when they were in need. The death penalty was different from any other sentence I had received in the past. I had avoided imposing on my family during previous periods of incarceration, but now I needed all the support I could get. But there were unforeseen problems: they were in as much pain now as they ever were; they were as uneducated about the death penalty as I was; they didn't have the money to get the kind of help I needed; and they couldn't bear to face me in such a position, knowing they were powerless.

I tried to educate my family and tear down all the fears that had engulfed them, so they would be able to cope as we worked through the different stages of the court proceedings, as well as the possibility of losing a loved one in this manner. No matter how hard I tried, I couldn't remove that fear and pain. When you look at families and the effects of natural death, or a member being killed as the result of an accident or even a murder, it does not compare to dealing with the fact that the very people whom you look to protect your rights, property and life, are the ones taking your loved one's life. It has a lasting effect upon a family.

As I sit and reflect upon the judge's words at my sentencing concerning my relationship with my son—that he will do just fine without my presence—I could cry and laugh at his ignorance and misconception of our relationship. I must admit that I myself didn't fully know the effects it would have on him, not until I received his first letter after a three year period had passed by. I knew he was not doing well in school or at home, but when I read that letter explaining what he was experiencing mentally, emotionally and physically, I had no choice but to come out of hiding and deal with this head on. I had left it to his mother, my mother and everyone else to explain what was happening with my situation, just as I had done in the past. Remember what I said earlier, that the death penalty is different than other sentences. It was impossible for them to explain, let alone guide him through this most difficult time of his life. At that stage of his development, he should have been dealing with the problems any child faces going into his teenage years, not wondering if the State was really going to kill his father.

I thought living and being educated to street life was hard, but imagine sitting down and explaining to your child that one day you will be executed by the State, and why he should not allow it to affect him in a negative way; that he should not hold anyone responsible for the act because it's due to your actions that you're in that position; that he should not hate people based on the color of their skin when he knows it is a white system killing his father. I can't compare anything else in this world to trying to explain this to your child while actually facing and living it on a daily basis.

Maybe I should send my sentencing judge a copy of my son's letter, so that he can see for himself, that though I may not have met his standards as to what a father should be, to my son I am the father he loves.

When I think of my wife I must reflect upon a verse out of the Holy Qur'an which states:

So, Verily with every difficulty there is relief: so verily with every difficulty there is relief.

Without a doubt, my wife is a blessing from God. I met her in my fourth year on death row, as I was seeking out support for death row prisoners from the agency for which she worked. Her presence had a very strong effect on me at our initial meeting. It was more than that physical attraction which usually attracts a man in prison. But as time passed and our inner natures began to mesh, the intensity of her willingness to aid our cause in a state where three of five support the death penalty drew me closer to her. I was able to open up and speak as I needed to speak concerning the death penalty and its effect on us. Like most people, she also needed to be educated

Abdullah T. Hameen

about the capital punishment, but her eagerness to learn opened many closed doors which had hindered our attempts to get outside support in the past.

The more we worked together, the deeper and stronger our love for one another grew, which led to my proposal of marriage on September 4, 1996. Accepting my proposal led her to the need for a support system to help her cope with the realities of death row which she would now have to live, eat and think on a daily basis. So a new form of education was needed in order for us to undertake our new journey. While at times this is a most difficult situation for her, she has been blessed with the strength that only such a situation could have revealed within her. My wife is highly educated and employable in many areas. While she came from a background that was somewhat removed from the world I existed in, she was able to understand my position, while at the same time maintaining that my actions were unjustified and that the taking of life is wrong on both sides of the ugly equation. It is such qualities that have laid the foundation of our entire relationship.

Now my wife and son have bonded and become each other's support system as this time of uncertainty unfolds before us all, and that adds to my willingness and ability to keep fighting, not only for myself, but for them as well.

In fighting for my life, I have reached out to every group, organization and agency that work on behalf of death row inmates. As I fought, I began to realize that not many people were in the business of helping death row prisoners, so my fight took on a whole new dimension. I began to fight for all death sentenced prisoners in Delaware. My first mission was to form a support group and begin to circulate information concerning the death penalty, both within the prison and outside. This led to the creation of Just Say "NO" To Death Row, a bimonthly newsletter. Secondly, we joined forces with B.L.A.C. (Because Love Allows Compassion), D.C.O.D.P. (Delaware Citizens Opposed to the Death Penalty), and D.C.J. (Delaware Center for Justice); now we also have C.C.S.C. (Concerned Citizens of Sussex County), all fighting to abolish the death penalty in Delaware, praise be to God! I have also filed a class action suit on behalf of all death sentenced prisoners and those awaiting trial, as well as future clients of premeditated murder at the hands of the State, which after almost a year of waiting is now on the way to being litigated. Also we at J.S. "NO" D.R. are in the process of proposing a bill to abolish the death penalty once and for all here in Delaware.

Until we can remember and acknowledge that all our roots for governing society have been derived from religious scripture, which has held man accountable for his deeds regardless of class distinction or ethnic hue, we will continue to fail as a race in our humane efforts. To do so in modern societies will always leave the door open for politics, classism and status to play an ugly and significant role in the imposition of the death penalty.

Abdullah Tanzel Hameen, born Cornelius Ferguson, was raised by his maternal great grandmother, and left home at the age of fifteen. He is incarcerated at the Delaware Correctional Center, sentenced to death by lethal injection. Mr. Hameen is married with one birth son, two stepsons and two grandchildren. He has an associates degree in accounting and business administration and is an active member of the Islamic community, member of Project Aware, co-editor of Just Say "No"to Death Row, member of Because Love Allows Compassion, and mentor and friend to any and all who need his advice or assistance.

SHAKEERAH HAMEEN

"Living With Death"

It's 3 p.m. and I have been busy all day, but as my day winds down, my thoughts return to death row. Don't get me wrong—they never actually escape—but as long as I stay busy, I can hide from them. You see, my husband is on death row, and every day, every minute, I live that sentence with him.

I am the victim that society would like to forget about because I have no rights. I don't have the right to hurt, because, after all, my husband committed a crime. The courts said they had no alternative but to sentence him to death. Was there an alternative, and if there was, would they have shown mercy? I have always felt the death penalty is a way for society to purge itself of its own failures, because had someone intervened earlier, would my husband be on death row today? The crime that brought Abdullah to Delaware's death row was an accident. No one cared or wanted to hear that, because my husband's past is not unblemished. He was the perfect sacrifice, the perfect candidate for death in the name of justice.

Abdullah led a very fast life style, and got caught up in the games of the street. He was someone who few people wanted to cross; because of their fear, his life had been on the line more than once. Abdullah was forced to carry a gun for his own protection, and on that fateful night, what he had for protection cost two people's lives: the victim's and his own. I can't go into the details of his case, because of where he is in the appeal process. I will say that if the courts had cared, they would have found that what happened was indeed accidental. But why should they care? After all, as the prosecutor put it, he was a prior convicted killer and he deserved death. The prosecutor didn't bother to explain that the charges from the first conviction were not first degree or intentional murder. He did not bother to explain that my husband was a juvenile at the time of the prior crime. No one looked into why this man was who he was or how he got there. Their only concern was death for death in the name of justice. What I find ironic is my husband was not alone, and his co-defendant only received fifteen years. Abdullah received two death sentences, forty-five years and six months in a half-way house. He was charged with felony murder and intentional murder, but was never charged with a felony. His co-defendant was only charged with first degree murder and was given leniency by the court. There appears to be an injustice there, but who am I to say that? After all, I have no rights.

Society is so quick to judge, so quick to want revenge, so quick to want blood. Capital punishment is an appropriate name because those with capital don't receive the death penalty. If you take a look at the many name-less faces on death row, you'll discover that not one of them was able to afford a dream team. I'm not saying that all their attorneys were incompetent, because at the moment my husband has an excellent attorney. Unfortunately, he didn't get him until now, and we are in the last stages of his appeals.

How have we as a society come to the point that we can kill our citizens? We cannot anticipate a perfect society, but have we forgotten that we need to make the effort? Society has erected the gallows at the end of the lane, instead of guideposts at the beginning. We've saturated our communities with guns and drugs, and we refuse to accept part of the responsibility for the high rise in crime. Our families have fallen apart, and it seems that each day we care less and less about one another. We don't see people as human beings anymore; we're just statistics.

I met Abdullah through my work, and I knew instantly that there was something good and decent about him. I saw a spark that others refused to see. I sensed in him a quiet strength and determination that instantly drew me to him. Over time, I gained a tremendous amount of respect for him because he is unselfish in his fight for life. He not only fights for himself, he fights for everyone on death row.

The man I love and the man I know is active in the Muslim community, and in Project Aware, a group that works with juveniles in the hope of deterring them from a life of crime. He is co-editor for Just Say "No" To Death Row, a bi-monthly newspaper. He is a caring father and grandfather, and he is a supportive husband and friend. He is, as society says, rehabilitated. Abdullah chose to change. No one forced him, and no one encouraged him.

When I visit with Abdullah, I don't see a monster. I see a man who has had a lot of hurt and rage in his lifetime. I see a man who is struggling to maintain his relationship with his family. I see a man who deserves a chance to live, because he can give so much to society. He can help kids not make the same mistakes he made.

His sixteen year old son constantly asks if his father is going to be put to death. How do I prepare him for that? How do I prepare myself for that? I go through each day trying to keep it together, and trying to stay strong. There are days that all I can think about is my husband being executed. There are times when I don't know which way is up, and how I'm going to get through another day. I sometimes feel like I am walking with death, and that it's going to jump out and attack me when I least expect it. Abdullah is a breathing, healthy young man that the state may escort to his death one day. How do we, as a family, prepare for that? Please know that we have not forgotten the victim or his family. We feel their pain, and we wish that what happened could be reversed, but it can't.

I don't want to lose this man, and neither does his family. We cannot bring back the victim, but is creating more victims the answer? I ask you to let my husband live so you can see the spark in him that I saw. Know him as I do and you will know his life is worthy to be saved.

Let's eradicate the death penalty and seek justice not revenge. Stop the death penalty so healing can begin and pain can stop. Let's find a way, together, to stop the killing. Killing is wrong, and killing in the name of justice is not justice. We do not help the victim by giving them blood, and we have truly failed, as a society, when we use the death penalty.

Please let's stop this walk with death.

Shakeerah Hameen graduated from Essex County College in New Jersey with a degree in Criminal Justice. She worked at the Network for Victim Assistance in Pennsylvania with victims of violent crime and as a rape counselor, and met her husband while working at the Delaware Center for Justice. Mrs. Hameen is currently employed at the Philadelphia YMCA, job training women in transition from welfare to work. A mother and grandmother, she volunteers her time to organizations committed to abolishing the death penalty.

THE FORTUNE SOCIETY, NYC

"The Death Penalty"

JESSICA SCANNELL

Dear Julie,

Enclosed are the final essays from four young Latino men, (ages 16-21), who participate in Fortune's Education Program. They came to Fortune for various reasons, as mandates by the courts or terms of probation. These students' reading levels range from 5th to 9th grade. They have been working with me and other tutors for 4-6 months. In that time they have increased their skills tremendously; some raised their reading levels by more than two grades. Their classes meet twice a week for two hour sessions. Their common goal is to stay out of jail, get a G.E.D. and afterwards a job that could support a family. Two of the students have one year old sons.

These writings are a result of over a month of work. The classes watched films, read both narrative accounts and statistics on the death penalty. We had many discussions, some of them heated. It was interesting to see how their ideas on the issue evolved. In the beginning their stances were cut and dried. However, the more they learned about the death penalty, the more complicated it was for them to state their opinions. These essays are the result of many drafts of writing, perhaps the most they have ever worked on one piece. Seeing the final, typed version of their work surprised and motivated them. At the onset of the project they didn't think they were capable of putting their ideas on paper in this way. They proved themselves wrong and are proud of the final product.

I also facilitated a discussion group of 15 young Latinos and African-Americans, ages 16-25, at Fortune. I wrote the words "Death Penalty" on the board and asked for the first thing that came to their minds. Here are the responses: doesn't deter crime, gas chamber, rapist, electric chair, bullshit, pain, revolution, murder, guns, violence, judgment, lethal injection, capital punishment, unjust, firing squad, victims, money, doesn't prove anything, people deserve to die (for revenge), who is God?, two wrongs don't make a right, race, social class, punishment should fit the crime. The discussion that followed was intense. We talked about the death penalty and race. Clients tied our current system of legal execution to slavery times and lynching. It was obvious that these young people do not believe that the criminal justice system is fair. The overwhelming opinion was that a person of color and low economic standing has far less of a chance to receive a life sentence than a white person with money, especially if the victim was white. Although they made many interesting points in the discussion, the one that sticks with me was the silence at the end of our group when I asked what we, opposing the death penalty, could do to change things. There was no hope that they had any power to fight the injustices they saw and experienced. It is my hope that projects like yours will inspire them in some way.

Thank you so much for this opportunity. Please call me if you need additional information.

Jessica Scannell

NOEL BRUNO

My opinion is that the death penalty should not be used because the people that be on the list are mostly the Puerto Ricans and the Blacks. If they only knew that white people be doing bad things too. It is not fair because the white people get away with a lot of things. One of the things I'm talking about is when they (white people) buy a bag of drugs, or rob someone, they are more likely to get away with it. The system is unfair because the whites get over and racism is real bad. There are a lot of white cops that don't like Puerto Ricans. They make us go through the system for bullshit reasons, like planting drugs in our clothes. They are always trying to fuck us over, because they believe that we are the ones who do the crime in this world.

If you do the crime, you do the time, it depends on what you do. Let's say you kill someone. I understand that you gotta do time for that. But sometimes the innocent people get locked up for no reason. Let's say that a person who did not do the crime gets the death penalty. That's not right. Because the person who did the crime gets to chill and lay back for the rest of life.

The system is cruel. Like what happened in the movie we saw, "Dead Man Walking." The thing he did was wrong, he and his man were not thinking about the consequences. It is not okay to rape a person. That means they could get no love from a girl, probably they were perverts. Women don't like that stuff. But only one guy got the shots [lethal injections]. They did not know who really did it. They should have given both guys the same time [in prison]. But I guess it's not like that. One guy got what was meant for both, that is a disgrace.

They should not have the death penalty. Innocent people die. The real people who do the crime get away with it. Within the system there is prejudice. It hurts family, loved ones, and society.

ROBERT LOPEZ

I think that the death penalty is not fair because nobody deserves to get killed. An example of those who do not deserve to die are those two young teenagers that threw their baby out in the garbage container. I think if they get the death penalty it will be unfair because they didn't know what to do with the baby. They were nervous, terrified. They didn't know what to do. So they can't be blamed too harshly.

In thinking of the death penalty I have learned that it is hard to decide who lives and who dies. I don't believe that it is up to me or any person to decide who dies and who lives. It is only up to God or some other higher power.

BENJAMIN JIMENEZ

I think that the death penalty is some thing that is very wrong. The reason why I think that the death penalty is wrong is because I don't believe in a human being killing another. If he did wrong let God take care of it if he deserves to die. Otherwise put him in jail to protect the people.

TONY VAELLO

In my opinion the death penalty was supposedly created to make an example of those who murder or commit other gruesome crimes. I would like to state an argument against the death penalty. The death penalty is not suitable for many reasons. The three main reasons are that it's a waste of money, it does not deter crime, and most importantly, I don't believe the State (or anyone) has the right to take a person's life.

In my eyes the death penalty is not needed to reduce crime. It has been statistically proven that the death penalty does not necessarily reduce crime, homicides, and other serious offenses. In 1975, there were 648 homicides in Manhattan alone. In 1994, there were 330, that's a reduction of more than half the homicides in Manhattan in less than two decades.[1] The reason I'm using these statistics is to stress the fact that the reduction of homicides happened without the use of the death penalty in New York State. I, myself, as an ex-felony offender, did not think about facing the death penalty before I did the crime or even after. In my past experiences I've learned that people don't weigh out the consequences before they act.

That's only one reason why the death penalty is not needed in New

York and other states throughout the country. Think of this, just to execute one inmate in North Carolina the state paid $2.16 million, more than enough to imprison a man for two lifetimes[2] I couldn't get too many facts, but I do know that one incomplete case cost California taxpayers nearly one million dollars.[3] Think about it, we as taxpayers are paying so much money so that someday one of our own family members or even a friend could suffer this horrific death. That is what we as taxpayers are paying for.

I don't believe that the state should decide who lives or dies. The 1987 Stanford Law Review study identified 350 cases in this century in which innocent people were wrongly convicted of crimes for which they could have the death penalty. Twenty-three were actually executed, (eight in New York).[4] There have been times that the police stopped me and wanted to bring me in for crimes I did not commit. What if you fit the police description? Could you imagine if they had brought you in for murder and sentenced you to death and murdered you, only to find out afterwards that you weren't the true killer? Would your position on the death penalty change?

Instead of wasting tax payers' money to murder, we should spend it building new schools so we could educate our youth. The public officials instead of scaring people out of committing crimes should offer real options to committing crime like jobs, treatment programs and educational programs. Police arrest people, judges convict people and states murder people who are innocent. It may not happen everyday, but the question is are we willing to let this happen even once?

Footnotes

1. Morgenthau, Robert. "What The Prosecutors Won't Tell You." NYTimes, February 7, 1995

2. NAACP Legal Defense Fund, "How The Death Penalty Really Works," n.d.

3. Verhovek, Sam Howe. "Across the U.S., Executions are Neither Swift Nor Cheap," NY Times, February, 22 1995 B2

4. Morgenthau, Robert. "What The Prosecuters Won't Tell You," NYTimes, February 7, 1995

PAMELA CRAWFORD

"My Brother, Ed Horsley"

My name is Pamela Crawford. I am the sister of the late Ed Horsley, former death row inmate, executed on Feb. 16, 1996. Right now I am still dealing with my grief, trying to move on with my life and hoping there is something I can do to make a difference and make some changes in our society. I would like to share a little of who Ed was and what he was to me and my family and how his long incarceration and eventual execution affected us.

Ed was born in Charlotte, NC to the late Edward Horsley and the late Juanita Roundtree Martin, and he lived there until he was 15, when he got in trouble with the law. At the time of his death, he was 38 years of age. He was one of five siblings, one of the younger ones—kind of shy and laid back—a lot of times even pushed back in life. He was picked on at a very early age because a lot of people felt like the odds were against him from the very beginning. My father's life was taken away from Ed before Ed's life even began. My mother was seven months pregnant when our father was killed by his brother in a fight.

Ed grew up in a very poor neighborhood with an alcoholic mother. His grandmother worked and tried to support her grown alcoholic daughter and her four children which later on became five—a single parent and an older black woman with hardly any education, trying to do the very best for the family.

When there was no food at home to eat, Ed made it possible for us to go on living. He went out and shoplifted, stole food and money to pay rent. We would get eviction notices. Ed was at home and he would tell my grandmother he was going out. He would then steal or do anything he had to do to get the rent money. The rent lady can remember that the little boy would always come to pay the rent. No one sent him. He was still a youngster, but he was pushed into being an adult, taking on responsibility. A lot of times when the other children were thinking about getting their plates and going to the table, Ed was thinking about what to get to go on the table. I can even remember sitting at home in the dark because the electricity had been shut off. So he had to grow up at an early age. Then, after that, he felt obligated—

that it was his duty and job to make sure that things at home were taken care of. Because of the situation we were in, my brother Ed got into drugs and crime at an early age—that was his way of survival. His personality changed. I didn't know the extent of it until he was caught.

We had neighbors and other adults around that witnessed what was going on in our life but sometimes in the black community they say it's being nosy, so nobody got involved and Ed went on to a life of crime.

I had my share too. I had my time. When I was 14 I went through a shoplifting spree and stole everything I passed. I thank God that someone gave me a chance to make it right. He saw a little girl inside—he was a white judge, but he had a lot of compassion. Even now his eyes say something to me. They say that he believed in me. He told me that he trusted me. This was one person who believed in me and turned me around.

Ed was more unfortunate than the other children. We got an opportunity to turn our lives. He was not given the same opportunity. If he had, I think he would have had a chance.

I feel strongly that he was doing what any parent would do. He saw it as a protection of his family. He was sincere but he was sincerely wrong in the way he thought he should go about doing it. That was all he knew, so he used what he had to work with. And he didn't have any other skills. He thought whatever he needed for his family he should get by force. It was the wrong way, but he didn't see it as wrong or right at that time. He saw it as survival. Because of that he ended up paying with his life. It was a tragedy and it was like a nightmare, because it is something that you can never, never imagine happening in your family, especially here in the United States.

I think if someone had told Ed," Tonight is going to cost you your life," it would have made a difference. Don't ever think it can't happen to you.

Like I said, it could have happened to any one of us. I had an experience where I was talking with a friend and she was shot to death. The girl who shot her said she really wanted to shoot me. We had had a disagreement about some children and a ball, and she went in the house and got a gun and shot and killed my girlfriend. When she did that, she dropped the gun. I picked it up and was going to aim it at her. I'm so thankful that I thought first. I didn't shoot.

She went to prison and served her time. She had to leave her children for a while, but she came back. We met again under different circumstances and we were able to hug and talk about the tragedy that took place in our lives and the effect it had on both of us. She is a better human being now. I loved my girlfriend very dearly, and I was upset, of course, but I don't hold it against her. I have seen where she came back and did a good job raising her children. Her incarceration and training in prison really helped her and motivated her. Now that she is back on the street she is a plus to society.

I have seen both sides. My uncle killed my father. My mother never got over it. I watched her die of a broken heart. She was an alcoholic and I watched her go through terrible abusive relationships. It all went back to the fact that my father was not there for her. But nevertheless I never saw my uncle as anything but a human being. He took my father's life, but if they had taken him from his children, they would have suffered the same pain that I experienced. I didn't want that for them. I wanted him to be able to turn around. He served his time and went home and raised his kids. He is a good man in the community now. He has something to put back. He sent his kids to college. He spent a lot of time with his neighbor's children as well as his own. If they had taken his life, nothing would have been accomplished. It would have left four kids without a father, just like our family.

I think that Ed got the sentence he did because it was a black person killing a white person. In the case of my uncle killing my father and this woman killing my friend, it was a black killing a black. The sentences were short and these people had a chance to be rehabilitated and come back and raise their families and be a part of society.

Money played a major part in Ed's defense. Money determines whether you live or die. That has been proven time and time again. If you are poor and can't afford to do a lot of things yourself, you don't have a chance. It wasn't just a racial issue. Prisons have been made for poor people. I don't think they have created one yet for a rich man.

If you don't have enough money and you commit a crime, you are going to prison, you are going to do hard time. If you are poor you don't have much chance of getting out either. I think more people need to be educated about America. Over here in America we are putting our people to death, and then across the water we are sending our men over to kill people for killing people. So if they turn on us and come here to kill us for killing our people, we are going to have a whole lot of dead people. I think we need to start at home finding a way to keep our own people alive.

A lot of kids don't understand. They get frustrated with the way society is. They feel like they are pushed. They get a message of violence and they look around in society and what they see is that killing is right. Our government says it has the death penalty to send out a message that we are not going to tolerate this. We are going to execute people. We are the role models for the young. If we are killers, which is what we are, and we are their role models, what can we expect from them? What kind of message are we sending to the children? The kids here are in more trouble than the ones across the water. Over there they know there is a war going on.

Here in the U.S. our kids are more confused. We supposedly don't have a war going on but they see it as a war. They see people being killed. My kids make pictures with their uncle standing here at 11 o'clock full of life. An hour later he is dead. Here is life; here is death. This is not because someone came across the water to kill him; this is because the United States chose to say that his time was up. It doesn't fit. It is confusing to adults, so you can imagine what children are thinking about this. They don't understand.

Had Ed's case been moved to North Carolina, he may have been given a different sentence. He may even have had a fair trial. I think in Alabama the odds were against him from the start. Once he was accused, they didn't want to hear any more . The experience I had with the governor made that clear. When I arrived in Alabama to meet with Ed's attorney, we were going to meet with Governor James about a stay of execution. The lawyers had some new evidence they wanted to present to him, but he said before I even got there, "The sister can come but my mind is made up and I won't talk to her." He made that statement and he did just that. He refused to talk to me. We went down there and sat in his office. He never came out. He never responded. The night of the execution a limousine had pulled up in front, and one of the kids said, "Uncle Edward, there's a limousine. That might be Governor Fob." Ed said, " There's no way on this earth to even think that. That's the hearse."

The state appointed attorneys were a joke—nobody ever took his case seriously. They would go into court because they had to, to stay within the law, but they were never really interested. The original attorney who called and told my mother that Ed had been arrested in Alabama never said he had been accused of murder. He said, "He killed a girl down here in Alabama. And he is going to be executed." He never said, "if he is found guilty." He didn't say anything about if he did or didn't do it. That was the person defending him, the person who was supposed to believe in him. He also had tape recordings that were made right after the arrest. He told my mother, "You don't want to hear the tapes because he is on there crying like a little wimp."

I had the opportunity to meet that same attorney in court four years ago and the lawyers for Ed were cross-examining him, asking him how he had defended Ed, and he gave such raggly answers that I got up and left the courtroom. I couldn't believe that he was a professional attorney. He was supposed to be for Ed, but no way was he for him—not then and he never had been. He wasn't secretive about his feelings. He never tried to hide them. He never had communicated with the family about anything until court day, and he very seldom cross-examined any of the witnesses or questioned evidence; he just sat there and beat on the table with his fingers like "come on, let's just get this over with." The jury was all white. At one point his attorneys said he should have been brought back to North Carolina because that is where the alleged kidnapping took place. Alabama said no way would they even consider that. I think it was because they thought that if they took him back to North Carolina, he might get a lighter sentence. He was never charged with kidnapping.

As I grew older, I began to understand what had gone wrong that led to my father being killed. I didn't use that as a hatred in my heart. I used it to make sure that my children understood how things like that happen and that you have to work to make sure that it doesn't happen anymore. I'm so grateful that I didn't take that sorrow and turn it into hate. I took it and applied it to my life and used it to get on with my life. It was something bad that happened and our father was taken away from us at an early age. A lot of people say, "You should be upset with your uncle. If he hadn't killed your father, Ed wouldn't have had to take over the family responsibilities while he was still a child, so you should look back at your uncle." But that's like trying to drive an automobile looking backward. There's no way you can go forward looking backward. I don't look back like that. I look forward. I'm sure that is what my brother would have liked to do. I don't go back and bury my father every day.

Ed just had a bad life. He had a terrible life. It made me look at other people. Sometimes people are put in bad situations. When he went to prison, he had not studied his books. His reading and writing were not good. He taught himself how to read and write. He studied law. He got permission to tutor other people in prison. I was so proud of him for being willing to put something back. His personality changed from being rowdy to being calm and so gentle. He'd talk with me about when we were children and our mother was gone all the time and he would emphasize making sure my children didn't experience that.

After my mother died, Ed really beat himself up. He knew that she started back drinking because of his situation. She was planning to start a new life, but she just died—Feb.15 the year before him. He lived a year and a day after. When she suddenly died, he went on a guilt trip. He couldn't really deal with his grief and his love because of being incarcerated. We had to get her buried and then get there for Ed. He needed to grieve.

Surely if you commit a crime when you are a youngster you do have a choice whether you are going to change or stay locked in that particular situation, and I think that society should look at these people as people and stop looking at them as a crime. Ed was never addressed as a person. It was always the crime. After you commit a crime you take on a new identity. Society isn't willing to see you as a human being anymore. You are not the person you were born. You lose your name and pick up a crime. That's your title. People are not willing to address that issue and try to make changes. People are afraid of changes. When it comes to the death penalty, people aren't willing to look at it and be sure it is the best thing. The U. S. army has a slogan, "Be the best that you can be"...that is until it comes to the death penalty, then you do what you want to do.

But until you have the experience of sitting down talking with someone in perfectly good health, of sound mind—you are sitting there watching them time the hours they have left on earth—until you experience that you can't imagine what it feels like. It feels like no other feeling I've had in my life, and I would hope nobody would have to experience that feeling. You can't describe it. There's nothing to identify it with. When you tell someone you love them, you can't tell them, "I wish you well," because there is no healing or forgiveness for them. They're going to be executed. A lot of people don't understand what electrocution is. Electrocution is something that burns your insides. I'm sure that if you've ever been burned, you know what it feels like. It's a terrible feeling. So I can just think what being electrocuted must feel like. What is that person thinking about in those last hours and minutes? That last morning they wake up they know they are going to be executed that night. When their eyes pop open what do they think about? "Well, I just thought that this is the last morning my eyes will pop open." That is something to deal with all that day. I watched Ed, my brother. He was not a sweet eater. He ate candy all that last day. At one point I asked him, "Why are you eating candy like that?" He said, "Why not; I'll never taste it again." We talked about things that happened when we were children, mistakes that were made, good times shared as well as bad times, what could have been that would never be now. He laughed with the children. He would ask what time it was, how much time was left. "How many more hours do I have?" We tried to do something to take away some pain. The kids had a lot of questions because they didn't understand what was about to happen and why. They wanted to know why he was going to leave us right then and why they couldn't come back to visit him. He was trying to deal with that as well as the fact that he was soon to walk out of the room for the last time and walk toward his death. My understanding is that when he went in to sit in the electric chair, he sat down very calmly and stretched his arms out to be buckled to the seat.

Ed was the reason that I decided to do something for me. I needed to work on being a better person and trying to contribute something to society. He would constantly call me whenever I was in the hospital or having a bad time, and he would always have something encouraging to say. I felt like I should be comforting him, but he would call me and say, "Pam, what you need to do is to try to apply something different to your life. You really need to take good care of yourself." If I was living in a bad situation, he'd say, "You don't need to do that now. You need to do something positive for yourself." Or when I was going through something with my children, he would always call and talk to those children. He would encourage them: "Don't do that. Do you see where your uncle is today? I would have loved for someone to have taken out some time or somebody to care enough about me, to have shared with me—'Ed, you don't have to do that.' You see, my situation was different, and that's why I'm saying to you—I don't want you to end up here. I don't want you to end up a label not a name."

Ed told me, "Life is good and life is precious and I want you to enjoy it and live it to the fullest, but by the same token, who is watching the kids? Somebody needs to be available when the children need you. Always put aside some time for your children—family time—be sure you do that." I applied that to my life. I make sure I put aside time for them. I make sure that I am involved in their lives. I make sure that if they need to talk, I'm not just their mother but their friend as well. I haven't had any experience with my kids being incarcerated. They've done very well in their areas. I think that Ed talking to them has made that possible. They listened to what he had to say because he was talking from a prison cell, and he made them see how important it was that they didn't end up behind those prison bars. People don't forgive you when you step behind bars or when you step outside what society will accept. They don't ever come back and look at you as a human being from that point on.

Ed told them that talking things out gets you the right answer—the answer you are looking for vs. quick decisions. I applied that also to my life. Ed talked a lot about quick decisions being the wrong decisions.

He was next to the youngest child, but was pushed into the role of the oldest child and that was true even later in life. He picked up our father's role. You would always have thought he was the older brother and I was the younger sister. He took over the leadership. A couple of times I sent him a father's day card, saying, "You are not my brother, but my father." He'd laugh and say, "I'm not trying to be your father. I'm just trying to help you out the best way that I know how." He was the only person I could talk to about our mother's alcoholism. He always seemed to call me at the right time. He knew the right words. One time when I took her to the hospital and was going on with him about all my problems with her, he said, "Stop. You are her daughter, not her mother. You need to talk to her out of love—share with her your concerns. After you do that, then you need to go on with your life, go back home, go inside, make sure that this does not happen to you and your children, but don't close her out as a person."

I guess when something like this happens to a family a lot of things change in your life. At one point I was so upset, I realized that I didn't want to be Pam anymore because Pam was hurting so badly that I was trying to get away from her and become a new person. I started with cutting all my hair off; I thought that would take away the pain. It didn't work. I was needing to feel that closeness with my brother one more time. I would lay down at night hoping that I could at least dream about him. I've never had a dream since February 16—no kind of dream. I go to sleep with the electric chair and I wake up with the electric chair. My life got affected by the decision of the State. They didn't just execute Ed. They executed a whole people that are still trying to get up out of the electric chair. I'm determined to get up. I'm determined to go on and do the very best that I can, to help the next person that I can help.

You keep hoping it's a dream and that you'll wake up. I'm still hoping I'm going to wake up and have the dream be over. For a long time, when the phone would ring, I'd think it was going to be Ed. Then I'd realize that he isn't among the living anymore. They stop the person when they execute him, but it starts a new chapter for the family. People don't understand how the family, the children are affected. It's a lot to ask children to go through.

It's been really tough, especially when my kids were around 10 and 11. They would get in fights at school. Other kids would pick on them. My kids would cry a lot. When I would take them to visit Ed, they'd start crying and halfway back they were still crying. They knew what death row meant. I'd ask why they were crying and they'd say, "Because they are going to kill my uncle." It was very hard on them all the years Ed was incarcerated, and my kids were punished. It was like torture going to see him, see what prison was, knowing they were going to carry out the execution.

The kids had problems sleeping afterwards. They knew he had been executed, but I wouldn't let them see him dead because of the way he looked from the burns. They would cry at night, couldn't sleep. The littlest was still dealing with my mother's death, and then her uncle was killed. She started saying she wanted to die so she could be with her grandmother and her uncle. She carried those problems on to school. They had her see a doctor. He started talking with her because she was bed-wetting again. Kids deal with things they don't understand in different ways. She wanted to know why everyone was crying, why things like that happen? She expected a grown person to be able to fix it. She wanted to know, since I went down to the prison all the time, why I couldn't stop it.

My granddaughter doesn't understand why we can't go see Uncle Ed anymore. I tell her he isn't there. There are a lot of questions to answer for little children. They really suffer a lot back in our community. When the wreath was on the door, a lot of kids didn't understand, wanted to know how he got killed. They wanted to know what execution is. Why do they do it? If the person knew they were going to die? Did they cry? These are questions that little minds have—Was he scared? Did they tie him up? What did he think about it? They ask things to try to understand. One little boy wanted to know if they put a sack on his head and swung him from a tree. It was also talked about in school because of the newspapers. One little boy wrote a paragraph about the execution—he wanted to know what the people who do the execution do after its over. Do they have to go to jail? Another wondered if the executioner was a hit man. He was told they were state workers, and then he said, "If they are state workers then they should go to jail."

It's like dying every day. I feel somewhat like death row inmates who feel that they are already dead. I can't get any sense out of it. I'm still trying to understand what happened and I have a problem dealing with that and then I have to try to explain to my children. I don't have an answer for them. I feel helpless when it comes to explaining to them how life is taken away like that, and especially when it is legal to do it that way. Those are questions that my children have for me. "Who answers to my Uncle Ed's death?" When I tell them "society," they want to know who is society? I tell them that is the people in the U.S. They want to know "Does that mean that we killed Uncle Ed, because we are people in the U.S.?" It makes it difficult for me as a parent to try to explain. Then there are my grandchildren. You're talking about a whole other generation. This thing is passed down from generation to generation. We are teaching them that killing is wrong, but then they look back in their family tree and see that in this case right here it is society that has permission to kill. It's okay for some people to kill and not for others. It confuses them. They want to know which is it? If it's wrong, it's wrong, if it's right, it's right. You can't say it's half wrong and half right. Because a little mind doesn't understand that. I don't understand it. I'm sure I won't ever understand it.

In terms of effects on our family—my older brother doesn't want people to know he was related to Ed because he says it cost him a job. They connected his name to Ed's and people at work got scared of him, so he doesn't want anyone to know that Ed was his brother. My case is different. I am proud to be Ed's sister, and I would stand up at the White House, on top of the fence or on top of the world and I would say that Ed was my brother and I loved him very dearly. I supported him. I still love him. I believe in him. He was a human being. He was just like your brother is to you. There is no difference. He was my brother.

This has affected my health. I have problems with my eyes because of my diabetes. Stress has made my sugar real high. I've had migraine headaches. At one point I was given sleeping pills because I couldn't sleep and they affected me too much. One brother couldn't be there for the execution—he couldn't take the stress and because of his alcoholism, he now has cirrhosis. He can't get over the loss of Ed to our family—he had stopped drinking, but he has returned to it. Our eldest brother and our baby brother—

they cry it out. The second brother drinks it out. It has really uprooted and upset our whole family. Our mother was driven back to drinking and died 11 months before Ed. What it does to an everyday life is that it's like being punished every day for no reason.

A death sentence should be taken very seriously because when you take a life, you can't give it back. It's forever. Instead of trying to get rid of things maybe we should try to fix them. I'd like to see people more educated on what a death sentence is. How many people are involved. When Ed sat in that electric chair, by no means did he ever sit in that electric chair by himself. He had three brothers and one sister—a host of nieces and nephews. A piece of us sat in that electric chair too. He wasn't the only one who suffered from this. We are still suffering. They executed him but they execute us every day because we can't make any sense of it. We don't see a beneficiary. It's just a circle of hurt that won't go away. In my case, I know it took a toll on my health, my way of thinking, my lifestyle. I didn't feel like I could hold onto my job anymore. I didn't feel like I could do well in my job. I had this pain, and I spent time sneaking away to cry. I needed to resign and I did, on February 20, four days after his execution. I basically live my life day by day, trying to cope and make some sense, and put together what I can to make a living. I don't want anyone else to experience that pain.

Human life kept me from going in the direction of vengeance. People are people; they bleed the same as I do, they cry the same—for that reason I could not get consumed by vengeance. The victim's family (the other side of the victim's family because I certainly am a victim too) said that after the execution they would feel better. I don't have anything to look forward to in terms of feeling better. There was not just one murder. There are two dead people now. There is not just one family hurt—there are two. There are children hurting that had nothing to do with it. There are people that have died with broken hearts. People have forced themselves into an early death because of the pain. It's a long chain. It goes on and on and on. I don't see a stopping point. I don't see who benefits.

It tears a piece of your heart out. You can't begin to imagine what it's like. Thinking about them pulling something down over his eyes. What it must be like to walk to the chair. You can't imagine what kind of pain it is to have somebody walk away from you, telling you that they love you but that society has decided that it is time for them to go.

If Ed could have met with the victim's family directly, it might have made a difference. He expressed a desire to do this and tried to arrange it, but his attorneys advised him that it was not a wise move. He also did an interview on the radio and apologized in public. That message went to them if they were listening. At that point he knew he was not going to get a stay of execution. All he wanted was forgiveness from them, but he got no response. That was a message to him that he had to be executed. They did not wish to hear what he had to say. As far as they were concerned, he was not a human being. I hate that it is that way. They don't believe in mistakes. They don't believe in apologies. They don't believe people can be rehabilitated.

Outside the prison, after the execution, the fact that there were people in favor of the death penalty was almost as hard to deal with as the hatred of the victim's family. I don't think people let go of the vengeance after an execution is over. Some people were there because someone in their family had been killed, and the person who did it had already been executed, but then they seemed to look around to see who else could be executed, so they live every day looking for the next death. It's like a serial thing. They thrive on somebody having to die. They even shouted at my children and grandchildren. They said, "One down and a hundred to go," referring to others on death row. That frightened my children. I tried to explain to them why the people were screaming at them. They couldn't understand why people didn't like their uncle. They thought it was that people disliked them. The accused's family has to deal with things like this. They feel like they did something wrong because they loved their loved one.

When people yell at children, it is usually because they have done something wrong, so that is how the children viewed it. They wanted to know what they did wrong. They saw some people crying and some laughing. They didn't understand. You don't know what to say to them. You have to stand back and let them figure it out. But when you leave them like that they may come up with the wrong answer.

People knew about the crime but didn't know the person. So Ed lost his identity to crime. While in prison he had grown from being a confused teenager into a fine human being. I watched my brother go from being slow to speak and not even understanding a lot of things to being a very, very intelligent young man and very caring about other people and also remorseful about the things that he had experienced early on in life. He was trying to put together what he could do to backtrack and get it right this time. I watched him for 19 years on death row. I watched his personality change as well as his appearance, and it bothered him that society said that people on death row cannot change. He worked really hard at becoming the person he was when he was executed. He was more concerned about other people than himself. He hardly ever said anything about himself. Even after he had an execution date he had asked that his family not be told until the last minute because he didn't want us to go through that grief. Instead of thinking about someone to share that grief, he was more concerned to spare us as long as possible. It wasn't until two weeks before the execution that I actually knew that he had a date.

Sometimes I think about what really happened down there. It's like a pain that comes in your stomach. It's a hurt that comes deep, deep down; it's like a stomach cramp. It is the most cruel thing that can happen to a human being. You are burning a person alive.

One of the hardest things was sitting there and trying to prepare to say goodbye—hoping the clock would stop—trying not to send him away sad, trying to do what he asked of us—it took everything I had within me to say goodbye.

I asked him if he was afraid to die. He said he didn't have the right answer to that because he had never been dead. "Like anybody, you feel afraid of the unknown, but I don't honestly know if I'm afraid of death."

He kept saying, "Will this make a difference?" He talked about the mother of the victim, hoping this was going to help her get on with her life. He said, " I don't want to die but if this will help her..."

He said he had made his peace with God. He said he felt like he had come to earth, born into the world for a season, but then was in prison from so early an age, he didn't have a life after that. He didn't know what normal things were like— going to a supermarket or having a driver's license. He felt like he was just here and didn't accomplish anything—that he was in the world but wasn't—dead and buried at 38.

A lot of things have changed. My children are the next generation to come from Ed or from our family tree. We are doing everything possible to assure that history doesn't repeat itself. We are trying to be good citizens and trying to be a plus to society. That was the dead man's wish. That was what Ed hoped for and wished for us. I'm really putting in a lot of time with my children to make sure. I have found a way to work at home. I'm devastated, I'm scared that my kids may have to do some things to survive with me not being there. I want to make sure that I'm there for them even if it costs me. I'm afraid that it might eventually cost them more if I'm not there, so I have just reordered my life to make sure that this doesn't happen to another one of my family members—that the nightmare doesn't con-tinue on— that we survive and make it through this.

I believe in human life, and the person that pulled the switch on my brother, as much as it hurts, I would have no problem showing love for that person. I would love them the same way as my neighbor. That's who I am. That's who my brother was. And I forgive them for what they have done. I would just like to see us come up with some way of making sure that no other family has to go through this because what it does is you end up with a whole group of victims, a whole group of people hurting, crying, having a hard time with society.

I go to sleep at night standing outside Holman Prison. I wake up in the morning, and I'm still standing. I can't put any sense to it, so it's like something that haunts me every day. But I don't use that for bitterness. I use that to try to find out what I can do to make a difference. What can I do to contribute something to society other than killing? I want the killing to stop. It's not a good feeling for blood to run 24 hours a day. Killing. Killing. Killing. Killing because of killing. Killing because someone else kills someone else so killing is the answer. Society is telling our children that killing is the answer and I think they are getting the wrong message. Killing is not the answer. What I would like to see happen for our people and our society is for us to come together and write down some opinions on what we can do to stop the killing. We need to come up with some answers that would be good for society, good for the next generation, something that we all could live with. We say we are concerned about life, but killing is not life. Killing is death. I am so sick of killing that I don't know what to do. No answers. Nobody is talking about answers—other solutions when a crime is committed to make sure that the person pays for the crime and there is restitution for the victim but not more killing. I am totally against killing. I don't care who is doing the killing. I don't care whether it is me or my children or the government. Killing is wrong—whoever is doing it. There is no right way to kill.

I think we've had enough hurt. It's time for us to go through the healing process now and to make sure this doesn't continue to happen.

Pamela Crawford lives in Charlotte, North Carolina. Her brother, Ed Horsley, was executed February 16, 1996 at the Alabama State Prison at Atmore. Ms Crawford operates a day care center out of her home and is a mother and grandmother.

178

"Once we remove that out of her system, she'll run much better."

Christian Snyder - "The X-Ray"

DR. ARMOND H. START

"Physicians and the Death Penalty"

Physicians have been confronted by the issues surrounding the death penalty and state ordered executions for many years. Physicians deal with life and death issues as part of their responsibility to their patients and to the society in general. In any discussion of the death penalty and executions, the medical profession is drawn into the debate of physicians' involvement or participation in executions. While there has never been a survey of physicians' attitudes toward involvement in executions, it is safe to say that there is a division among physicians on this subject. Many physicians will not publicly state their views while, privately, voicing the opinion that it is necessary and appropriate for physicians to assist in a final judgment and sentence, whether that be by lethal injection, by electrocution, or by lethal gas. Historically, physicians have been involved in executions. The guillotine developed by two French physicians was commonly used to execute criminals in France.[1] In 1987 a physician study favored electrocution or a drug overdose rather than hanging. The physicians at that time were objecting to the public spectacle of hanging which often was not carried out in a professional manner.

In 1980 the AMA House of Delegates adopted the following resolution: [2]

1. An individual's opinion on capital punishment is the personal moral decision of the individual.

2. A physician as a member of a profession dedicated to preserving life when there is hope of doing so should not be a participant in a legally authorized execution.

 3. A physician may make a determination or certification of death as currently provided by law in any situation.

In 1992 the AMA House of Delegates[3] again spoke to the issue of physician participation and capital punishment. In the twelve year period since the resolution of 1980, physicians were reported to participate in executions and the House of Delegates believed that it was necessary to define precisely and specifically what the term prohibition from participation meant.

The resolution adopted in 1992 specifically outlined what actions by the physician would constitute physician participation in execution. The resolution also specified what actions did not constitute physician participation in execution. Following the action of the AMA House of Delegates, all state medical societies and state medical licensing boards were provided a copy of the AMA action. This information was distributed under the auspices of the National Center for Correctional Healthcare Studies at the University of Wisconsin Medical School. All state medical societies and all state licensing boards were informed that participation by physicians in state ordered executions would be considered unethical behavior and subject to disciplinary action by the state professional society and/or the state medical licensing boards. In spite of the widespread dissemination of these actions, the United States Attorney General, William P. Barr, announced on November 30, 1992 that the federal executions would require the presence of at least one physician.[4] The proposed regulations would also require a physician or another qualified person to declare death.

Physician involvement in executions became a significant issue for the medical profession when the death penalty was reinstated in the United States. In 1972 the Supreme Court declared all death penalty laws unconstitutional. In 1976 the Legislature in the State of Oklahoma rewrote the execution statutes to conform with the guidelines outlined by the 1972 Supreme Court decision. Oklahoma became the first state to legislate state executions by the lethal injection method. Previously, the State of Oklahoma had a statute requiring execution by electrocution. In developing the new statute, the Senate author of the legislation determined that it would cost approximately $75,000 to repair the electric chair. In addition, the author received information that if the execution would be carried out by gas, the state would be faced with a $300,000 cost to build a gas chamber. The Senate author, in consultation with physicians, wrote into the newly modified state execution statutes the requirement that execution would be carried out using a lethal dose of a short acting barbiturate, a muscle paralyzing agent, and a drug to paralyze the heart. The physicians advising the Senate author intended that this methodology would be more humane and of little cost. It was represented that the short acting barbiturate would cause an intense sleep and that the muscle paralyzing drug and the drug paralyzing the heart would cause the death while the person was asleep. The statute containing this provision was passed by the 1976-77 state legislature and signed by the governor.

In July of 1977 I transferred from the Oklahoma State Department of Health to the Oklahoma State Department of Corrections. At the time of the transfer, I was the director of Communicable Disease Control for the Oklahoma State Department of Health. The Department of Corrections was under a court order to implement a health care delivery system in the State prison system. The work effort required an implementation of a health care delivery system that met the AMA prison standards. During the process of implementing the system, I was requested by the director to write the policies and procedures by which a person would be executed under the newly passed legislation. At the beginning I believed that writing the policies and procedures for execution were part and parcel of writing the policies and procedures for the delivery of basic health care services to the inmate population. During the process of thinking about the procedures and discussing the procedures with prison officials, I became increasingly uncomfortable with the medical staff becoming involved in the lethal execution process. I realized that a physician could not be involved in any manner and any activity associated with execution. I became convinced that this was unethical behavior for a physician, even though it was a legal procedure. I sought consultation and advice from the State Medical Society physician leadership in how I might approach this problem. With the support of the physician leadership, I informed the prison officials that I would not participate in any activity dealing with the lethal execution process. I refused to write policies and procedures that I was directed to write by the director of the Department of Corrections. I became a very unpopular employee in the Department of Corrections because I refused to participate in this process. The militaristic mind set of a Department of Corrections requires loyalty and the following of orders. I was viewed as not being loyal and guilty of not following direct orders. I concentrated on implementing the health care delivery system and brought a resolution to the AMA House of Delegates through the Oklahoma State Medical Association. The Oklahoma delegates to the American Medical Association introduced the resolution to the AMA House of Delegates in 1980, and the House of Delegates adopted the resolution as indicated in the earlier part of this chapter.

While Oklahoma was the first state to pass legislation that required execution by the lethal injection method, the state of Texas was the first state to actually carry out the procedure. I became the Medical Director of the Texas Department of Corrections in July of 1983. Lethal injection had already occurred in the state of Texas prior to my arrival. According to the information that I received, physicians were involved in carrying out the procedure. I made it very clear to prison authorities in the State of Texas that neither I, nor any member of the medical staff, would participate in any aspect of the execution process. During my tenure as medical director from 1983 through 1986, lethal injections were carried out in a systematic fashion. To my knowledge, no member of the Division of Health Services participated in any way in this process. I distanced myself from any discussion regarding the lethal injection process. Information came to me that the

Department of Corrections contracted with physicians outside of the prison system to assist them in this procedure and that the mechanics of the lethal injection procedure were managed by non-medical personnel.

Morality

A significant percentage of our society, physicians included, are confused between morality and ethics. In this particular section I would like to address the issue of morality of the death penalty. The basic discussion of morality involves the issue of whether state ordered executions are right or wrong. There is a significant difference of opinion on this issue and many physicians sincerely believe that it is right to execute a person for certain crimes. For these physicians, the death penalty and becoming involved in the execution process, does not present a problem. A physician as a member of society has the right to his or her opinion regarding the morality of state executions. In my official capacity as medical director of the state prison systems in Oklahoma and Texas, I avoided stating my personal views in regard to the rightness or wrongness of the death penalty. The reason is because the questioner frequently follows with a question regarding the morality of abortion. While there may be some similarities between abortion and the death penalty in the minds of some people, there are very distinct differences and the death penalty debate is frequently clouded by a discussion of the abortion issues. It is my personal opinion that the death penalty is wrong. As a member of the faith community, with the ability to monitor the discussion over the past 20 years, I have come to the conclusion that state or government ordered execution is an immoral act.

It is very difficult to intelligently debate the death penalty issue. The atmosphere usually becomes charged with an attitude of vengeance, anger, hostility, and efforts for political gain. The individuals that I have met in my professional career who do not support the death penalty are usually kind individuals who present an attitude of forgiveness. While I believe very strongly that a person must be held accountable for his or her behavior and that society has a right to punish by incarceration certain kinds of crimes, I do not believe it is right for a state to take the life of a person as an act of vengeance for murder. There is ample evidence that a person's behavior and lifestyle do change with increasing age. I became convinced that the majority of inmates on the death row unit in Texas could be released and would not commit further crimes. The process of aging and maturation within a structured environment has a significant impact on future behavior. It appears to me that it is wrong to take someone's life who is sincerely sorry for past criminal acts and displays every indication that a significant lifestyle change has occurred. Many of the men and women incarcerated for life become model prisoners and have a significant positive effect on the total population of incarcerated people. It is not true that a life sentence without parole is a wasted life. Many individuals faced with the reality that their lives will be spent in prison adapt to that environment and become productive in terms of supporting many of the activities of that institution. Many inmates on life sentences form the basic work force that maintains the laundry, grounds, food service, etc. These individuals do make a contribution to the operation and maintenance of the facility. Wardens of maximum security prisons frequently state that the best behaved prisoners are those that are serving a life sentence. Those who maintain that a life sentence in a prison is a wasted existence usually have never been in a prison nor have any idea of how a prison is managed.

Ethics

Physicians through their professional society have declared that activity of a physician in the execution process is unethical behavior. The AMA House of Delegates in 1980 and again in 1992, passed resolutions in unambiguous language that any activity of a physician in the implementation of the death penalty would be considered unethical behavior.[2,3] Furthermore, unethical behavior by a physician requires a review by the State Licensing Board in terms of a license to practice medicine or disciplinary action for violating the ethics of the profession. Medical ethics is frequently defined as that professional behavior that is not prescribed by law. There is no law that prohibits a physician from involvement in a state ordered execution. The medical profession has reached a consensus that participation in executions is unethical behavior.

For many centuries physicians have had a social contract with their patients. This social contract was first articulated in the oath of Hippocrates which states in part, "I will prescribe regimen for the good of my patients according to my ability and my judgment and never do harm to anyone. To please no one will I prescribe a deadly drug nor give advice which may cause his death." The 37th session of the United Nations General Assembly adopted a resolution on principles of medical ethics which required the protection of prisoners and detainees against torture and other cruel, inhumane, or degrading treatment or punishment.[5] The resolution further goes on to state that "it is a contravention of medical ethics for health personnel, particularly physicians, to be involved in any professional relationship with prisoners or detainees the purpose of which is not solely to evaluate, protect, or improve their physical and mental health."It is quite clear in the resolutions of the medical profession on this procedure that the role of the executioner is a proper role of law enforcement professionals and it is their responsibility alone. The AMA's executive vice president Todd stated at an exhibit of documents on physician participation in Nazi Germany's crime against humanity, "When the healing hand becomes a hand inflicting the wound, the world is turned inside out. We physicians must be the first to say no to the ever present danger. Doctors must never again become agents of the State. No, first and foremost, doctors must always serve as the agents, the advocates not of the State, but of our human patients."[6]

It does not require the skill or the medical expertise of a physician or other health care provider to carry out an execution. The process of execution, whether that be by hanging, electrocution, firing squad, or lethal injection, can be implemented by a number of individuals who are not involved in the health care delivery system. There are many individuals in our society who are adept at starting intravenous fluids who are not part of the health care delivery system. These individuals are found in research laboratories, veterinary medicine, and ex-armed forces paramedics. It does not require a health care provider to write a prescription to acquire the medication for lethal injection. The same process of law that gives the provider a license to practice medicine is a law that permits the State to acquire the medication from the pharmacy. It does not require the skill or expertise of a health care provider to calculate an overdose of medication. This can be easily discerned by anyone with a high school diploma.

Before Dr. Kevorkian introduced his "suicide machine" on national television, he was marketing his "suicide machine" to departments of corrections who were charged with the responsibility of carrying out execution using the lethal injection methodology. Dr. Kevorkian's sales pitch to departments of corrections was that the inmate himself or herself would trigger the onset of the lethal chemicals into their blood stream and therefore would not involve the actual participation of any employee. While some states require a physician to sign the death certificate on all deaths, this maneuver can be accomplished at some time and at some distance from the actual execution site. In most cases, however, a public servant is permitted to sign the death certificate, either a coroner or a medical examiner. If the word legislator were substituted for the word physician in all death penalty statutes, I believe that there would be little enthusiasm for carrying out the death penalty. The purpose of involving physicians in this process is to sanitize death. It would seem that the physician involved in the process of execution would somehow make it more legitimate and more easily acceptable. It is my strong belief that all health care personnel should not be involved in any aspect of implementing the death penalty. It is not necessary and it should not be required of any health care professional to be involved in this process. As Dr. Eugene Feingold, Ph.D., J.D., President of the American Public Health Association, has stated, "The participation of health professionals in an execution adds a deceptive tone of humaneness to the execution. Executions are not humane. The proposed regulation and thinking

behind it are a corruption and exploitation of the healing role
sonnel."[6] I believe very strongly that the patients that we serve
that we are committed and dedicated to the preservation of li

186

Public Policy

Physicians must oppose the death penalty because it is bad public policy. In my view there are basically nine reasons why the death penalty should not be a part of a civilized society.

1. The death penalty is not a deterrent to murder. There is no scientific study that has produced evidence that the death penalty deters violent crime. In fact, the murder rate in states with the death penalty is almost twice that of states without it. I have observed that the people who commit murder are usually not rational in terms of their cognitive behavior at the time they commit the crime. Many of them are intoxicated with drugs or consumed by out-of-control passions and/or anger. These individuals do not equate their behavior with consequences. Their thinking process is so disturbed and disoriented that the consequences of death don't occur to them. In a 1995 national poll of chiefs of police, 82% believed that murderers do not even think about possible punishments.

2. In the State of Wisconsin, the Wisconsin Bar Association and the Wisconsin State prosecutors are opposed to the death penalty. In the view of the lawyers and prosecutors there is no reason why the state of Wisconsin should rescind its 140 year policy against the death penalty. The Wisconsin Bar Association has produced materials under the heading "six reasons Wisconsin can live without the death penalty."

3. A true life sentence without parole does not equate with a meaningless existence. Persons can be productive and make a contribution to institutional life. Many inmates who realize that their entire life will be spent incarcerated make a decision to make the best of it and become active participants in the life and culture of the prison, which in the view of many wardens is a positive factor in the proper management of the institution.

4. The criminal justice system is a very imperfect system. There have been a number of individuals who were condemned to die who later were found to be innocent. Between 1905 and 1974, 23 persons were executed in error. Between 1973 and 1994, 54 persons were released from death row as innocent or probably innocent. Over 90% of death row inmates are indigent and are assigned over worked, under paid, under staffed, and/or inadequate counsel. In most states there simply is no formal procedure for hearing new evidence of a defendant's innocence prior to his or her execution date. After the trial, the legal system becomes locked in a battle over procedural issues rather than a re-examination of guilt or innocence.

5. The death penalty is applied disproportionately to minorities and the poor. Of the approximately 20,000 persons committing murder in the United States in each year, the 200 or so who are sentenced to death are not necessarily those whose crimes are the most atrocious or vicious. Race, income, quality of legal counsel, and geography all play large roles in the imposition of the death penalty. Ninety percent of death row inmates have no money. A study of the Texas judicial system demonstrated that 73% of persons convicted of capital crimes with court appointed attorneys were sentenced to death, whereas only 35% of defendants with private attorneys were sentenced to death. While blacks and whites are victims of homicide in almost equal numbers, 83% of the 221 persons executed since 1976 had white victims. Until 1994 in this century, there was only one instance where a white person was put to death for a murder of a black person and he was serving a life sentence for 7 other murders. In 1990 a study by the U.S. General Accounting Office concluded that there is "a pattern of evidence indicating racial disparities in the charging, sentencing, and imposition of the death penalty."

6. There is a great difficulty in determining a mental disorder. In many cases there is serious disagreement among mental health experts in determining whether an individual is "mad or bad." While the incidence of violence is not increased in the mentally disordered population, it is possible that a mentally disordered person may commit murder and the mental disorder not be recognized as a contributing factor. Many individuals with a border line mental retardation cover up their deficiencies by aggressive anti-social behavior. In addition, mental disorders and particularly psychiatric illnesses have a relapsing pattern that may play a role in that individual's specific behavior. A civilized society should not be involved in the execution of its mentally disordered population.

7. The cost of execution far exceeds the cost of incarceration for life. The most comprehensive study in the country found that the death penalty cost North Carolina $2 million per execution over the cost of a non-death penalty murder case with a sentence of imprisonment for life. In Texas a death penalty case costs an average of $2.3 million; this is about three times the cost of imprisoning someone in a single cell at the highest security level for 40 years. Florida spent an estimated $57 million on the death penalty from 1973 to 1988 to achieve 18 executions. That is an average of $3.2 million per execution.

8. The implementation of the death penalty is a mechanical nightmare. State officials who are charged with the responsibility of carrying out the death sentence are frequently faced with great difficulty in obtaining individuals to participate in the process. I have discussed the difficulty in recruiting health care professionals in the execution by lethal injection. The

process is very secretive and it involves a medicalization of death. If one is in a state that utilizes lethal gas, there is always a mechanical problem in terms of gas concentration and whether or not gas is capable of producing instant death. In those states that carry out the death penalty by electrocution, there is an issue regarding the capability of the electric charge and the degree of burned flesh that results from this process. The mechanical problem involved with hanging involves a discussion regarding the length of the rope based on the weight of the individual. The majority of people, when faced with an alternative to the death penalty, prefer life without parole plus restitution. It is the disagreeable aspect of the death penalty that I believe cause 44% of the people surveyed to prefer life without parole plus restitution to the execution process.

9. The carrying out of a death sentence requires individuals working for government to be at risk for unethical behavior. As state employees, many health care providers are intimidated into being involved in the process because of loyalty and because they feel obligated to carry out a legal procedure as part of their duties. The long delays awaiting execution (up to 10-15 years), subject the individual to a high degree of psychological torture. Health care providers are confronted with the treatment and management of these patients. In addition, health care providers are frequently confronted with situations that require life saving procedures only to have that procedure become ineffective because of the subsequent execution process.

In summary, it is my opinion as a physician, that the majority of physicians in this country oppose the death penalty on moral, ethical, and public policy grounds. As the State Bar of Wisconsin has stated, "the death penalty—Wisconsin can live without it."[7]

Armond Start graduated with an M.D. from the University of Michigan, and, after serving in the Air Force, got an M.P.H. from the University of Oklahoma College of Health. He received his Board Certification in Pediatrics in 1964, and served on the faculties of the Univ. of Wisconsin-Madison Medical School and the Univ. of Oklahoma College of Medicine. Dr. Start served as Medical Director and/or Consultant for the Departments of Corretions of Texas, Oklahoma, and Wisconsin. He was a member of the audit teams for the American Correctional Association's Commission on Accreditation, and a correctional medical consultant or expert witness of the U.S. Department of Justice, as well as at the DOCs of many states.

References

1. Weiner, D.B. "The Real Doctor Guillotin," JAMA 1972; 220:85-9.
2. Current opinion 2.06 of the Council on Ethical and Judicial Affairs. 1980.
3. "Physician Participation in Capital Punishment," Council on Ethical and Judicial

Affairs. Resolution 5, I-91. Dec. 8, 1992.

4. Department of Justice. "Implementation of Death Sentences in Federal Cases: Final
   Rule," Federal Register 1993;58(11):4898-902.

5. Resolution adopted by the general assembly 37/194 principles of medical ethics. 37th
   session of the United Nations. 1983.

6. "Health Professionals Oppose Rules Mandating Participation in Executions,"
   JAMA 1993; 269:721 -23.

7. "The Death Penalty: Six Reasons Wisconsin Can Live Without It," State Bar of
   Wisconsin 1996.

Clifford Boggess - "Escape from Death Row"

Beyond Imagining

Lindsay Graham Bannister - Wife of A.J. Bannister, Death Row Inmate

Anne Coleman - Mother of Frances Coleman, Murder Victim

John Yarbrough - Former Police Officer, Former Death Row Inmate

LINDSAY GRAHAM BANNISTER

"The eyes of the world are fixed on this case...This case will serve as a window through which others will judge the merits of the judicial system in the state of Missouri..."

Judge Myron H. Bright of the United States Court of Appeals, in the Eighth Circuit, wrote these words as part of his ten page dissent in the capital case of **Alan Jeffrey Bannister v. Paul K. Delo**, filed November 14th, 1996. I am married to Alan Bannister, and this is as much his story as it is mine.

Three and a half years earlier, I had arrived in the United States from Great Britain. It was a blisteringly hot August afternoon when I landed at Lambert International Airport in St. Louis. The savagery of the heat was surpassed only by the oppressive humidity which enveloped me as I walked across the parking lot of the airport. I was in Missouri to travel to Potosi Correctional Center, a maximum security prison around 70 miles from St. Louis. There, I was going to meet Alan Bannister, the man with whom I had been corresponding for the previous seven months.

In January of 1993, I had watched a documentary shown on BBC2 called "The Execution Protocol," a film which was thought-provoking, disturbing, educational and compelling. It examined the method of execution employed at Potosi Correctional Center—lethal injection. The narrative of the film concerned white collar staff whose responsibililties included the planning and conducting of executions, and three death row inmates; Alan was one of these men.

In common with many Europeans viewing the film, I was forced to confront my own ignorance. I felt somewhat ashamed of the pre-conceived notions I'd hitherto had of the stereotypical "death row inmate." Here was Alan, a man who displayed all of the attributes which I, and many others in society, would have never associated with a death row inmate. He was able to verbalize in an articulate, rational manner, his feelings concerning capital punishment, lethal injection, and his own mortality. He had an amazing clarity of thought and expression, his sentiments were immediately accessible, combining an honest subjectivity with consummate objectivity and an element of pragmatism which could only have been borne out of years of experience in the penal system.

In short, he was the complete antithesis of everything which I had ever imagined a death row inmate to be. He struck me as atypical, or perhaps he was the exception which proved the "rule"...

Alan J. Bannister, or C.P. (Capital Prisoner) #24, had been on death row since the age of 24; he was now 35 and so was I. To many people, this was arguably the only thing which we had in common. After all, we came from different countries, diverse cultures, and our life experiences were dramatically dissimilar, yet wholly reconcilable.

I believe that, for all of us, there are times in our lives when what few bonds unite us become infinitely more durable, stronger and more meaningful than those which (seemingly), separate, distinguish and distance us.

In the past three and a half years with Alan, I have known more happiness than at any other time in my life. These years have also been the most emotionally charged, stressful and, at times, painfully destabilizing.

Paradoxically, the agony of uncertainty has consolidated our relationship, and strengthened our resolve; we know that we must make every moment count. When a life is at stake, we don't waste time on trivialities. Our enemy is the death penalty which, in any context, goes hand in hand with social ignorance, and ignorance will always be exploited by unscrupulous and ruthless politicians.

I came from a country which had long since recognized that capital punishment was a brutal anachronism, that it had absolutely no place in late twentieth century Britain. In 1965, a private Member's Bill to abolish the death penalty for a trial period of five years was passed. The abolition of capital punishment was confirmed by Parliament in 1969. The public had grown increasingly aware, not only of the barbarism of the death penalty per se, but there had also evolved an acute sense of social anxiety, apprehension and disillusionment regarding the fallibility of the judicial/legal systems, the police force and other allied organizations.

Moreover, the sheer finality of a death sentence had become offensive to the collective consciousness of the nation. A posthumous pardon was of no comfort to the families of an executed prisoner who was later exonerated and proven to be innocent. Clearly the safeguards within the judicial system, which were supposed to obviate tragic irreversible miscarriages of justice, were simply insufficient and unreliable.

As with any system or any organization which is managed/administered by human beings, mistakes will always be made; no system will ever be without defect. However, if, when errors are made, their cumulative effect is to cause the death of another, then, as civilized, intelligent beings, we are duty bound to seriously question the worth and legitimacy of that system. Additionally, the crime statistics in Britain spoke for themselves. The existence of the death penalty as the ultimate "sanction" had no bearing whatsoever on the incidence of serious crime; as a deterrent, it was clearly ineffective.

So, to a society already questioning the value and virtue of the death penalty, the logical and ethical next step would be to abandon altogether the archaic practice of executing those found guilty of murder in the first degree.

To this day, no country in Western Europe embraces capital punishment, and no country in Western Europe has experienced a subsequent breakdown in the social order, let alone witnessed an explosion in serious criminal activity. It is clear that a society can function and can progress without something as retrograde and socially dysfunctional as the death penalty.

Ironically and sadly, the United States continues to execute those found guilty of capital offenses, continues to resist calls for the abolition of the death penalty, yet continues to condemn, vociferously, human rights abuses wherever else in the world they are perceived.

The statutes of a given state bestow the odious privilege of conducting state sanctioned murder on the prison authorities. And we elect the very politicians who support the death penalty; we give them a mandate to perpetuate the killing, to perpetuate the myth that state sanctioned murder is a just and fitting punishment.

I deplore the intrusion of politics into any debate which involves the life of another person. Where there are politics, there is political ambition; where there is ambition, there is opportunism and manipulation.

Here in Missouri, many members of the voting public have become passive, malleable and too easily persuaded of the need for the death penalty. These people will continue to be held hostage by their own ignorance unless or until the politicians, the media and educational establishments present these people with the truth. The tired old rhetoric which may sound appealing and plausible enough on the election platform would lose all credibility if the voters were educated and exposed to the truth about capital punishment. We should never stand idly by and permit others to define the boundaries of our knowledge and understanding. If we do, we are inviting intellectual manipulation by others. As we all know, vacuity of the mind is a godsend to those obsessed with their own personal political agenda, who cultivate public fear and then have unlimited access to the media. Adolf Hitler recognized the relative ease with which a populace could be indoctrinated. A diet of constant propaganda which exploited fear itself, along with the monopolization of the media, guaranteed the success of the brainwashing.

The exploitation of public fear and insecurity remains the passport to political success, at least as far as the death penalty is concerned. Tendentious and offensive as this is, there is no avoiding the unpleasant reality that political ambition has acquired an ugly bedfellow in capital punishment, ugly, but remarkably effective. There are valuable votes to be had with the easy allure of capital punishment. It has become dangerously attractive to a public which submissively allows itself to be seduced into believing that the "eye for an eye" philosophy is an appropriate response, the only solution to serious crime.

The penal system itself, at least at Potosi Correctional Center, attempts to degrade, dehumanize and demoralize its captives—often it does so with remarkable success. It does so in an insidious, calculated manner, which, for so many, culminates in the ultimate form of punishment—death itself at the hands of the prison officials.

State sanctioned murder, masquerading as capital punishment, is morally bankrupt, gratuitously cruel and counter-productive. A death sentence immediately negates the remote possibility of rehabilitation. If we are in earnest about the humane confinement/treatment of offenders and the potential for their ultimate return to society, our penal policy should not start off from the premise that a given individual could not, under any circumstances, have the potential to return to society as a responsible person who has unequivocally, positively changed for the better.

It would appear that in those states which consider the death penalty to be indispensable, there is a profound failure to grasp the concept of personal reform and remorse of an offender. Forgiveness and rehabilitation have been superseded by a vicarious social revenge and the systematic, needless destruction of life in execution chambers throughout the United States.

"Homicide—Legal" is the sinister misnomer used by the coroner and the prison authorities to describe the cause of death of an executed prisoner at Potosi Correctional Center. It conveniently prevents the process of execution from being termed "murder" (by definition, a premeditated act), and therefore absolves the perpetrators of any culpability.

Alan came to within an hour and forty-five minutes of being executed in the hospital wing of the prison in December of 1994. No inmate at PCC relishes the prospect of a visit to the hospital there. Far from being a place of care and healing, it is synonymous with death and despair; the execution chamber is within mere feet of the treatment area.

The "holding cell" is a suffocatingly tiny ante-room adjacent to the execution chamber. In it, occupying less than half of the floor space, is a metal cage with close knit mesh—a holding cell within a holding cell—where 24 hour supervision is made easy with the assist of 24 hour fluorescent lighting and 24 hour video surveillance.

All physical contact between the condemned man and his family is strictly prohibited. Any attempt made to move close to, let alone to touch, one's husband, father, son, etc. results in the termination of that visit. And in case anyone is in any doubt as to how near to the cage they may venture, the prison authorities have thoughtfully painted a line on the floor of the holding cell beyond which no visitor must step, reach or lean.

A serious execution date is issued approximately six weeks prior to the actual execution. The condemned man is immediately taken out of "general population" and placed in Adminstrative Segregation. Loosely translated, this means that he is placed in an isolation cell, has his contact visits with his family taken away, and may only talk to and see them from behind glass, on the institution's telephones. He has no physical contact with anyone and loses all other telephone privileges (with the exception of attorney calls) completely.

This is all part of the much vaunted Missouri Execution Protocol. The callous rigidity of these rules defies all standards of common decency and compassion. The vigor with which this arbitrary protocol is enforced betrays the extent to which the Department of Corrections has become bereft of any humanity.

The nightmare of the five days which Alan spent in the holding cell in December of 1994 is still fresh in my mind; recounting it inevitably brings the pain of it all back into sharp focus.

Alan's execution was set for 12:01 am on December 7th, 1994. He had been incarcerated for just over a decade, for a crime which had involved an accidental shooting during a fight. Pivotal to the excessiveness of his death sentence was an initial catalog of legal incompetence and ineffectiveness, coupled with numerous constitutional violations. All of this was the subject of a filmed documentary about Alan, his life and the case which had brought him to death row. Entitled "Raising Hell—The Life of A.J. Bannister," this film brought the facts of the case to the attention of an international audience of over 40 million people. Public concern and outrage concerning the injustice of the death penalty in his case reached an unprecedented level. At last, the public could see for themselves how the justice system had betrayed and abandoned Alan right from the very beginning, and that its consistent failure to remedy its own mistakes suggested very strongly that it had also lost sight of its own raison d'être. Alan was within days of paying the ultimate price.

There was no escape from the mental torture which intensified as December 6th drew closer. The inability to touch, or even see him properly through the close meshed metal screen, compounded an agony which few people, unless they have actually experienced it, could ever truly understand.

Even now, in 1997, I'm not sure if I can convey the full extent of the pain, tension, and heartache which all of us involved were forced to endure. For me, the memory of those days is extraordinarily vivid, yet the mental torment is almost too vivid to describe.

We were all locked inside our own personal hells—reaching out for Alan, wanting to comfort him while not adding to his distress by openly displaying fear and despair.

The physical and mental exhaustion which worked its way through me was not offset in the slightest by "sleep." It was a shallow, restless, semi-conscious slumber, which invariably gave way to the real nightmare which resumed on waking.

There were fleeting moments when it seemed inconceivable that Alan might be executed. At other times there was a crushing realization that the most deadly scenario of all was perfectly conceivable.

Those of us outside in the muddy, windswept field adjacent to the prison were given the news that the U.S. Supreme Court had upheld the stay of execution by 6-3. However, the prison authorities neglected to mention this to Alan for nearly an hour after we had received the news.

Potosi Correctional Center has recently (in the past two years) given greater definition to the meaning of "institutional depravity" than at any other time in its short eight year history.

With the change of Superintendents in 1995, came numerous disturbing changes. One of the most shocking developments took place in 1996 when the Department of Corrections successfully managed to ban the media from all Missouri's prisons. A controversial court battle ensued. Although ostensibly a blanket media ban, it was actually aimed at Potosi Correctional Center, or rather at its inmates, and Reverend Larry Rice.

Rev. Rice had been highlighting many of the men's stories and showing filmed interviews with the inmates on his own television network. For once, the public was being exposed to more than one version of "the truth." Condemned men now had the opportunity to explain their cases to the viewers, discuss their fears, their families, etc.

It soon became obvious that Rev. Rice had managed to project these men as human beings; they weren't all saints and they certainly weren't all innocent. It was the mere fact that the public was actually getting to "know," or at least listen to, these men, and understand that maybe, just maybe, there had been a miscarriage of justice in a particular case. This proved to be the last straw as far as the Department of Corrections was concerned.

Official paranoia reared its ugly head and the Attorney General of Missouri informed the media that "...death row is not a movie set..." This was an interesting sentiment coming from someone who had never hesitated to contact the media when it suited his purposes, or whenever he felt the need to subject all of us to his repugnant pro-death penalty invective.

The ultimate hypocrisy of the Department of Corrections came about mere weeks after the media ban was in effect. It deemed that the "ban" did not include those members of the media who declared their support of capital punishment. The unfairness and illegality of this double standard didn't alter anything at the prison; the objective had been to silence the inmates, and this had been achieved.

The media ban at Potosi Correctional Center is particularly sinister. In order for society to make an intelligent, informed decision about the issue of capital punishment, it must be made aware of all of the relevant information. And all the relevant information does not start and finish with incessant monologues emanating from the office of the Attorney General or the Department of Corrections.

Dissemination of information increases our understanding of social issues, it does not diminish it. The public/the voters need to see and read exactly what happens inside our prisons, particularly our maximum security prisons—already shrouded in mystique and secrecy.

Those incarcerated may have lost their freedom, but this should not mean that we become deaf to their voices, that we overlook human rights issues, that their points of view are somehow invalidated because they are at the mercy of the State/Department of Corrections. If we do ignore them, then we will only be exposed to one version of "the truth," and this version will come from career jailers and others who have made a lucrative business out of the misery of both victims and perpetrators.

I have been fighting to save Alan from execution for the past three and a half years. We have in operation a network of intensely devoted, highly motivated individuals from all over the world. Without their help, it would have been impossible to establish and maintain any momentum.

Amicus curiae (friend of the court) briefs, have been filed on Alan's behalf by human rights organizations from France, Sweden, Holland, and England. They remind us that "the eyes of the world" are indeed fixed on this case, that the injustices within the case, are, at least to the Europeans, too grievous to be left unquestioned and unchallenged.

As a lifelong opponent of capital punishment, I have found the adjustment to life in a country and state which condone and encourage this barbaric practice immensely difficult.

Global awareness and abhorrence of the death penalty are comforting. However, until the people of the United States are able to identify this issue as the political weapon which it undoubtedly is, the rest of the world may have to be content to look on, merely as a concerned "spectator" to a "game" whose rules it regards as unacceptable, cruel and indefensible.

Alan's lawyers have been working tirelessly to avert a tragic miscarriage of justice, but there is only so much they can do when the justice system within which they work is fraught with iniquities.

At this point in time, there is little standing between Alan and the execution chamber. As this book goes to press, the stay of execution upheld since 1994 remains in place, but we don't know if or when it may be dissolved. If it is, it will be yet another of the body blows which we have sustained over the past few years, but it will not signal the end of hope—it will not signal the end of the fight; it will serve to intensify our motivation and determination.

As long as we have men like the Attorney General Jay Nixon, justice will continue to be frustrated. For Mr. Nixon, the pursuit of "justice" is subordinate to the pursuit of an execution date for everyone. The governor of Missouri, Mel Carnahan, has stated that he has "an abiding faith" in "the system." That puts the onus on those seeking a commutation of a death sentence to prove that mistakes were made of sufficient seriousness to warrant his intervention.

We would all like nothing more than to have an "abiding faith" in the system of laws here in Missouri. But in order for this to happen, the system must treat us all fairly in return. Thus far, the system has failed Alan, just as it has already failed countless others who have been incarcerated and executed, even in cases of actual innocence.

Alan has never claimed to be entirely innocent of a crime, quite the contrary. He knows that he has taken a life, he knows that nothing will bring back the man who died; never a day goes by without the inescapable feeling of remorse. The absence of premeditation, along with numerous other issues, establishes categorically that the death penalty in Alan's case is far from just.

These are amongst the subjects discussed in the book which Alan wrote and which was published last year, called <u>Shall Suffer Death</u>. The title is the words used on a warrant of execution, a poignant reminder of the fate which may await him still.

Over the years, Alan had been extremely outspoken about the death penalty, the penal and justice systems, politics, etc. This has not endeared him to the Department of Corrections, and as recently as December, 1996, he accumulated more "conduct violations" in one month than he has had in 14 years! This is not mere coincidence; it is part of an orchestrated campaign of harassment, as transparently obvious as it is infantile, and if the consequences of these fabricated "violations" were not so serious, they would be laughable.

However, the Department of Corrections is determined to isolate and keep Alan incommunicado with the outside world. They are aware of the fact that it has been his ability to communicate with others which has contributed to his survival thus far. With an execution date looming, what better way to reduce his chances of success and minimize the "risk" of any repeat of 1994 (his stay), than to handicap him in terms of his ability to communicate with others whose help and support he needs?

He has had all contact visits withdrawn for 6 months (commencing December, 1996), his telephone privileges have also been withdrawn until at least April of 1997, when his cell confinement should also come to an end. Neither I, nor his mother, his family or friends, can talk to him on the telephone, let alone see him.

One of the heinous conduct violations which precipitated these excessive punishments was: "Disobeying an Order," i.e. dialing his attorney's telephone number, rather than letting a guard do so. Another violation was for being in possession of "contraband;" this time a cigarette lighter was found in the mattress of the cell he had just been put into. The cumulative effect of these violations has been to keep Alan out of general population for as long as possible.

In conclusion, it's clear that the forthcoming weeks are going to be critical. As Judge Bright observed, the Eighth Circuit Court is hamstrung in terms of being in a position to offer relief; this is so in spite of the fact that:

"Several of Bannister's allegations go to the heart of perceptions of fundamental fairness in the criminal justice system...The right to be free from governmental interrogation after receiving appointed counsel...The right to a competent attorney during sentencing..."

The court is prevented from examining the merits of Alan's claims, not because it chooses to ignore them, but because of certain "roadblocks"..

"Procedural barriers prevent this court from addressing several of Bannister's claims...If these issues remain unaddressed, Missouri may execute a man without offering him a fair trail or competent legal prepresentation...Because this court cannot address those issues on their merits, we must rely on other authorities...either the United States Supreme Court or, if not, the Governor of Missouri...to review the record and address Bannister's contentions."

The death penalty is a premeditated act, "dignified" and legitimized by statute. Perhaps it's time for all of us to try to rise above the primal thrust for revenge, because, as Dr. Martin Luther King Jr. reminded us, in the final analysis: "The eye for an eye philosophy leaves everyone blind."

Lindsay Graham Bannister

Lindsay Graham Bannister was born in Scotland and raised in England where she attended Essex University and received an Honors degree in Sociology. She worked for the British government, and was a social worker. In 1993, she moved to Missouri and married death row inmate Alan J. Bannister. Mrs. Bannister coordinates an international campaign to save her husband's life, and to increase awareness of his case. Mr. Bannister came within two hours of execution in December 1994; as this book goes to press, the Stay of Execution which was upheld in 1994 remains in place.

ANNE COLEMAN

My name is Anne Coleman. I am the Delaware State Abolition Coordinator for Amnesty International. I have to tell you that Delaware is the number one per capita in the U.S. in executions. We have executed eight people in the last four years, three of them this year. I came to be Amnesty's death penalty coordinator quite by accident. But I think I'd best start by telling you that I am not a bleeding heart liberal. I believe in accountability. I believe you have to be responsible for your actions. I also oppose the death penalty. I always have and I always will, except for one day in my life.

It was September 22, 1985. I was living in Buffalo, NY. My three children, all in their early twenties, had gone off on their own. Unfortunately, Tim had to return home after developing a brain tumor while serving in the Army. He was undergoing radiation therapy. My husband, Claude, was recovering from cancer surgery. My youngest, Daniel, was a sergeant in the Army, stationed in Hawaii. My daughter, Frances, was working as an occupational therapist in Los Angeles.

The phone rang in the afternoon, and I picked it up. It was my niece, who said, "Frances is dead. She has been shot." I don't remember screaming, but I know I did. I do remember saying, "Where is Summer? Is Summer all right?" Summer is my daughter's child, who was two years old at the time. Since both my husband and my son were sick, I had to make my way to Los Angeles by myself, and I can tell you, sitting on that plane, I was thinking, "When I get there, if I can find out who killed my daughter, I am going to kill them myself." That was how angry and how frustrated I was. It was the loneliest time of my life. But that was not the normal me. That was me, the mother, the one who was full of rage, waiting to wake up because I was positive that this was only a dream.

Daniel met me when I landed in Los Angeles. He had been put on emergency leave from the Army. Together we went to the 77th district station. I asked the detectives what happened to my daughter. We were told that it was none of our business. They said they don't discuss crimes with third parties, which includes family members of the victim. I was told that I wasn't allowed to ask any questions. They were the people in charge of asking questions. I was lucky that I had a violent crimes coordinator assigned to my case. She told me exactly what it would be like. "If someone hasn't been arrested in four days, most likely, unless there is a snitch or they pick up some finger prints, you will never know who killed your daughter." Sadly, to this day, that is still the case. I don't know who killed her.

We went home from the police station to my niece's house, and about five hours later the police arrived. They had been to the autopsy and they had brought her purse and car keys. They threw them across the room at me and said I'd better pick up the car: "It's costing you money." I wish I had never picked up that car. I wish I had never seen it again. My daughter was shot in the car. She bled to death—the bullet going through her lungs, her heart, and her aorta. She drowned in her own blood. The car had been towed to the police pound; it was September and quite hot, and it smelled really, really bad. My son Daniel said that he never, ever could forget that smell. He couldn't get rid of it. Wherever he was, he would smell that smell. In fact, the smell of that car and the attitude of the police, being too busy to find out who killed my daughter, had made my son very, very angry, and he wanted revenge.

After six days of taking care of business, I managed to get back to Buffalo. My daughter's body was already there, and the wake was the very same day. We went about our business, burying my daughter. But Daniel became angrier and angrier. He wanted to kill the people who murdered his sister. My son, who had made E5 sergeant in three years, started to become a non-functional member of society. Over the next two years and nine months, his need, his desire for revenge really took over his life. He thought at one time that he would go buy an Uzi and go to the Coliseum in Los Angeles and mow down as many people as he could because he thought he might be able to get the person that killed Frances. And the other people really didn't matter because he might have killed that person. But you know we can't do things like that, even though the Constitution says we have the right to bear arms; we certainly don't have the right to go around killing people.

Two years and nine months after my daughter was buried, I was back at the very same cemetery to bury my son, Daniel. He had finally gotten the revenge that he needed, but the only person he could take revenge on was himself. He had nowhere else to channel his feelings about a need for justice. Although the death certificate says, "cause undetermined," in my heart I know that he took an overdose of antidepressants deliberately. So I had to bury two children from one bullet. But I also saw how bad revenge can be.

After my daughter's death, I inherited my daughter's child, Summer. She is now 13. Seven years to the day after my daughter died, her father died of "natural causes." He had always refused to answer any questions about what happened to Frances. We were now free to adopt Summer and could leave the state of New York. It also meant that Summer has to live the rest of her life with the fact that both of her parents died on the same date.

We moved to Delaware. One of the things that happened soon after our moving was that there was an execution scheduled. I had never lived in a state where they had executions. New York had not had them all the time I lived there, so it was a new experience for me. At first I thought, "I'll just leave the State while they are doing this." But the "We the People" in me said, "No, it's wrong. I can't tolerate this." So I called the newspaper and asked where the demonstrations would be held. They said, "There aren't any here in Dover. You could go to Wilmington, which is more liberal." This was surprising since Dover is the state capital. So Summer and I went down to the governor's office building by ourselves, and we demonstrated that afternoon with home made signs. Through going there that one time, I met many people who opposed the death penalty. A couple of weeks later, I went to an assemblyman's hearing on capital punishment. The Ku Klux Klan were there as well as clergymen, lawyers, and this one small black woman, a lady called Barbara. She got up and she said, "I'm in so much pain. It hurts me so much. My son is on death row and I can't stand it, because it is not just my son that is being punished—it's my grandchildren, it's my children, it's me. We have nightmares every night about when they are going to kill my son. I'm non-functional, and I don't know how to work anymore."

I know what that feels like from losing my own two children. I also realized that I couldn't live with what she was going through. I think I would go crazy and probably take matters into my own hands. Sadly, there are over 3000 families in this country in the same situation as Barbara. She went on to say, "I wish I could give the daughter of my son's victim a hug." I walked over to her after the meeting and said, "I have a daughter who needs a hug. You can give her a hug."

Barbara and I have become very, very good friends. She and I go on The Journey of Hope, which is the annual journey of Murder Victims Families for Reconciliation. We go all over the country speaking about the death penalty. At one point she asked me if I would go with her to see her son on death row. I agreed to go to the Delaware Correctional Center to see Robert. His question to us was, "Just what are you going to do for all the other families of death row inmates that are hurting just like my mother and our family?" She and I thought about his question for a while and we made appointments to see every other person on death row in the state. At that time there were 14 of them. I have to tell you that some of these people are pretty nice people who made a terrible, terrible mistake; others I wouldn't want to be around—but I've met them all.

One of the people I went to visit was a man called Billy Bailey. He was one of 23 children, from a very poor family—sharecroppers. Billy's mother died when he was six months old. Billy's father remarried almost immediately and it turned out that the stepmother had absolutely no use for the children. She beat them severely. The younger ones raised the very smallest ones. Billy learned to steal like the other kids did—food from people's houses, food out of people's fields—in order to survive. When Billy was ten, his father died at the age of 75. Billy was abandoned in the cemetery by his stepmother, along with his sister who was two years older. He was brought to Wilmington, Delaware where the abuse continued. In the records, the State says that he was socially deprived and socially retarded. They didn't say that he was mentally retarded—just socially. He thought that he had to steal everything that he wanted. And I'm not talking about gold jewelry. If he needed food, he would go into a store and take it. That was his way of life. It continued to be his way of life into adulthood.

Delaware has long had a "three strikes and you're out" law. When he got his third strike, they said they were going to put him in prison for the rest of his life. He went on a drunken rampage and killed an elderly couple.

I believe you have to be accountable for your actions, and I have no problem with Billy Bailey having to spend the rest of his life in prison. In fact, prison was the first real home Billy ever had. The Billy Bailey that was sentenced to death in 1980 was not a nice person. When I first went to meet him, I was really very frightened because I thought I was going to meet Hannibal Lecter. The newspapers had made him out to be such a person. In fact, what I found was a little man, 5'3", walking through the door with his eyes downcast, wondering if I had come to assassinate him. As I went in, the sergeant at the gate was incredulous. He said, "You are going to visit Billy? He hasn't had a visitor in over ten years."

Over the next two years Billy and I became pretty good friends. We used to talk a lot, and he really couldn't believe that the State of Delaware was going to kill him. After all, the first nine years of his incarceration, he had said he wanted to die. They said, "No you can't." Then seven years ago something changed his mind and he started fighting to stay alive. By that time the State began to try to execute him. Billy had been the foreman of the woodwork shop at the prison for over six years. He produced over $15,000 of work a month in labor for which he was paid thirty-five cents/hour. He was fully rehabilitated. He never expected to leave the prison, but he wanted to work and was contributing to his upkeep. As I said, I am not a bleeding heart. I agree that he should have stayed in prison for the rest of his life.

On the 12th of December, I was in court with Billy when the judge said, "You'll hang by the neck until you are dead, and may God have mercy on your soul." He also read an execution order for lethal injection, and the State of Delaware tried very hard to make Billy go along with lethal injection, because that is absolutely routine now. Billy would not. He said, "I will not participate in my own execution. They sentenced me to hang. They have to hang me."

Billy was housed in the maximum security unit. In maximum security they are locked away 23 hours and 20 minutes a day in a single cell with a door and a hole under the door where they push the food in. There are no bars. It is a big metal door. If you want to speak to someone across the hall, you have to lie down on the floor and shout through the hole. You are not allowed a TV but you can have a radio and books. You are out of your cell for 40 minutes a day. You are permitted one 45 minute visit and one phone call a month. The state of Delaware has executed four people who were what they call consentual in their executions, because they just couldn't stand living like that anymore. They wanted to die rather than to spend the rest of their lives in maximum security. For those who think prison is like a country club, funded by their tax money, I can only say that I wouldn't want to be a member of that club.

I had an appointment to see Billy on the 13th of December. When I arrived, Billy told me, "They are not going to let you visit me any more. The warden says he doesn't want you to come again." It took me seven weeks to get permission to visit Billy another time, and only through intervention by the governor's counsel, who was able to convince the warden to allow me one visit. I had to keep my hands flat on the table the whole time. I was with him when his attorney called on the 20th of January to say that the Supreme Court had refused to grant a stay, and that he would, indeed, be hanged.

He was hanged just after midnight on the 25th of January. He was standing on top of the gallows out on the prison farm when the witnesses arrived at ten minutes to twelve. The wind was howling so hard that my son got a wind burn. That's how cold it was that night. So I have always wondered how he managed to stand on those gallows without trembling. The two guards at either side of him were wearing masks, the kind of mask that the assassins wore at the 1972 Olympics, kind of tight over the face. They stood beside Billy. One hand was tied behind his back; the other in front of him. At 12:01 the execution order was read. Billy was asked if he had any last words. He said, "No, sir." A hood was placed over his head, and the knot of the rope was placed behind his left ear. He was dropped down at 12:04 and was pronounced dead at 12:15. The witnesses saw him twirl six times in one direction and a couple in the other. Then a curtain dropped down, and no one knew what happened after that. It took eleven minutes hanging there for him to die, which, to me, seems like cruel and unusual punishment.

Six days later we were back for another execution, this time by lethal injection. I didn't feel that I could deal with another right then, and I was going to stay home. But I went to my mailbox that day and there was a letter from the next candidate for execution, thanking me for being his friend and for helping his family. So I had to go back again.

David is another person sentenced to death in Delaware. Four years ago this man stabbed his wife. Then, with his wife, his two children and two of his neighbors' children inside, he set fire to the house. He was found not guilty of stabbing his wife and killing her. He was found guilty of killing the three children that burned in the fire. Undoubtedly, he has to be punished for the rest of his life. But Delaware has a thing called a jury override, and the jury override means that when a person is convicted of a crime, and the jury has said that they are guilty, they also get to decide the penalty; if the penalty is supposed to be death, it used to be that 12 people had to agree to that punishment. Now it is jury override—the judge can override the jury and determine the penalty. At the penalty hearing, the man's surviving seven year old son said to the judge, "I love my daddy. I need him. Please don't kill my daddy. I need him." Now if that 7 year old child, who was the victim, the only surviving victim, can forgive his father, even though he knows that his father has to spend the rest of his life in prison, what are we saying to that little boy when we "know" better than he does what he needs, and that we have to have justice for the victims. His father must be killed. This boy is certainly the victim, yet no one is listening to him. Marcus is now 11. He still lives every moment with the fact that his father is going to be killed. I sometimes take him to prison for his monthly visit, and Marcus sits there talking to him just like any other child would talk to his father. He loves him. He has forgiven him. He knows that his dad has to spend the rest of his life in prison. But who are we going to punish if we execute David? David will be dead, but Marcus will be paying for that for the rest of his life, and Marcus' children will certainly be paying for it, too.

Another prisoner, Jim Clark, was executed April 19, 1996. He had asked me to be a witness. I had been his only visitor in the year that he was awaiting his death order. Sadly, the State told the judge that my known association with anti-death penalty groups made me a security risk. They said I might expose his execution team. James was alone on the day of his execution. His case might make you think a lot about what the State is really accomplishing when it executes someone. He had consented to his execution, and right before he died he shouted to his lawyer, "Jerry, hey, I'm free. I have no more pain." The State simply succeeded in carrying out his own suicide for him.

Now the State of Delaware has a law that came about after a fourteen year old killed a ten year old child. The fourteen year old was charged with

1st degree murder and was tried as an adult. The State Supreme Court ruled that the State had made an error and that he would have to be released when he was eighteen. He was released at that time. Immediately, the Assembly went into emergency session and passed a law which states that if anyone fourteen or younger is killed by someone four years older, the accused is subject to capital murder charges.

Recently, I was on the Geraldo show. With me on the program was a woman who had been in California at the execution of her son's killer. It was now two months later. She said, "I am so angry. They promised me I would feel better. I waited 15 years for this man to die, and now I have no one else to hate. I have no one to hate and I am so angry." It turned out that everything she had been able to blame on her son's killer no longer had an outlet. I had a nice talk with her, and I have a friend who is in contact with her on a regular basis. She feels she was cheated by the prosecution because they told her she would feel better after this man's execution, and she really doesn't. She feels she could have put the tragedy behind her a long, long time ago if he had been sentenced to life in prison. She would have known he was going to spend the rest of his life in prison, and she could have gone about getting her life together.

The other people I would like to speak about are all the family members of people on death row. I have met so many of them all over the country. Can you imagine how your parents would feel if somebody walked up to them and said, "On the 9th of July I am going to kill your child, and there is nothing you can do about it." How would you feel? This is what family members of death row inmates go through on a daily basis. I have to tell you that my feeling upon losing my daughter was pain, and I have come to learn over the last few years that pain is pain, and it doesn't matter where the pain is coming from because we can't weigh it. The mother of a death row inmate has as much right to feel pain as the mother of the victim, and I know she feels as much pain as I do.

Finally, I want you to think of these statistics. There are approximately twenty-five thousand homicides a year in this country. About 1%, or 250, of these homicides get prosecuted as capital crimes, punishable by death in states that have the death penalty. Out of the 250 people convicted we execute approximately 50, or 20-30% a year. So of 25,000 people murdered each year, executing 50 doesn't make any sense, because we are picking and choosing who we think are most vulnerable—not who committed the most heinous crime. My daughter was just as precious to me as you are to your mother, and that, I think has to be the factor—that every human life is precious. We have to consider that "We the People" are the ones who are losing when we execute someone. We the People, not the execution team that is killing someone. Every time a State executes someone it is in my name, and

Anne Coleman

I object strenuously to that.

Anne Coleman is the State Death Penalty Abolition Coordinator for Amnesty International. In 1985, her daughter, Frances, was found shot to death. Later, grief and frustration over his sister's death resulted in the suicide of her son. Ms. Coleman steadfastly opposes the death penalty and works with the families of death row inmates in Delaware.

JOHN YARBROUGH

I
Is the Death Penalty Equally Applied to Convicted Murderers in the United States?

It would seem that if the United States Government or the states have the legal and moral right to take the lives of convicted criminals, the imposition of death would be played out on a level field. First, let's examine what actually determines whether a convicted killer or other criminal will receive a sentence of death.

The initial consideration is the location of the crime. Some states have a death penalty statute, some do not. If the crime is committed in a non-death penalty state, the person responsible for the crime will not die at the hands of government, no matter how heinous his acts. A great number of persons are thus spared the possibility of receiving the death penalty based solely on the state the crime was committed in.

If the crime is committed in a state with capital punishment, the decision of whether or not to seek the death penalty lies with the District Attorney or one of his or her staff. Obviously, some prosecutors are more in favor of the death penalty than others. Criminals fortunate enough to have committed their crimes in a county or jurisdiction with a prosecutor opposed to, or with mixed feelings about, the imposition of the death penalty may well escape the death chamber, based on who is prosecuting the case.

In considering the first two determinates of who gets the death penalty versus who does not, common sense will tell you that basing the decision on where the crime occurred and who is prosecuting the case does not afford all the citizens of this country equal protection of the law as outlined and guaranteed by the U.S. Constitution. Perhaps someone can explain to me why murdering a police officer in Massachusetts is a lesser crime than murdering one in Texas.

Speaking of police officers, the next determinate of whether the criminal will be subject to death is, in many states, who the victim was. In Texas and many other states, it is a Capital offense to kill a police officer, a fireman, a person under the age of five years, etc. In Texas, for example, you could receive a lethal injection for killing a five year old child, but no worse than life in prison for killing a six year old child. If there is some rationale for that, it escapes me.

In many states, the taking of another person's life alone will never subject you to capital punishment. There must be another, specific underlying crime involved before the Capital statute is triggered, i.e. murder in the course of a robbery or burglary. In the Lone Star State, a person can be executed for a murder committed in the course of committing kidnapping. He cannot be executed for a murder committed while perpetrating an extortion.

The taking of another person's life is not always considered murder in the legal sense either. If a person runs over your spouse or child while driving under the influence of alcohol, it is never a murder case. While it probably couldn't matter less to you whether your loved one was killed by a drunk in a car or a teenager with a gun, it is a vital legal consideration.

Let me outline the various possibilities in Texas when one person takes the life of another. The least serious unlawful killing is negligent homicide. If through your negligence alone you act in a way that results in the death of another, you face a maximum of one year in jail.

The next step up the ladder is involuntary manslaughter. If you kill someone, but you didn't really mean to, you face a maximum of ten years in prison. This is followed by voluntary manslaughter. If you kill someone, but do it in the heat of passion from a reasonable cause, you face up to twenty years in prison.

The highest murder without a death penalty attached is simply called murder. This is where a killing is committed intentionally and knowingly.

A Capital murder is also committed intentionally and knowingly, but another factor is involved. A specific underlying crime must have also occurred, i.e. robbery, burglary, rape, kidnapping or arson. Or a specific person must have been killed, i.e. a law enforcement officer or child under the age of five.

Returning to more specific determinants of who dies and who lives for their crimes, we must consider gender. It is rare for a prosecutor facing a Capital trial to seek death for a female defendant. In Texas, there are over four hundred men on Death Row and only five women. While it is true that more men commit Capital crimes than women, it is also true that prosecutors are reluctant to have a woman's blood on their hands. And, should a prosecutor seek the death penalty, a woman is less likely to be given death by a jury. Let's look at a few examples of this.

Kristi K. and two male companions conspired to kill her father and step-mother in order for Kristi to inherit the family's wealth. All agreed that Kristi's idea and she solicited the boys to carry out the murders. I would argue that Kristi was equally culpable. Kristi received a life sentence from the jury. Both boys sit on Texas Death Row. All were average teenagers with no prior criminal history. The only variable in their situations was that Kristi was a female.

Ricky G. and his wife Sharon were involved in multiple homicides. Sharon participated in two murders, helping stab the victims to death. Ricky received two life sentences and one death penalty. Sharon's harsh punishment was ten years probation. She did not serve one day in prison.

Even more disturbing to those of us who feel all should be treated equally by the criminal justice system, are cases in which co-defendants, very often the wives or girlfriends of the person on trial, turn state's witness and avoid prosecution all together. A very good example of this is the Sattewhite case in Texas. The female in this case had just been released from prison for murder. She and her boyfriend robbed a convenience store and killed the cashier. Both claimed the other was the killer. The murder weapon, a gun, was found near the female in the get-away car. Yet the prosecutor granted the female, who was out of prison on parole, complete immunity to testify that her boyfriend was the killer in this case. He had no violent past history, but he now sits on Death Row while his ex-con partner goes about her life in society. No one may ever know who the killer was, but under Texas law, even if Sattewhite was the killer, both are equally responsible.

All things being equal, two other classes of people are more likely to die at the hands of the state than others. These are minorities, especially blacks, and poor people. Regarding minorities, you must consider that the southern states with their record of bigotry are the most pro-death penalty states. Texas and Florida lead the nation in the number of people executed since the reinstatement of the death penalty. Other southern states also kill with more frequency than their northern counterparts. Georgia, South Carolina, Alabama, Louisiana and Arkansas all execute a fair number of convicted killers.

To be poor means you rely on the state to furnish your attorney. You get what you pay for. A person with a hired attorney is far less likely to die than one with an appointed attorney. Unfortunately, it is still true in the south that to be black often means to be poor. To be black, poor, male and facing an all white jury in the south is a monumental step toward death at the state's hands. It is only slightly better to be white, poor, male and facing the same jury, but there is no doubt that blacks have borne the brunt of the severest punishment available to the citizenry and continue to do so to this day.

There is one final factor that must be mentioned regarding the actual application of the death penalty. While many states have and use Capital laws, some flinch when it comes to actually carrying out the sentence. California has a lot of people on death row, but they have proved slow indeed in carrying out the ultimate punishment.

The truth of the matter is, regarding the death penalty, that it is not equally applied. It has been said that you could take a stack of murder reports, throw them up in the air, and be as likely to pick up one that resulted in a death penalty as you would be if you carefully studied the facts of each case and then tried to guess the punishment given.

There are also persons who are exempt from the death penalty. While there are variations from state to state, generally juveniles, insane persons and people with diplomatic immunity cannot be executed. The age at which you become an adult varies from state to state, as does the definition of what constitutes insanity. Nationality can also exempt you from death in some cases. For example, a Mexican citizen can commit a capital murder in the U.S., flee to Mexico and be guaranteed of no extradition to the U.S. and no Capital trial in Mexico. Many other countries, especially those with no death penalty, will not extradite their citizens to the U.S. to face Capital charges.

One other problem arises from time to time regarding the death penalty and that is time itself. If a person committed a murder during the time the U.S. had no death penalty or before a statute was changed to include certain acts as Capital crimes, no death penalty may be sought. This is becoming less prevalent as Capital offenses are enlarged by the states.

On the Federal level, we only recently had Capital crimes added to the books. Surprisingly enough, only the U.S. Federal laws allow death to be imposed on non-killers. This seems likely to change, but presently only in Federal court can a large drug distributor receive death as a possible punishment.

When the Supreme Court reinstituted the death penalty, it stated pretty explicitly that it expected the ultimate punishment to be reserved for the "worst criminals who commit the worst crimes." This would lead you to believe that people who had previously committed violent acts, gone to prison, failed at rehabilitation attempts, gone back out and committed horrible murders would be the persons given the death penalty. This simply is not true. The death rows of this country are filled with first time offenders who in one scared moment pulled a trigger. While no one can condone their acts, they are far from the worst of the worst committing the most horrible murders imaginable.

In Texas, if a person is convicted of a capital offense, punishment is determined solely by the jury and there is no authority for the trial judge to override the verdict or punishment if the trial was properly conducted and sufficient evidence put before the jury for their findings. The possible punishments are life in prison with forty years minimum before parole eligibility, or death by lethal injection. In order to impose death, the jury must answer so called special issue questions unanimously in the affirmative. Even one juror can save a defendant's life by giving a negative answer to one of the special issue questions. This theoretically would allow a juror to prevent death, but there is a catch. The jurors are told to simply answer the questions without regard to whether death will be imposed, although it is those very answers that determine life or death.

One of the questions posed is, "Is there a probability that the defendant will commit future acts of violence?" You might think this means it is virtually certain that he will. But the jurors are told that this means "any probability, which is nothing more than a possibility." You might further think that acts of violence refers to violence against persons—such as death, injury, rape, etc. But jurors are told violent acts can also be acts against property, i.e. burglary is a violent act against a person's property.

You also might think the best indicator of future behavior is past behavior. Has this offender failed at past rehabilitation attempts—a life long criminal, a three time loser, etc. But the jury is also told, "Consider this crime itself." It may be so terrible it alone indicates probable future violent acts.

Since murder is inherently violent, you may wonder why the question is even asked. Anyone who has killed has certainly proved himself capable of violence. The reason it is asked is because at the time the law was written, the state legislature was well aware of the Supreme Court's instructions regarding what it would accept in drafting a lawful constitutional death statute. In looking for "the worst of the worst," the intention was to narrow the death penalty to society's perennial bad boys who had killed someone after a seedy previous history. As I have stated, this simply is not the case and we continue to push the death penalty to its legal limits.

II
Calvin and Craig

Whether you favor or oppose the death penalty, I would like to relate situations that resulted in the death penalty being given and ask if you agree with the death verdicts. Remember, each of these people will die for the crimes described unless their cases are reversed, and most have exhausted nearly all appeals at this time.

Calvin B. was a security guard in Houston. His roommate was also a security guard and Calvin's lover. The relationship became abusive and Calvin left, not even pausing to take his personal belongings in fear for his safety.

Shortly after leaving, Calvin found another roommate and told him of his previous relationship. Calvins's new friend told him that he would go with Calvin to gather his belongings from his previous residence. While in the process of loading his property, the former roommate arrived home and confronted Calvin and his new friend. The new friend was a seventeen year old teenager, an adult in the state of Texas. The seventeen year old and Calvin's former lover got into a fight and it ended with the former roommate being stabbed to death by the seventeen year old. Calvin was not the killer.

Because the prosecutor decided Calvin was the older of the two, should have anticipated a killing might occur, and should not have entered his former residence, he was prosecuted for Capital murder. The teenaged killer was given a sweetheart offer. "Testify against Calvin and no charges will be filed against you."

Calvin was convicted under "the law of parties" (you can be responsible for another's crime under some circumstances), and the only question left was—would he die or get a life sentence while the killer walked free.

In arguing to the jury to kill Calvin, the prosecutor said, "This man is a homosexual. Life in prison is not punishment to him. He will be around men. He will like that. You have to give him the death penalty." They did just that.

There was never any question that Calvin was not the killer. It is pure speculation that he should have anticipated a murder would occur. I doubt a life sentence would have been the big party the prosecutor painted for the jury, but one thing we do know. The non-killer in this case is sentenced to die and the killer walked free for helping this happen.

Calvin once told me, "As bad as he treated me, had I any idea he would be hurt, much less killed, he could have kept my things." Should Calvin die for this crime?

Craig O. sits on Death Row in Huntsville, Texas. Craig was working as an informant for the Federal Drug Enforcement Agency (the DEA). He had just completed an assignment in Florida that resulted in the breakup of a large cocaine smuggling operation. Craig earned his living by working as an agent for the DEA; his pay was based solely on the results he achieved.

Craig was sent to Houston and told to await instructions for his assignment there. He was told to stay at a motel near the Astrodome. Arriving in Houston, Craig took a taxi to the Astrodome area and checked into a seedy motel. He noted that what appeared to be drug dealers and prostitutes were loitering about the motel parking lot.

Entering his room, Craig immediately turned on the heater as it was a chilly winter night in Houston. The heater would not work and Craig called the front desk. They told him they couldn't fix it at night and he'd just have to do his best to stay warm. He was also informed that most patrons of the motel only use their rooms for a couple of hours.

Walking to the lobby to straighten this problem out, Craig saw several drug buys being made. At the office, he was again told to take his room "as is" or get out. Craig then noticed that a Houston Police car had a traffic violator stopped in front of the motel. He decided to ask the police to take him to another motel.

As Craig approached the police unit, he noticed two officers were in the car along with the traffic violator. Craig approached the driver's side of the car. What happened then is in conflict between Craig and a Houston cop.

Craig says he approached the driver and was told to "wait a minute." He interjected, "I'm a DEA operative, and the cop said very loudly, so loudly the druggies on the motel lot heard him, "Oh, you're a DEA snitch, huh, well hold on."

This scared Craig, as he might later be trying to buy drugs for the DEA from some of these same people. Craig began backing away from the police car. As he did, his coat flew open and his gun was showing. (He kept a pistol in his waistband.) The cop saw the gun, jumped out and opened fire on Craig; Craig fired back. One cop was killed. Craig was shot in the stomach and, after a life-saving operation, he lived to face trial, conviction, and the death sentence in a Houston courtroom.

The police officer who lived said Craig asked for a ride, got angry at being told to wait, and that Craig pulled out his gun and shot first. Personally, I think that Craig's story makes the most sense. Why would a police operative open fire on two police officers over something as trivial as the surviving officer reports?

The truth probably lies somewhere in between these two stories. Both saw movement towards a gun, both fired in fear for their own lives. Maybe this was manslaughter, but Capital murder? I don't think so. The only factor that made this a Capital case was that a policeman was killed. But if the cop was aggressive or if his intentions were misunderstood, should this be a case where the death penalty is meted out?

One has to wonder, if there had been one cop and two DEA operatives and one DEA agent was killed, would the cop be on trial? Probably so. Craig was working with full permission and under direction of a police agency himself. So, theoretically, the cop could himself have been in trouble if he lived and Craig's story was the one believed.

But Craig killed a Houston cop, in Houston, and the case was investigated by Houston police with a Houston patrolman as their witness. This case should have been handled by an agency with no connection to the slain officer or the surviving witness officer. Craig faced a badly stacked deck of cards.

III
Walk a Mile In My Shoes

I was taken to the Diagnostic Unit of the Texas Department of Corrections in February of 1991. The other nine inmates who rode on the bus with me from Cleburne, Texas would remain at the processing center near Huntsville for several weeks while the Classification Committee decided the most suitable prison unit to send them to.

It would not be necessary for me to be classified, as I had only one place that could house me—Death Row at the Ellis I Unit located only a couple of miles from the Diagnostic Unit.

Within an hour I was fingerprinted, photographed, given a haircut, checked for tattoos, sprayed with a delousing soap, showered and clothed in Texas prison "whites" and a pair of cloth shoes. Two guards armed with high-powered rifles and sidearms shackled my legs, handcuffed me, and threw me in the back of a panel truck.

It was drizzling rain and ice and there was no heater in the truck. Upon arriving at the Ellis I Unit, the truck parked at the rear of the unit and I was let out of the rear of the truck.

My short sleeved shirt and cloth shoes (similar to house slippers) did little to keep me dry or warm. My leg shackles kept me from moving one foot more that six inches in front of the other. I was made to walk around the entire prison unit, more than a mile, before being led shivering with a runny nose into the gate the truck had first parked at.

The guards were a male and a female. Upon entering the prison building through the kitchen, the male guard spoke for the first time. "Are you a vegetarian?" he asked.

"No," I replied.

"Well, you soon will be," he said.

Walking into the long hallway that extends the entire length of the prison, I was led past inmates in the non-death row part of the prison. Of the 2000 inmates at Ellis I, only 350 or so are on Death Row.

"Fresh meat," I heard one inmate say, to the laughs of his cronies.

"Death Row," I thought. "Let's see—there are about 300,000,000 people in the USA and less than 3,000 people under sentence of death. About one in every 100,000 people. Twelve people decided that I'm one of the most horrible people alive and not deserving of life itself."

Ten years before, I sat in front of my television set watching a demonstration at the Walls Prison Unit. The Walls Unit is where the actual execution of Texas prisoners takes place. Hours before the lethal injection is given, the living corpse is driven from the Ellis I Unit into the city of Huntsville to the Walls Unit.

This was a different type of demonstration I was watching. The death penalty had only recently been reinstated by the Supreme Court and Texas was proud to be in the forefront of killing society's worst offenders. The demonstration was a pro-death penalty affair, held mostly by prison guards who were off-duty and wanted the world to know "us Texans don't treat killers kindly."

"Right on," I told my wife. "An eye for an eye. It's about time we started getting rid of these guys again." My wife, a cop like me, smiled and said, "Yeah, it's about time."

It really pains me now to think of all the people that I was with at Ellis that have been executed. It was really an awakening experience to find after a short time that there were some pretty nice people there. I don't know what they were like 10-15 years prior, when they first were arrested, but Steve and Mark were two of the best people I ever knew. And living 24 hours a day for over a year with someone, you get to know them pretty well. It's not like in the free world. It's a constant exposure to each other in close confines and you see people at their best and worst. There is no "faking it."

Sadly, most of the time on death row, I was next to the Death Watch Cell and spent the last day with many who were killed. It was an experience I'm not sure I can describe. Some hope for a last minute reprieve, some get it, some don't. Some know "this is it." All appeals have been exhausted and the Texas governor very rarely gives a stay of execution.

To me, letting a person who is perfectly healthy sit and await sudden death with full knowledge it's going to occur is a lot crueler than the spur of the moment killings most death row inmates were involved in. How many made their victims sit and contemplate their deaths? All killing is wrong, but planned killing of knowing victims by the State takes the prize for meanness.

IV

Into God's Hands

(Hail Mary, full of grace)
There are no courts left to go to, that was the last place.
(The Lord is with thee)
The Governor didn't call, I waited to see
(Blessed art thou among women)
There are five in the waiting room, I believe all kin,
(And blessed is the fruit of thy womb, Jesus)
Show them you're a brave man, don't make a fuss

John Yarbrough

(Holy Mary, mother of God)
As they roll out the gurney, look at your folks and nod
(Pray for us sinners)
We may have lost, but your family are winners
(Now and at the hour of our death, Amen)
It will only hurt a little, when they stick the needle in.

(Our father who art in heaven)
Do you have any last words, son?
(Hallowed be thy name)
Like finally accepting the blame
(Thy kingdom come, thy will be done)
They said you shot him with a gun.
(On earth as it is in heaven)
Why not just say you're sorry, son?
(Give us this day our daily bread)
In less than fifteen minutes you'll be dead
(And forgive us our debts as we forgive our debtors)
His mother said he was the only child of hers
(And lead us not into temptation)
You can't change things, what's done is done.
(But deliver us from evil)
Killing you will make things level
(For thine is the Kingdom)
An eye for an eye, a son for a son
(And the power)
Your casket's waiting over by the tower
(And the glory forever, Amen)
They'll release your body to your next of kin.

(The Lord is my shepherd, I shall not.....)

John Yarbrough graduated from Tarrant County Junior College and the Texas Christian University. He holds an A.A. degree in Law Enforcement, a B.G.S. in Criminal Justice, and advanced and instructor certification from the Texas Commission on Law Enforcement. Mr. Yarbrough was a Fort Worth Police Officer from 1967-85 and held the rank of Detective Lieutenant. He was Chief Deputy of the Wise County, Texas Sheriff's Department from 1986-89. In 1990, Mr. Yarbrough was convicted of capital murder and received the death penalty. In 1991 he was sent to Death Row at the Ellis 1 Unit near Huntsville. His case was overturned in 1993 and he received a life sentence. He continues to maintain his innocence and is currently involved in trying to obtain a new trial. A book is being written about his case.

Billy G. Hughes Jr. - "Lady Justice"

PERRY JOHNSON

"Killing Murderers Is No Answer"

But the trouble is that in order to carry out the death penalty one needs an executioner. The executioner is, or becomes, a monster, and on balance it is better to let the monsters that exist go on living rather than to create others. —Errico Maltesta

With three hundred already dead, and thousands waiting to go, executions seem to have become as American as apple pie. They are immensely popular—polls consistently show that between 70 and 75 percent of Americans support capital punishment. And where the populace goes politicians are sure to follow—or rush to the front and lead.

Support for capital punishment seems to have become virtually the litmus test for being tough on crime. Any candidate for office who has ever voiced a reservation about the death penalty is likely to become targeted in attack ads as a friend to murderers. Congress got on this bandwagon recently by passing a crime bill that, among other things, expanded the number of federal crimes that could warrant death from one to 47. Similar examples can be found in many states. But does capital punishment really merit such widespread endorsement? After much difficult and troubled weighing of the actual consequences of the death penalty, I think not.

It is exceedingly difficult to consider this topic rationally and dispassionately. I must confess that when I watched the unrepentant and defiant contempt of Richard Allen Davis upon receiving a death sentence for his savage murder of 12 year old Polly Klass, a voice within me whispered: *An efficient sanitized execution is too good for him; better that he should rot in prison in fear of his fellow convicts who treat a "baby rapist" as the most contemptible among them; and, yes, let him survive even that to die old and shriveled in his cell, followed by an ignominious burial in the shadow of the prison's wall.* And this would in fact be his fate were he sentenced in Michigan—my state.

So each of us feels outrage over such monstrous acts, and our helplessness to save the victim or comfort the bereaved leaves us with emotions that cry for vengeance. But the question we must ultimately ask and answer as members of the body politic is what a civilized society should and should not do in dealing with these feelings, and with these offenders.

During my 33 years in corrections, I have reviewed the grisly details of many homicides—sometimes because I was responsible for supervising the murderer in prison, sometimes because the murder itself was committed there. I have personally known prisoners who later became victims of brutal killings. I have experienced sorrow and anger over the senseless prison slayings of loyal employees. I have come to know many murderers well who were serving out their adult lives in prisons, some as responsible, productive human beings, others as impossible management problems.

The conclusion I have reached is that some of these people, like Richard Allen Davis, fully deserve to die for their crimes, but that we, as a civilized society, should not kill them. We should not because the death penalty fails the two tests against which any just sanction must be measured.

The first is that the sanction must be in our public self-interest. In this instance that means that we protect our own lives by taking that of another. In my profession, public protection is a primary responsibility. Therefore, if I had grounds for believing that the execution of a convicted murderer would save the life of even one innocent person, I would be obligated to endorse that sanction.

But capital punishment does not save lives. Few issues in criminal justice have seen as much research over the last 50 years as the deterrent impact of executions, and I am aware of none in which the evidence weighs so heavily on the negative side. There is even a real possibility that some murderers see execution as a martyrdom which will provide a dramatic end to a life of hatred directed toward themselves and others. Utah's Gary Gilmore may be one such example.

But, it is sometimes said, even though an execution may not deter others, it at least prevents the freeing of one murderer to kill again in a few years. A common enough argument, but in Michigan, which has not executed anyone in nearly a century and a half, we have no record of any person commuted from a sentence of first-degree murder who repeated that crime. Most first-degree murderers die in prison and those few who receive executive clemency have either served many years or are terminally ill. Their record after release from prison has been exemplary. So the claim that we need capital punishment for our own safety will not stand scrutiny; life imprisonment is adequate for that purpose.

The second proper test of any penalty exacted by a civilized society is that it can be applied with assurance of justice and fairness. Capital punishment clearly fails this test as well.

It fails a test of social justice in that it has been disproportionately applied to minorities—the race of both the offender and the victim are factors in that determination. Research on death row prisoners has consistently shown that this disturbing aspect of the way in which the death penalty is actually administered remains a problem even today.

There also is the ever-present possibility—and over time the certainty—of the ultimate injustice: the socially approved execution of a person who is in fact innocent. Despite all judicial safeguards, some persons serving prison terms for murder have been subsequently found to have been wrongfully convicted. When that discovery is made, a prison term can at least be abridged, but a life cannot be restored.

Even Supreme Court Justice Harry Blackmun, who for more than 20 years voted to enforce the death penalty, finally concluded that it could not be administered consistently and rationally. In his dissenting opinion in the Collins case he declared: *Even under the most sophisticated death penalty statutes, race continues to play a major role in determining who shall live and who shall die. Even the most sophisticated death penalty schemes are unable to prevent human error from condemning the innocent. Innocent persons have been executed.* He went on to say: *From this day forward, I no longer shall tinker with the machinery of death. I feel morally and intellectually obligated simply to concede that the death penalty experiment has failed.*

It is ironic that the post-Blackmun Court has now, apparently indifferent to the flaws cited by Justice Blackmun, and, according to some members, acting with unseemly haste, agreed to expedite executions by limiting appeals from death row inmates. Apparently we are so eager to get on with the killing of the 3100 plus on death row that we are willing to reduce safeguards against execution of the innocent. To paraphrase George Bernard Shaw, indifference to guilt or innocence when executing our fellow man would seem to be the essence of inhumanity.

Some argue for capital punishment on the grounds that it will save money. So far it is just the opposite—it costs more. This has been reported in every jurisdiction where it has been looked at. In Texas, for example, a typical death penalty case is said to cost taxpayers more than two million dollars, which is three times what they have to spend to keep a prisoner in even the highest security level for forty years. Recent efforts to streamline the process may eventually change that, but even if that is possible, the taking of a human life should not be based on so shallow a reason—and, as noted, shortening the process increases the likelihood that an innocent person will be executed.

Once we recognize that the death penalty is neither a just nor effective response to murder, then vengeance alone is left as its justification. Several years ago, Canada's Pierre Trudeau asked this question: *Are we so bankrupt as a society, so lacking in respect for ourselves, so lacking in hope for human betterment, so socially bankrupt that we are ready to accept vengeance as a penal philosophy?*

I am convinced, therefore, that capital punishment fails all tests as an effective and just response to even the most serious of crimes. But there is a stronger reason yet why we, as a civilized people, should not kill even the most heinous and undeserving of criminals. That is the brutalizing effect which the death penalty has on the public which imposes it. Deliberate and pointless killing cheapens the value of human life. The ultimate message we give by exacting this penalty is that it is all right to kill out of anger or for vengeance. But that, as it happens, is what every unrepentant murderer I have ever known believes.

Perry Johnson's career in corrections has spanned 37 years. He holds a BS degree in police administration and a MS degree in corrections administration. He served as Director of the Michigan Deptartment of Corrections for 12 years. Since retiring, he has been an internationally known corrections consultant and served a two year term as President of the American Correctional Association. He received the ER Cass Award, the highest tribute given by the ACA to a corrections practitioner. Mr. Johnson is a partner with a corrections consulting firm, and an adjunct professor at MI State University's School of Criminal Justice.

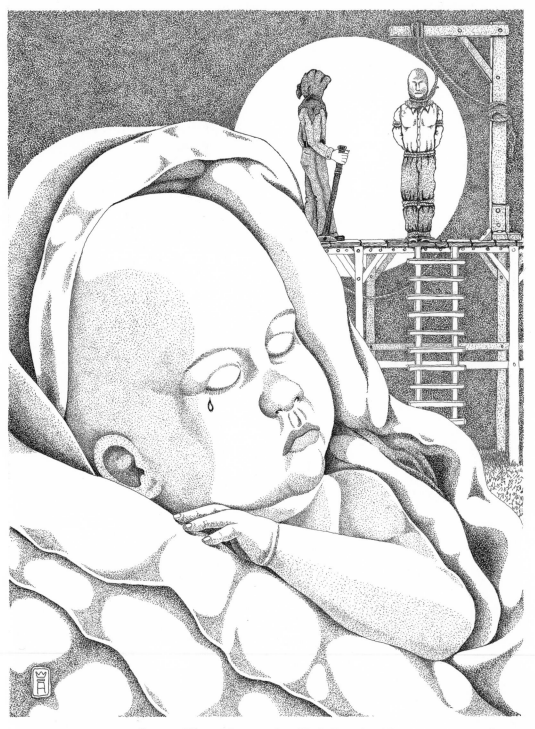

Steven King Ainsworth - "Is It Destiny?"

The Luxury of Hope

Rev. Joe Ingle - "A Few Days in the Life of Aaron"

Hon. Henry B. Gonzalez - "Calling for a Constitutional Amendment to Abolish the Death Penalty"

Gene Hathorn - "Death Knell"

REV. JOE INGLE

"A Few Days in the Life of Aaron"

I received a telephone call from the public defender's office of a mid-size Tennessee city. Their client had requested to see a minister and they wondered if I would be willing to talk to him. The young man who was their client was 22 years old and in the beginning of jury selection for his death penalty trial. I asked for a few details about the situation.

Aaron was accused of burglarizing a home. In the process of seeking to find $550 for a friend so he could pay the rent, he was surprised by the victim who grabbed him. Aaron, who had a knife in his hand which he had used to cut the window screen, stabbed the man repeatedly and fled the scene with his buddy who had been the lookout on the front porch. Aaron had turned himself in and confessed to the crime. After hearing the essentials, I agreed to pay a pastoral call on Aaron at the county jail.

On Thursday, January 23rd, I drove in a ferocious winter thunderstorm to the jail. The investigator on the case was kind enough to meet me and introduce me to Aaron. Aaron and I sat in a small room, actually a large closet containing prisoners' jumpsuits, and we began to talk. Aaron looked down at the table and was reluctant to speak, and I gingerly began to establish a bridge of communication. His flat affect was of one who is seriously depressed. Aaron had been in the jail for two years and eight months awaiting trial, and his complexion was washed out of color, a chalky white. The orange jumpsuit was a bright contrast to the pallor of his skin.

Knowing I had worked with the condemned since 1974, Aaron was curious about Tennessee's death row and asked me what it was like and who was there. We talked about the reality of death row as opposed to the myth. Gradually, he relaxed and began to open up about his situation. Through tears he recounted the night of the crime. He wished he had been the one who had been killed. I encouraged him to cry, assuring him it was all right, and he wept quietly for a few minutes. We talked for almost two hours and closed with a prayer.

The lawyers on the case followed up the next day, asking me if I would be willing to see Aaron again since he had appreciated the visit. They also asked me to consider testifying in the mitigation phase of the sentencing hearing, if Aaron were to be found guilty of first degree murder. I agreed to do both and had two more visits with Aaron as the trial continued over the next week.

The district attorney was relentless in portraying Aaron as a premeditated, cold blooded killer. Aaron's "friends," who were involved with the crime, were pointing their fingers at him, as so often happens in these cases. The victim's family wanted revenge. And Aaron was clearly guilty. The jury went out to deliberate Thursday afternoon, January 30th. They returned with a verdict at 3:30 Friday afternoon. They found Aaron guilty of premeditated and felony murder.

The verdict was hard to take. I had come to know this young man, to see that he was really just a kid. Entering that house, he meant no harm to anyone, but he had overreacted and killed someone. He was ill of remorse and guilt. I have worked with many people who have killed someone; Aaron was among the least likely to be a premeditated killer. The district attorney had sold the jury his story. The defense team, who had done an excellent job, were hoping that the jury's length of deliberation on the guilt/innocence might have meant they were coming back with second degree murder. The verdict was a blow. The judge indicated sentencing would take place on the following day, Saturday, February 1st.

I had shared my visits with Aaron with my family. My daughter, eight year old Amelia, included Aaron in her bedtime prayers. "And God bless Aaron and nobody but Aaron!" The theology was a bit off, but the sentiment was genuine.

Saturday morning saw the victim's family take the stand. Aaron's mother, aunt and I waited our turns in the corridor of the courthouse. The court recessed for lunch. Our turn would come beginning at 12:30. I taught Aaron's niece and nephew, who suffered from cerebral palsy, how to play "I Spy," the children's game. Finally, I was summoned by the bailiffs, the last witness for the defense in mitigation.

The defense lawyer led me through my resume and then began asking me about my relationship with Aaron. My main contribution was to simply share the humanity of this young man with the jury—for them to realize his genuine grief and sorrow over what he had done. I sought to place that in the context of the Christian faith, in order for the jurors to sense they were called to discipleship by God. The State may well indeed seek to kill someone, but a Christian is not bound to honor that request because we have a higher calling. There was no cross examination of my testimony. I remained to hear closing arguments, and after the instructions from the judge, the jury went out to deliberate its options: life, life without parole and death by electrocution.

Joe Ingle

The jury began to deliberate Aaron's fate at 4:30 p.m. on Saturday, February 1, 1997. The emotional roller coaster ride from hoping for second degree on Thursday to facing death on Saturday was utterly draining. Aaron had told his family not to be in the courtroom when the jury returned with the decision. He had also asked his lawyers if he couldn't just go ahead and get the death penalty and get it over with for his family. The tension was wearing on everyone.

On the night of February 1, at 10:30, the jury returned with its decision. The foreman read the decision of the **State of Tennessee v. Aaron Light**. Aaron was sentenced to spend the rest of his life in prison without the possibility of parole.

When Aaron's lawyer called to thank me for assisting in the case, I remarked to him, "There is no joy in this case, is there?" We agreed there was none. But there was consolation. Aaron would not be walking from the holding cell in Building 8 to the electric chair at Riverbend Maximum Security Prison. Thank God for that blessing.

("Aaron" has been used as a pseudonym in this essay.)

Joe Ingle founded and served as executive director of the Southern Coaliton on Jails and Prisons. He was nominated for a Nobel Peace Prize in 1988 and 1989. Reverend Ingle is an ordained minister of the United Church of Christ. He continues to minister to death row inmates in Tennessee.

HON. HENRY B. GONZALEZ

"Calling for a Constitutional Amendment to Abolish Capital Punishment, House of Representatives, Friday, June 30, 1995"

I rise today to introduce a joint resolution proposing a constitutional amendment to prohibit capital punishment within the United States. I believe that the death penalty is an act of vengeance veiled as an instrument of justice. Not only do I believe that there are independently sufficient moral objections to the principle of capital punishment to warrant its abolition, but I also know that the death penalty is meted out to the poor, to a disproportionate number of minorities, and does not either deter crime or advance justice.

At a time when South Africa's highest court, in the first ruling of the new multiracial Constitutional Court, has just abolished the death penalty—on grounds that it is a cruel and inhumane punishment that does not deter crime but which does cheapen human life—as part of the post apartheid quest for democratic government and a just society in that country, we should give up to no lower of a standard in our continuing effort to uphold democracy and justice in our land.

Violent crimes have unfortunately become a constant in our society. Every day people are robbed, raped, and murdered. We are surrounded by crime and yet feel helpless in our attempt to deter, to control, and to punish. The sight of any brutal homicide excites a passion within us that demands retributive justice. We have difficulty comprehending that which cannot be understood. Mr. Speaker, we will never comprehend the rationale of violent crime, but the atrocity of the crime must not cloud our judgment and we must not let our anger undermine the wisdom of our rationality. We cannot allow ourselves to punish an irrational action with an equally irrational retaliation—murder is wrong, whether it is committed by an individual or by the State.

Violence begets violence. I cannot help but wonder if the vigilante executions that are becoming more frequent in our country, whereby citizens arm themselves and mete out capital punishment for crimes such as "tagging" as happened in California and recently in my own district in San Antonio, and for knocking on one's front door and acting disorderly as happened in Louisiana, and numerous other incidents where property crimes are met with a lethal response, are a direct result of the atmosphere of violence embraced by our Federal and State governments as a proper response to problems. Indeed, I wonder whether the overall escalation of violence in our society perpetrated by criminals can be traced to the devaluation of human life as exhibited by our governments.

The United Nations Universal Declaration of Human Rights states, "No one shall be subjected to torture or to cruel, inhuman or degrading treatment or punishment." The death penalty is torture, and numerous examples exist emphasizing the cruelty of the execution. Witness Jimmy Lee Gray, who was executed in 1983 in the Mississippi gas chamber. During his execution he struck his head repeatedly on a pole behind him and had convulsions for 8 minutes. The modernization to lethal injection serves only as an attempt to conceal the reality of cruel punishment. Witness the execution by lethal injection of James Autry in 1984. He took 10 minutes to die and during much of that period he was conscious and complaining of pain.

Despite the obvious mental and physical trauma resulting from the imposition and execution of the death penalty, proponents insist that it fulfills some social need. This simply is not true. Studies fail to establish that the death penalty either has a unique value as a deterrent or is a more effective deterrent than life imprisonment. We assume that perpetrators will give greater consideration to the consequences of their actions if the penalty is death, but the problem is that we are not always dealing with rational actions. Those who commit violent crimes often do so in moments of passion, rage, and fear—times where irrationality reigns.

Rather than as a deterrent, some studies suggest that the death penalty may even have a brutalizing effect on society. For example, Florida and Georgia, two of the States with the most executions since 1979, had an increase in homicides following the resumption of capital punishment. In 1984 in Georgia, the year after executions resumed, the homicide rate increased by 20 percent in a year when the national rate decreased by 5 percent. There can be no disputing the other evidence—murders have skyrocketed in recent years, as have State executions. The government cannot effectively preach against violence when we practice violence.

The empty echo of the death penalty asks for simple retribution. Proponents advocate that some crimes simply deserve death. This argument is ludicrous. If a murderer deserves death, I ask you why then do we not burn the arsonist or rape the rapist? Our justice system does not provide for such punishments because society comprehends that it must be founded on principles different from those it condemns. How can we condemn killing while condoning execution?

In practice, capital punishment has become a kind of grotesque lottery. It is more likely to be carried out in some States than others—in recent years more than half of the Nation's executions have occurred in two States—Texas and Florida. My home State of Texas led the Nation in 1993 with 17 executions, more than three times the number of executions in the State with the second highest rate. The death penalty is far more likely to be imposed against blacks than whites—the U.S. Supreme Court has assumed the validity of evidence that in Georgia those who murder whites were 11 times more likely to receive the death sentence than those who kill blacks, and that blacks who kill whites were almost 3 times as likely to be executed as whites who kill whites. It is most likely to be imposed upon the poor and uneducated—60 percent of death row inmates never finished high school. And even among those who have been sentenced to die, executions appear randomly imposed—in the decade since executions resumed in this country, well under 5 percent of the more than 2,700 death row inmates have in fact been put to death.

It cannot be disputed that most death row inmates come from poverty and that there is a definite racial and ethnic bias to the imposition of the death penalty. The statistics are clear, as 92 percent of those executed in this country since 1976 killed white victims, although almost half of all homicide victims during that period were black; further, black defendants are many times more likely to receive the death sentence than are white defendants. A 1990 report of the General Accounting Office found that there exists a pattern of evidence indicating racial disparities in the charging, sentencing, and imposition of the death penalty. In 82 percent of the studies, race of victim was found to influence the likelihood of being charged with capital murder or receiving the death penalty. Similar statistics can be found in my area of the country with regard to individuals of Mexican-American descent; in fact, similar practices once prevailed with regard to women. The practice was to tell the murderer to leave town if he killed a Mexican-American or a woman, as the feeling was that the murder must have been justified. We may have moved beyond that point, but not by much. It is as much a bias in favor of "haves" and at the expense of the "have-nots" as anything else.

Racial and ethnic bias is a part of our Nation's history, but so is bias against the poor. Clearly, the ability to secure legal assistance and to avail oneself of the best that the legal system has to offer is based on one's financial status. The National Law Journal stated in 1990: "*Indigent defendants on trial for their lives are being frequently represented by ill-trained, unprepared court-appointed lawyers so grossly underpaid they literally cannot afford to do the job they know needs to be done.*" The American Bar Association has admitted as much.

The legal process has historically been replete with bias, as well. We have a history of exclusion of jurors based on their race; now, the Supreme Court has sanctioned the exclusion of multi-lingual jurors if witnesses' testimony will be translated—this is particularity significant in my area of the country, in San Antonio. Further, we have executed juveniles—children, actually, as well as those with limited intelligence. Only four countries besides the United States are known to have executed juvenile offenders in the past decade: Bangladesh, Pakistan, Iraq, and Iran. That's some company to be in.

There are moves on in Congress to speed up the execution process by limiting and streamlining the appeals process. But when the statistics show how arbitrarily the death penalty is applied, how can we make any changes without first assuring fairness? If the death penalty is a fair means of exacting retribution and punishment, then isn't fairness a necessary element of the imposition of capital punishment? There are no do-overs in this business when mistakes are made.

The imposition of the death sentence in such an uneven way is a powerful argument against it. The punishment is so random, so disproportionately applied in a few states, that it represents occasional retribution, not swift or sure justice. My colleagues, I implore you to correct this national disgrace. Nearly all other Western democracies have abolished the death penalty without any ill effects; let us not be left behind. Let us release ourselves from the limitations of a barbaric tradition that serves only to undermine the very human rights which we seek to uphold.

The evolution in thinking in this area has progressed in nearly all areas of the world except in this country, where the evolution halted and even began reversing itself in recent years as the Federal Government has moved to execute Federal prisoners and States such as Texas have accelerated State executions. But among our country's most highly-educated and highly-trained legal specialists, the evolution has been restarted. Former Supreme Court Justices Lewis Powell and Harry Blackmun came to the conclusion in recent years that capital punishment constitutes cruel and unusual punishment. Congress should pursue the line of thinking espoused now by these legal scholars in recognizing that capital punishment is unconstitutional and that this should be declared in a constitutional amendment. I urge my colleagues to join me in this effort.

Henry Gonzalez is a member of the United States House of Representatives from the state of Texas. He has introduced a resolution for a constitutional amendment to ban capital punishment in every Congress for ten years, but it has never been acted upon.

GENE HATHORN

"Death Knell"

The chants, buttressed by gaiety and drunken laughter, ring through a rainy night outside the death house in Huntsville, Texas, and those eerie utterances bespeak a lust for blood unlike any I've ever seen. As a lifelong Texan I am quite familiar with the population's adherence to the precepts of what they call "frontier justice." Of course I can't hear the chants, because I am in my cell some fifteen miles from the death house, but I can feel them as they vibrate through the ethers to reach my heart and scornfully pluck its strings. I have been a resident of death row for over ten years, and this night another of our number, barring an unlikely reprieve from a benevolent jurist, shall be poisoned to death at the direction of a warden who claims it is his job, mandated by law, to initiate and preside over the most premeditated type of killing imaginable. The warden will nod his head toward a window with a one-way view, buttons will be pushed to begin the flow of poison, and outside, apart from a smattering of anti-death penalty protesters, a tumultuous roar will emit from those participating in a ghoulish celebration of death. Another soul seeks its path in whichever world lies beyond, and again Texas-style punishment has been meted out.

Texas recently performed its 100th execution, a milestone which was observed with much interest and fanfare by the media, and of those 100 men I was personally acquainted with 95. A sad legacy indeed for a man who, despite his hopes and pleas for a cessation of the wanton madness, has witnessed a hardening of public attitudes toward death row inmates, and the retrogression of laws intended to guard against the capricious imposition of the death penalty. As an example of the more rigid attitudes, victims' rights advocates recently persuaded the Texas Board of Criminal Justice to sanction the viewing of executions by the survivors of condemned inmates' victims. Behind the push to allow the viewing of executions was the twisted belief by victims' survivors that watching the man die whom they believed killed their loved one would lend a sense of "closure" to their healing processes, but in this case one may exchange the word "revenge" for closure. Not until the bereaved survivors see the death throes of the object at whom they have directed their wrath, actually see him suffer as he gasps for his final breath, will they feel that he has paid an adequate price for his misdeed, and only then, with the perverse scent of vengeance still in their nostrils, will they attain the closure they claim to seek. It does not satisfy these people that various killers have been removed from the streets and placed in prison where they can't cause further harm, and when the depths of this hate are considered pragmatically, with proper attention given to the implications for society as a whole, one shudders.

We on the Row bear witness to these appalling developments and wonder if the social pendulum will ever swing to a point where the inherent humanity of every person is acknowledged, and if so will we live to see it. The system itself, after great pains have been taken therein to ensure that the direst of straits prevail for death row inmates, through the mediums of shortened appeals and speedier executions seems to negate this possibility with disconcerting finality. Our blood, offered by a cadre of politicians who make their living pandering to the fear and hysteria of their constituents, is the only prize the public deems acceptable, thus the likelihood of a death row "savior" emerging from the tempest of reason to reform attitudes in favor of compassion and true justice appears remote, if not unthinkable.

On occasion I have encountered the question: What makes you, a death row inmate, deserving of compassion? Being a death row inmate does not automatically make one a bad person, as it is common in the lives of all people to make mistakes of varying degrees, and none have thus far managed to transcend this unfortunate affliction of humanity. I readily concede that there are people on death row who probably should not be allowed to experience freedom ever again, but what, aside from the ephemeral solace offered by revenge, is gained by killing them? The arguments and statistical evidence in support of abolition are legion, so I won't rehash them herein. I will, however, point out that alongside the nefarious fellows mentioned above lives a greater number of the retarded, the mentally ill, and the outright insane, not to mention a significant number of guiltless people who, because of their financial status or just plain bad luck, could not prove their innocence at trial. Yet they sit here year after year in extremely hot and squalid conditions in the summer, extremely cold and drafty ones in the winter, being abandoned by wives, mothers, and friends, eating prison food that is routinely infested with insect parts or human hair, and being issued one roll of toilet paper per week—God forbid someone catch a cold or the flu and need to blow his nose more than once or twice, because, to save his toilet paper for more pressing needs, he must resort to using his cell towel, or perhaps his bedsheet, as a handkerchief. Sometimes one chooses a drug-induced haze to alleviate the agony of living in this hostile, oppressive, and predatory environment, and I dare say, especially when speaking of the innocent: Who can blame them?

Living on death row, at least for those who manage to maintain their sanity, would seem like a page torn from the book of surrealism were it not for the fact that the pain and misery are too tangible, too cloying, to be the bastard product of incongruous musings. Yet there are days when I find myself questioning the most elementary concepts of reality, wondering if anything I've experienced over the past decade had actually happened, and pondering the possibility that the frayed thread suspending me above the sword of dementia may finally be ready to snap.

The American Criminal Justice System, specifically the part which pertains to capital punishment, is a shambles and no one is imbued with a high enough purpose to change it, for it is easier and more politically feasible to maintain the status quo of justice by sound byte. Recently I read an article which illustrates the glaring discrepancies and whimsical idiosyncrasies generally utilized in our justice scheme. It spoke of a man who had been charged with murder, was tried and convicted, and sentenced to ten years in prison. After serving only three months of the ten-year term the man was granted "shock probation" by his sentencing judge, who happens to be someone I've known since early adolescence. Shock probation entails the release of a person who has served but a fraction of his sentence, the idea being to give someone who has never been to prison a taste of prison life to "shock" him into staying out of trouble once he is released.

Then I began to focus on the similarities between the man who was released on probation and myself, and was amazed at how stark they are. Both he and I are from the same area, both were charged with murder, both were first offenders, and both were fathers of small children at the time of our convictions, the latter being a pertinent consideration in the judge's decision to afford the other man leniency. Now the probationer is with his family, playing with his children every day and sharing passion with his wife, and I am still on death row. Why? Sadly, I have the answer: He was a prison guard convicted of beating an inmate to death, thus, because in the eyes of many he did society a favor, he should be granted a second-chance to prove his worth as a human being. Here the similarities between us end.

The hatred and apathy showered on death row inmates by politicians and unenlightened people notwithstanding, there is an even greater force that often imposes its will into our lives, and it is Fate. The diabolical nature of its lightning strikes can make the brightest of moods evaporate in a matter of seconds. About two weeks ago an acquaintance took great pride in telling me that he had just seen his first grandchild in the visiting room. "She was only eight-days old and so tiny," he said. "No bigger than a football!" Then yesterday the same man received from his attorney a letter in which was contained the news that his final appeal had been turned down, so the elation he felt at getting to meet his grandchild two weeks ago has been replaced by a miscellany of emotions, such as anger, a sense of betrayal, disbelief, and the inner reflection he is cosmically required to perform in light of his impending death. I've noticed that concession to defeat has made his shoulders a bit more slumped than usual, and I must watch from the shadows helpless and sedate, for, even though I feel sorrow over his plight, what words could I possibly say to ease his pain, to offer comfort in the face of the realization that he'll not see his new granddaughter reach the age of one?

This man, like any other, has lessons to teach, but our leaders do not want our lessons publicized because if what we say helps curb the violence someday, the powers that be will no longer enjoy the benefit derived from castigating death row inmates for political gain. Their scapegoats will be no more, and they, because they are working out the same life sums as we, despite their pride of counterfeit respectability and moral worth, will be forced to face and deal with issues of real concern to the voting public. The fact that they are shrewd enough to cover their own guilt with a polished coat will not sustain them forever, for their scorn and loathing of my ilk is mockery. Tear away the tinseled fabric of their reputations and the loudest among them would be found to revel in lust, deceit, and many other forms of secret sin. But for now death continues to flow on rainy nights, while chants of jubilation sicken the pure and arouse the foul of heart.

Sometimes when I allow myself the luxury of hope, I picture a scene in the snow covered mountains. I am sitting in a rocking chair on the porch of an old cabin, pipe in hand and a faithful dog lying nearby, watching the silent beauty of falling flakes as they gather on the ground and the receptive limbs of trees. The only sound is my breathing and the whisper of swirling white, but every so often I hear the distant crack of a bough too laden with velvet weight. As I sit there in jeans, hiking boots, a flannel shirt, and thermal underwear, thinking about the hot tea I'll have in front of the fireplace later, I honestly believe in my heart of hearts that, despite the pain, betrayal, and treachery I've experienced in my life, the world isn't really a bad place. Just the little corner of it in which I live, and I'll never be finished trying to change that for the better.

Gene Hathorn is an ordained minister who oversees Angelheart Ministry, an organization which donates stuffed animals to AIDS hospices, hospitals and other care facilities for terminally or critically ill children. He is Chairman of the Board of the Lamp of Hope Project, an educational organization overseen by death row inmates which provides education to the public about injustices inherent in the American criminal justice system, and which offers a forum for crime victims and survivors of murder victims to express their anger and their views on crime reduction. Mr. Hathorn is predominantly self-educated and a writer of poetry and prose. His poems were published in Trapped Under Ice: A Death Row Anthology [Biddle Publishing Co.]. He has been on death row for 12 years.

Christian Snyder - "The Solution"

TEKLA DENNISON MILLER

"Death Penalty Myths and Alternatives"

Convicted felons on death row were not a concern for me when I was a probation officer in Michigan in the early 70's. The news that the United States Supreme Court reinstated the death penalty in 1976 had little impact on me because Michigan is not a death penalty state. So, as with most people then and now, this issue had no face, no human aspect. I did what most of us do in an uncomfortable situation: I ignored it. As I progressed through the ranks, I realized I could not continue to ignore the death penalty issue, not only because it is morally wrong to murder in any form, but because of what I learned about the inequities of the criminal justice system. I discovered that as politicans and media massage our fear of crime, the death penalty myths harbored by the public represent much of what is wrong with this system.

1. The first myth is that the death penalty is a crime deterrent. To date, no evidence proves either the death penalty or prison deters crime. This area has been one of the most widely researched in the criminal justice system, and some studies show that more homicides occur immediately after a publicized execution. Sister Prejean, author of <u>Dead Man Walking</u>, reported that in 1987, immediately after the state of Louisiana executed eight people in 8 and a half weeks, the murder rate in New Orleans rose 16%. Most studies show that executions do not deter crime. A person committing a crime, especially a capital offense, does not analyze what sentence he might receive, because he operates on the premise he will not be caught.

In the United States, the murder rate is no higher in the states that do not have the death penalty than in those that do. In New York City in the first four months of 1992, the murder rate declined 11%, which was attributed to community policing. These studies indicate crime is not deterred by making humans expendable. However, renouncing violence as a means of resolving violence is a deterrent.

Imposing the death penalty takes resources away from crime fighting programs like community policing and public education. Further, punitive prison programs perceived to be deterrents, like chain gangs and boot

camps, have proven not to reduce recidivism or prison crowding as promised. However, prison programs like Project Horizon in Utah have reduced
recidivism by a third. It is a GED program combining tutoring, software and
video series, and focuses on assessment, job placement, family involvement,
and pre and post release support.

2. The second myth is that the death penalty is more cost effective.
This is a misperception, because capital trials require more expert witnesses
and investigators, longer jury selection, expense for sequestering the jury,
the expense of two trials (one for conviction and one for sentencing), followed by appeals in state and federal courts. Housing someone on death
row is also more costly because of the additional staff needed. Employees
take up the majority of prison budgets. Further, death row inmates cannot
offset expenses they incur by working.

Florida estimates it costs more than $3 million for each death sen-
tence compared to the cost of life imprisonment (based on 40 years) of about
$500,000. If California did away with the death penalty, they could save $90
million a year and use it for public education. A government official in Florida
said, "If the death penalty is ever abolished, it's not going to be on principles, it's going to be on dollars. If the public realizes they can't afford it,
then they'll abolish it." It saddens me that we, in a civilized society, allow
economics to decide who lives or dies. It makes more economic sense to
buffer against the problems that cause criminal and violent behavior because it is cheaper than prisons and executions.

3. The third myth is that the death penalty is a just punishment. The
perception is that people on death row are out of control barbarians—mass
murderers like Jeffrey Dahmer who commit the most heinous, cold blooded,
premeditated murders. The media and politicians perpetuate this untrue
perception because it sells more news and gets more votes. They use our
fears for personal gain. The truth is many cases on death row are there as the
result of panic murders by people who have had a history of being abused
children, who may be brain damaged, may be mentally retarded or insane;
they may even be our own kids. All of us can commit a panic murder or a
murder of passion. It happens in seconds without rational thought, and is
not planned.

The risk of being a victim in felony-type murders is two people for
every 100,000. Though this is two too many, it is roughly the same percentage that die of drowning or accidental poisoning. Compare this to the possibility of dying in a car accident which is 48 people per 100,000. We must also
examine who are the potential victims of violent crimes. Based on a report
from the Bureau of Justice Statistics (BJS), blacks are more likely to be victims

of violent crimes than whites. The young, especially between the ages of 12 and 24, are more likely to be victims than the elderly. BJS also reports that except for rape, men are more likely to be victims than women, and when women are victims, they know the offender 75% of the time. Further, persons living in urban settings and those with low family incomes are more likely to be victims.

I am not making excuses for murderous behavior. I am concerned, however, that our overreaction fueled by the media and politicians are leading us away from what should be done to solve the social ills in this country. Pouring money into prisons that do not work and executing a few prisoners are not the solutions.

Amnesty International recommends that attorneys spend no fewer than 500 hours on death penalty cases. Usually where there is a public defender or a court appointed attorney assigned to a death penalty case, the average number of hours spent is 50. It is well known that most of the people on death row are poor, because they get the kind of legal representation for which they pay. One public defender whose caseload averages 700 per year said the indigent defendant represented by an overworked lawyer ends up on death row. An indigent person is usually represented by a court appointed attorney who may only see his client the day before or the day of the trial after the accused has been in jail for months. Even a good attorney in this situation cannot give the same service to an indigent as to a paying client.

Although half of all murder victims are black, 85% of those executed or awaiting execution since 1977 were charged with killing whites. Only twice in the long history of executions in the U.S. has a white person been executed for killing a black. A black who murders a white is more likely to get the death penalty than a white murdering a black or a black murdering a black. Add to this that black defendants often face all-white or nearly all-white juries and this usually by design. The U.S. Government's General Accounting Office found the correlation of race to be a factor present at all stages of the criminal justice process. This includes the prosecutor's decision to charge the defendant with a capital offense or to go to trial rather than plea-bargain. Of the approximately 24,000 murders committed a year, 1% of murderers are selected to be prosecuted for the death penalty and this is based on who got killed. We rarely hear about a prosecutor going after the death penalty if the victim is homeless, poor, or a minority, because they are also victims of status.

Since 1976 when the Supreme Court reinstated the death penalty, at least 40% of the death penalty convictions have been reversed. It is believed that about 5% of the people on death row are innocent of the crime that put them there. Yet the public wants the appeals process limited because it costs too much. How would we feel if one of the innocent 5% were our child?

Should we limit appeals to someone like Bob who after 17 years on death row had his sentence reversed by the U.S. Supreme Court? He was acquitted in a subsequent trial after being found innocent beyond a reasonable doubt. It turned out the alleged victim died of natural causes.

A Stanford Law Review study revealed that during this century in the United States at least 417 people were wrongly convicted of capital offenses and of these 23 executed. They were killed in error, either because they were innocent or tried unjustly. Since the 1970's, at least 46 people have been released after many years on Death Row because they were discovered to be innocent. One of the most famous cases is Randall Dale Adams, a black Texas inmate who was freed in 1989 following twelve years on Death Row, after the documentary "A Thin Blue Line" proved Adams was not the killer. Clarence Brandley, another black Texas inmate, was released in 1990 after ten years on Death Row when two white prosecution witnesses admitted that a white man had committed the crime.

The inequities of the criminal justice system are further revealed in cases where co-defendants charged with the same murder are tried by different judges before separate juries and defended by different attorneys in the same courthouse. They sentence one to life without parole and the other to death. However, it is not always the person who pulled the trigger who gets selected to die, such as when one codefendent turns state's witness against the other and receives life without parole, while the other gets death. What made the state's witness less guilty—a politically advantageous death related conviction? How just is it that procedural default issues not raised at trial level cannot be reintroduced on subsequent appeals, even if new evidence shows justification for a new trial or that the accused may be innocent? We are allowing bureaucrats to decide life and death. One definition of capital punishment states, "those who lack the capital get the punishment." So, if we support the death penalty, we support a justice system that metes out one brand of justice for the rich and one for the poor.

4. Myth number four is that victims and their families deserve an eye for an eye. Of course we all feel pain when we hear about brutally murdered children. Rage fills us. We all want the murderer punished. Many want the accused killed. The media fuels our rage by making sure we know the victim and her family intimately. Yet, there are the other victims, beginning with the different ways both the families are treated, depending on the race of the victim. Though the criminal justice system is not known for its sensitivity when dealing with victims, it is even less sensitive to the needs of the victim's family when the victim is a minority.

Families of the accused are victims because the community ostracizes them, and the media scrutinizes and brutalizes them. Everyone forgets that the accused is also someone's loved one and sometimes is innocent. These families are often tried, found guilty and sentenced by public opinion even before the accused is.

Many victims' family members have said that watching the accused executed does not relieve the guilt or rid them of the rage they feel, and the execution does not bring closure. Yet they believe they betray the victim if they do not demand the death penalty. There are many victims' family members who do not believe in the death penalty because they refuse to perpetuate the violence.

Many public opinion surveys show that it is protection from criminals rather than executions that we want. This is especially true when we are shown that capital punishment does not deter crime, and when we are offered an alternative punishment of life without parole. Most agree if serious punishment is consistently meted out for serious crimes, our demands for retribution and safe communities are met. The key, of course, is consistency.

There is yet one other group of victims. These are the employees working on death row. They spend hours in training, exhaustive prior planning, thorough and extensive rehearsals and comprehensive pre and post trauma intervention programs. They also face an occupational hazard—getting to know the inmate personally. There are documented cases giving evidence that many people on death row make dramatic positive changes, so that at the time they are executed, they are not the same people who committed the crimes for which they were sentenced. Seeing positive changes in the man they must execute is a difficult part of the correction officer's job. Many leave their positions because they cannot cope with the stress of taking another person's life. Wouldn't we all be better off by letting these people serve life sentences?

Most of the executions in this country take place in the Bible Belt, because that population believes in an eye for an eye. Ghandi said, "If everyone took an eye for an eye, the whole world would be blind." I believe Ghandi.

5. The fifth myth is that executions are humane. If executions are so humane, why are they not public for everyone to see? Few supporters of the death penalty have ever viewed an execution. Many believe executions would be stopped if we were allowed to watch a person murdered.

There are documented cases in which serious errors were made in the execution process. For example, one prisoner caught fire in the electric chair and another was injected several times causing convulsions before he died. How humane are we when we spend money to keep a prisoner alive so we can kill him rather than let him die of natural causes? How humane are we when we force a prisoner to take tranquilizers to help ensure there are no mistakes, so the government can kill without problems? Are we humane when we prevent a prisoner's suicide so we can save him for his execution? Are the executioners humane when they give prisoners new clothes to die in so witnesses observe clean and sterile executions?

6. The sixth myth is that people sentenced to life in prison or mandatory, lengthy sentences rather than the death penalty can escape and commit new crimes and are more assaultive in prison than other prisoners.

Hearing of someone escaping from a maximum security prison is rare. The media and politicians make sure the public hears about the heinous crimes committed by an escapee or parolee. Yet they do not report that there are more than one million prisoners and that 90% of them will be released. Most prisoners serving life without parole do their time well. We managers prefer them to the "jitterbugs," the young prisoners who bounce in and out of prison for nonviolent and often drug related offenses. Jitterbugs are youngsters who are out of control and never learned how to manage their anger or curb their need for immediate gratification.

7. The last and to me the most important myth is that the death penalty makes our communities safer. This myth is based on the belief that if we permanently remove the alleged criminal from a community, he can no longer commit crimes. Yet of every 100,000 people in the United States, there are approximately 340 in state and federal prisons. One of every 43 adults in the United States is under the control of a corrections department, either on probation, on parole or in prison. There are more than one million persons in our prisons, and of those, over 3000 are on death row. Has this made our communities safer?

As our government slashes social programs, new prisons are built and more people are executed. When I started in corrections in the early 70's, using prevention programs was the norm. Then the recidivism rate was about 30%. Today, on the heels of the "get tough on crime" mind set which supports more prisons and few programs, the recidivism rate is estimated at between 60% and 80%. This prison building boom tells us that we humans are no longer good at taking care of each other. Executing or putting someone away in prison is easier. Then we do not have to deal with the social ills that put more than one million of our citizens in prison, 3000 of them facing death. We do not have to do something about poverty, or fund drug and alcohol counseling programs, or listen to each other. We do not have to do anything about these ills though it is cheaper and will make our streets safer. When our government executes someone, it is telling us that violence/murder is an easy solution for society's problems. When we have a problem with someone, we want to get rid of them, kill them. We are allowing our government to teach our children that the answer to violence is violence.

Though there are many programs that have proven to work toward the reduction of crime and violent behavior, we as a society must be willing to face our prejudices and devote time and energy to change attitudes about criminal behavior. On average, it costs about $50,000 per prisoner bed to build a prison, and upwards of $20,000 per year to keep a person in prison, and far more money to execute someone. As a society that claims to care about people, there are many programs and measures we can take that will help make our streets safe. Among these are:

1. Intervene with the young who are out of control by working with families at risk and by providing constructive community activities like midnight basketball and youth recreation centers. These programs lack funding because the public does not understand their benefits.

2. Provide education which encourages our youth to stay in school because they are challenged and enjoy it, not because it is the law. Sadly, we often turn down requests to fund new schools, equipment, and teachers' salaries. Yet we will fund prisons which cost more and reflect our failure to cure social problems.

3. Provide counseling in a variety of areas such as anger control, family violence, self worth, problem solving, conflict resolution.

4. Provide drug and alcohol counseling and prevention programs. Many people ask for help from programs, yet are turned away, because there is a waiting list, or they do not have the right insurance coverage, or they do not have insurance at all. Drug use among our youth has increased. Yet even before this rise, one out of three females in local jails is there for drugs. Programming is no easier to get in jail or prison, because funds are lacking.

5. Parenting and its responsibilities should be a part of our education starting at a very young age. No money or programs can replace positive interactions between parents and children. If we do not pay attention to this, more young people will make gangs their families.

6. Provide job training and provide jobs. Most people with jobs do not commit crimes

7. Stop relying on corrections and the criminal justice system to correct the failures of all the other social entities. On average, a prisoner spends three years in prison, usually after he is 18 years old; even if the corrections department could do anything in that short time span for this well formed adult, there are few preventive programs left in prisons which could help their reentry. So if the public continues to demand more prisons and incarceration, then they must also provide funding for legitimate habilitative

programs.

  8. Increase the number of police on the streets and support community policing.

  It comes down to where we want our money invested. Do we want our money spent on building more prisons which have not worked and are filled mostly with drug offenders? Do we want to spend millions of dollars to sentence a few to death? Do we really think executing a relatively few people a year will help us manage crime? Or do we want to spend our money on prevention? It is plain to me which spending plan will make our streets safer and communities healthier, because it comes to a choice between killing a few or helping the thousands of youth who are out of control. If we do not encourage prevention programs over incarceration and the death penalty, we will continue to lose generations of our children to drugs, gangs, prisons and death.

Tekla Dennison Miller attended Cazenovia College, UCLA and Oakland University in Michigan. She worked as a probation officer and a halfway house agent in Detroit, was supervisor at the first women's prison camp in Michigan, and warden at Huron Valley Men's and Women's Prisons. Ms. Miller was the first warden in Michigan to manage two maximum security prisons simultaneously. She is the author of The Warden Wore Pink [Biddle Publishing Co.], and a co-editor of the upcoming Frontiers of Justice, Volumes 2 & 3.

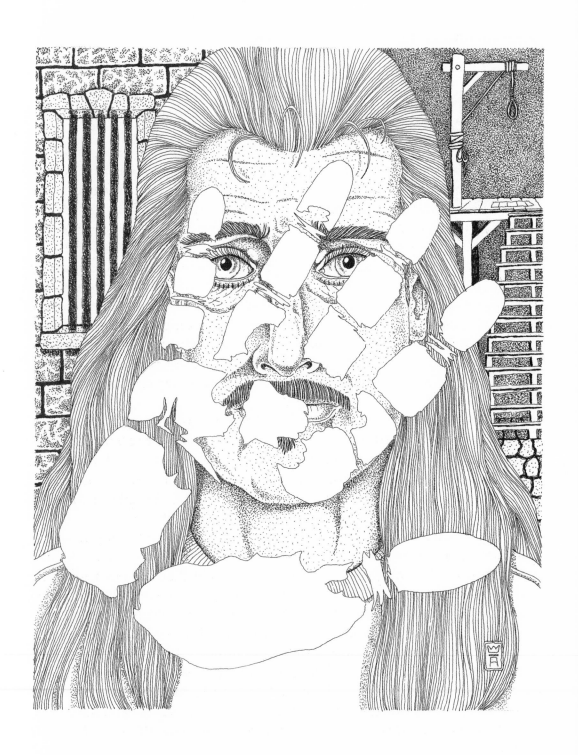

Steven King Ainsworth - "Vae Victis"

JOHN GAFFNEY

"Thoughts Inspired by an Execution"

Today I saw a man die. Yes, I know; you too have watched men die. But not like this. This one was different. He was hanged, hanged by the neck until he was dead. Hanged with a rope. He stood there, just stood there and looked at us. Then he spoke, very softly. Then something collapsed under his feet. He fell through a hole and died, died easily, with hardly a movement.

Last night when I walked home from work I had a little blue card in my shirt pocket. It might have been a theater ticket or a football ticket. But it wasn't. It was a ticket, all right though—a ticket to admit me to a room so I could see a man die. I took the ticket out of my pocket many times and read the words printed on it. This ticket is not like the others, I thought; this one is different. I have never had one like this before. I shall never have another. I didn't think this one was real. I wasn't sure what I thought. I was going to watch a man die.

When I woke the next morning, fifteen minutes earlier than was necessary, it was still quite dark. It was 6:45. I had planned to rise a few minutes past seven. When I was younger, I used to wake long before I should on mornings I was going hunting or on a camping trip; it was the same with this. I awoke and tossed about a little, wide awake. I thought of the next hour, the next hour and a half. A whole world waited there.

At seven I rose and drew back the shade to look out of the window. Outside the sky was overcast, gray and depressing. It was raining a little, not a great deal, just a little. And it seemed right that the sky should be overcast, that rain should be falling, especially that no sunlight should be playing anywhere about the streets or the hills or the sills. For today a man was going to die; sunlight would not harmonize, it would be sacrilegious.

It should not be that way, death a sad thing, but it is. We have made it sad. Death itself is not so bad always, not, that is, if we had left it alone. But we haven't. Instead we have added to death music, sad music, and flowers and coffins and an endless line of white crosses, and prayers and tears. Yes, indeed, we have made of death a sorry thing. And so the skies are dark and gloomy.

Somewhere once I read a few lines about death. I have read many lines about death but these impressed me and stayed in my head; they were simple lines too. They were something like this: "To die in the open air, no one staring at you, no black box, no beautiful, tormenting music, no well meant heavy words but just rain and wind and the ground and no more...would that not make of death a different thing?...It is the way they die...the great unhurried hosts of nature." That is what I believe.

I let the shade fall back into place, turned away and began to dress. While I put on my clothes, I had thoughts of him putting his on for the last time. It seemed so pointless to put on one's clothes to die. To tie your tie about your neck, to draw it up tight into a fine knot. To feel it about your throat, feel it like a rope. Hah! What might have been a laugh died away in a shiver, from the cold perhaps but more from my thoughts. When at last I had made myself ready to walk downtown to the office, I picked up the little blue ticket, placed it firmly inside my shirt pocket again, peered in after it to be sure it was there, and left the house behind me.

When I reached the office, Al was already there, looking over the early wires. He wasn't sitting down looking at them, he was walking about. It was ten minutes before eight. We were to be there before eight-thirty. Then they were to lock us in. Lock us in jail, inside, like him; but we would come out again, would walk out again and breathe the air into our lungs and see the overcast skies. For a few minutes the two of us—Al and I—went about the office quietly, talking a little now and then. Then we went across the street to get a cup of coffee. We had planned to do that. I would rather eat a little something I had said, and I repeated it now.

We didn't talk much while we drank our coffee and ate our rolls. Instead we watched the clock on the wall. Pretty soon a man across the room rose from his seat, paid his check, put on his coat and paused at the end of the counter where Al was sitting. They exchanged a few words, some almost too quiet for me to hear. When he had gone, Al said to me, He will be there too. He is one of the eight. Oh, I said, looking at the clock. It was ten minutes past eight. At eight-thirty they would lock the doors; no one would be let in then; no one would come out. We paid our bills and walked back to the shop. The rain had stopped.

Shortly we walked up the hill to the jail-yard. We loosened our coats and shook the moisture from them. At the big wire gate there were three or four men from the marshal's office. They were moving about in little circles to keep warm. As we passed through the gate, one of the men reached out a hand and we handed him our little blue tickets, just like entering the stands to see a game. Only this game was to be one-sided; the score was fixed.

We opened the door and stepped inside. It was dimly lighted in there and we saw a group of men standing along in a kind of haphazard row; most of them were holding their hats in their hands. Their coats were still on. They were silent. I was not familiar with this part of the building. This is it already, I thought momentarily. The stage is all set. We are in the very room. They have been waiting for us after all. Al thought the same thing for the first instant. He told me so afterwards. But we were wrong; a glance or two around the interior told us that. We heaved out our breath just in the relief that there would be a few minutes to take it easy. A man didn't walk into a room from the world outside and watch a man die. There had to be some formality, some walking stealthily from room to room, down dimly lit corridors, hearing strange sounds, seeing the shadow of the noose on the wall high up on the gallows. That's the way the movies had been and the movies are particular too.

We looked about and found ourselves in a hallway, the front part of which was an office. Toward the front, near the door we had just entered, was a roll-top desk with papers on it and more in the pigeon holes. There was a chair or two near it and in the corner a fire-proof filing cabinet. In the wall to the left of the desk was a door. Above the door it said Marshal's Office and inside a brighter light was shining. Above another metal-looking door it said Main Tank. Before we had time to see any more, a little man in shirt sleeves and wearing an eye shade came up and asked our names. We told him and he seemed immediately satisfied with what he heard.

Come in here and sign your names, he said, moving toward the marshal's office. We followed him in and the marshal was there, also in shirt sleeves and wearing a vest. On a table were three simple-looking papers, each one partially covering another. A man was signing his name. He was an attorney. If he didn't drink he'd be the best lawyer in town; that's what they say anyway. You can sign now, the marshal said, and Al picked up the straight pen and dipped its point into the ink bottle.

He signed once and made as if to put the pen down again. You're not through yet, the marshal said. There are three to sign. Al signed the other two and handed the pen to me. I thought at once that my hand was sure to shake a little. I hated that, for they would watch me. There was something about a time like this—they were sure to watch me. I started to sign the first one and I felt their eyes on my hand. It was trembling a little. Not bad though; probably theirs shook worse than mine. Deliberately, I took plenty of time. I put the one I had signed under the other two, slowly. I signed the others the same way. When I stood straight again, another fellow was there to sign; he peered cautiously over his glasses at the printed matter on the top paper. What's it say, Bill, he said to the marshal, half joking. How do I know I'm not signing your note? He went ahead and signed then, while we smiled at his joke.

Hardly anyone talked now. We just moved about, or stood still and looked at our watches. I made sure mine was wound and ticking. I was to note the time it took him to walk to the gallows, the time before he was pronounced dead. We needed that for the stories. The people would like that.

I laid my hat down on a little table toward one side of the room where I had noticed a couple of others. As I put it there, I saw a sort of chart or rack above the table. Written in chalk on the board it listed the number of prisoners: number of men, number of women. I think there were about forty altogether. I turned around again and just stood leaning against a post. I felt better when I leaned against something. It was warm in there and so quiet. I looked at the man to my left; I had seen him many times, but I didn't know his name. He works at a theatre. He looks around like the rest of us and after a while he looks at me, only half seeing me, and mutters, I'm not sure whether I'm going to like this sort of thing or not. His lips moved in a half smile. I said nothing.

Every now and then one of the marshal's assistants would pause in his walk past the main tank and peer through a hole in the wall. That is, I guess he peered through a hole; I couldn't see a hole, but he was doubtless seeing inside when he looked like that. Where is he? a fellow said, whispering to anyone who heard. Right in there, answered the man from the other daily paper; he motioned with his hand, which still held his hat, toward the main cells. Oh, the first man said, and as one we all looked toward the doorway. From the rear of the jail came the sound of several men laughing; then a few words in laughing voices, more laughter. Like men laughing at someone's joke over a breakfast table. We looked at one another and said nothing.

One of the two doctors was late. It was a few minutes past 8:30. The door was to have been locked by now. The marshal was cursing, angry. I was only disgusted with a fellow who kept nearly fifteen men waiting at a time like this. What's his phone number? said one of the deputies. He picked up a directory and found it. Yes, he was just leaving. He would be right there. So we stood and waited.

I grew restless again and began walking about. I paused near the marshal's open doorway. A deputy was at the filing case by the desk near the other door. He pulled open one of the drawers, reached in a hand and brought up a little ball of black cloth. He handed it to the marshal, who stood beside him. The marshal tucked it hurriedly up under his vest. That was the hood, I thought. And I wondered how many times it had been used before; never in this jail but somewhere else perhaps. I wondered who had worn it last, if it had been washed since then. I was sure it must have an unpleasant, musty smell. I sincerely loathed that black hood. I would not want it; but of course they would make me have it. If I didn't my eyes would be too ghastly afterwards; and my tongue....damn I loathed that hood.

In a few minutes there was a sound outside another door and the doctor had come. He was barely inside then when the marshal said, let's go. Let's take these fellows around to the other side. I picked up my hat, put it on slowly and marched outside with the others. We walked single file around to the side of the building. The gallows, I knew, had been erected under the big wooden stairway leading up to what had once been the courtroom. Now we saw a square of new-looking boards that had been tacked loosely onto the side of the stairs, covering what would have been the open side of the stairway. The deputies quickly loosened a couple of nails and the entire section of new boards fell away.

With that, we saw a space no larger than a small kitchenette. Inside, two benches, each long enough for four men to sit, had been placed in preparation. Without words we pulled our coats around us to avoid catching them on the sides of the entrance, stooped our bodies forward, and half-climbed into the cubbyhole.

I saw a water pipe at the far end of the second bench. I touched it and it was cold and wet. Water dripped from somewhere near its top. Sit here, I thought, and there will be something to hold onto if you need to. I looked at the watch on my arm and sat down. The men on the bench in front of me were so close my knees touched them. I was thankful it was almost like outdoors here under the stairs, cold, damp. In the movies it had always looked warm. You could feel faint there, but this was fine.

A few words went round then as we settled ourselves. Hasn't anyone a drink, said the attorney. No one had. Has he had anything to drink this morning, or any dope? somebody else said then. Not a thing, someone else said. The marshal said he ate a good breakfast, but he slept only about an hour and a half last night. He's taking it pretty well.

Directly in front of the first bench, there ahead of me, was a wire screening, big not fine wire with holes big enough for eggs to go though— big enough so that if you didn't think about it you forgot it was there. Below that was a pit perhaps twelve feet deep, formed by the stairway and the basement. The floor of the basement was of concrete. The concrete was black looking and wet. Opposite us, across the pit, was a little platform, about twelve feet by five feet; in the center of the platform was the trap and showing a scant few inches of itself around a wide plank nailed to the side wall was the rope. It looked new and thick and strong.

Off to the right of the platform was a door leading to the jail and the office from which we had come a few moments before. Now the sound of someone walking came from near the door.

The marshal appeared; this was to be the prologue, I thought; he was going to say a few words of greeting before the play began, before the curtain went up. But he didn't; there is to be no talking after he comes out, he said, and went off again. What did he say? someone asked, leaning forward. No talking after he comes out, I answered and at least two others answered with me. Then we all fell silent. We looked at our watches; I put my wrist to my ear and the ticking sound came back to me. It was 17 minutes before nine o'clock.

I looked first at the trap, then at the pit. It looked a long way to the bottom, and so damp and dark, like a dungeon. He would fall four feet, they had said. That was a long way, too. But now was no time to think of that for there was another sound outside the door.

Two clergymen appeared and took their places on the platform, just a foot behind the trap. I remembered a funeral I once went to then, when they came out so slowly and stood there so solemnly. "Would that not make of death a different thing...?" I swore to myself. Here they've come to mutter their senseless prayers which are no good; the church and God, they say, are tolerant and forgiving; they will stand behind this man about to die, they will mutter in his ear about God, and he will be forgiven and he will go to heaven. God! what manner of men is this? They who can forgive a man in death but not in life; while he stands there before them, breathing, speaking, his pulse moving in life, his hands bound to his sides, they will whisper about God and forgive him his sins. They know he is going to die and it will not matter then. He will be good. Could they not as well forgive in life? Is he a better man, is his soul better because he has given his life for his crime?

There were more sounds at the doorway. This would be it. First the marshal appeared, his arm holding someone else's arm, his body half-hiding another man. Then, slowly, so slowly, three of them were there, the marshal, a deputy, and between them, a man, a native, whom I had never seen before; he was *the man*. Then I learned I had been wrong about one thing; I had decided he would stand, not facing us, but sideways; but it was not that way. He stood there, not more than fourteen or fifteen feet away, looking at us. He looked as we had expected, like the full-blooded native he was. He wore blue serge trousers, black shoes, a white shirt, and a dark tie, well knotted and in place. His hands and arms were bound tightly to his sides with canvas bands.

Seconds ticked away; a few inches behind me, at my right side, water dripped, dripped and struck the boards. Like drops from a faucet, steadily, just so fast, no faster, but always steadily. I didn't want to hold onto anything, not yet anyway.

The marshal shook out another long canvas strap and stooped to adjust it about the man's legs. As he finished his task, he stepped back a little. Is there anything you would like to say, Nelson? he asked. We listened as we had never thought a man could listen, listened till our ears would burst, listened while we expected him to say nothing but hoped he would. We expected a brief negative nod of the dark head. But he spoke, his voice a half-sob, whispering, barely more: I am innocent of killing my mother-in-law, he murmured. I don't want to hang. I still say I am innocent.

His head was bowed forward; you could feel if not see the hot tears in his eyes, you could feel his trembling in your own body. Had I any thought of a man, a criminal, about to pay for his crime? Any thought of a disreputable and dangerous killer about to give his life for the one he had taken? No— nothing like that. Only that a man was about to die. That there, almost within reach, was a man, a man like ourselves, a man who somewhere had a wife, who had once slept an untroubled sleep, who had only the day before laughed and hoped for life.

I was aware of some particular feeling as I sat there then, some unusual feeling that was strange to me. Then it was vague and there was no time to fathom it. But now I know: it was the certainty, the sureness of it. I knew for the only time in my life that within minutes this man who now lived as I lived would be dead, a stone, cold and lifeless. Men have been stricken with fatal diseases and we have known they would die; we have held our buddies in our arms at the front and watched the last breaths spend themselves. But even then there had been hope and when not hope the awareness that death might stay away a while. Would it come now, or later perhaps? But there was none of that now. Nothing less than a miracle could save this fellow and there are no miracles in this life. We know no other. Soon he will be a stone.

From under his vest the marshal brought out the black hood. With a deputy standing on the other side, assisting him, he began to draw the thing onto the man's head. Now I thought of the funeral again, remembered that I had not felt too bad until the priest had appeared in his long black robes. I had seen those robes and tears had come. No tears came now, but still I hated the black, hated the hood. I thought, take it easy now, you fool, and don't be afraid you are going to miss something. Look away for a few seconds. So I dropped my eyes and looked into the pit, then up again.

They were having trouble with the hood. It was too small. Halfway on, its edge caught on the man's right ear. Fix my ear, he said quietly; said that, his last words, like a small boy about to be punished, who, with a half sob begs his parent to be careful not to break the toy in his pocket. Here was a striking bit of reality in all this dream. I learned about men and life as I heard him say that.

Now. All was ready. The marshal and his deputy stepped back nearer the clergymen. The marshal reached up and released the rope from its peg, began at once to place it about the man's neck. It looked even stronger now as it was drawn tighter about the man's neck. The noose looked as it should have looked; the movies had been faithful there all right.

John Gaffney

The marshal stepped back again, raised an arm toward his deputy, and his lips formed a half-audible okay. The deputy reached somewhere toward the back wall and at once a clicking noise began. It was loud in the quiet, widely spaced clicks which seemed seconds apart. Loud yet muffled, unmechanical sounding clicks. The water near me dripped on, drip, drip, click, click; drip, click, drip, click.

Then the clicking stopped with the louder sound of the trap's springing. There it was: the square of wood on which he stood fell away and he fell toward the pit, fell then swung. No extra movement, just swung, turning, turning, now right, now left. Like a stone on a string, a bit of paper on a cord held in the air for a kitten to leap at. For bare seconds no one moved; we stared, not blankly, not in terror, not sick; just sadly, silently, a little wondering.

We roused ourselves then to move a little, as the marshal and the others walked off the platform and started downstairs to help the doctors. The body swung, still some distance from the floor of the pit. Boxes were brought over and one of the doctors climbed up finally and then said one word: dead. We looked at our watches again. Six minutes had gone by since the clicking had stopped. It was 8:56.

Directly we heard men outside our cubbyhole and the nails were drawn out. The partition fell away and we crawled out into the cold air. We stretched and brushed off the backs of our coats. All the witnesses leave the yard, the marshal said. As we went through the big gate, a long slender hearse turned up the driveway. It was jet black, the blackness shining even without sun.

Al and I hurried toward town again, barely talking. We trembled a little perhaps, but there was nothing else unusual. It was not so bad. In the bar to which we made our way we ordered scotch and soda; easy on the soda, said Al, and I felt the same way. We drank and returned at once to the street. The rain had begun again. Al turned up the street, back to the shop, while I made my way toward the waterfront. A boat was whistling and there would be people aboard. People who moved and did not turn and twist like a rock on a string. I had watched a man die; these would be living.

John Gaffney grew up in Juneau, Alaska, went to the University of Idaho and served as a War Department official in World War II. He was a journalist for 26 years on a variety of newspapers, from "leg man" to editorial page editor, and spent 8 years supervising a staff of editors and graphic artists in publications at Cornell University. He is the author of On the Record [Audenreed Press], a collection of his newspaper columns of the same name. At age 21, Mr. Gaffney was a newspaper reporter in Alaska who was a formal witness to the execution by hanging of a Ketchikan man. His reactions to that event were written on the night of the execution, November 10, 1939, and are reproduced here unedited.

ABOUT THE ARTISTS

Steven King Ainsworth has been on San Quentin's Death Row for 17 years. His artwork has been published in periodicals throughout the country, and his poetry and art appeared in <u>Trapped Under Ice: A Death Row Anthogy</u> [Biddle Publishing Co.]. "During my twenty plus years of incarceration I have always been drawn to artistic endeavors in order to alleviate the boredom and stress of confinement. The therapeutic value of art and the act of creating something positive in a prison environment is immense."

Clifford Boggess, incarcerated on Death Row at Huntsville, Texas, is entirely self-taught as an artist. "I couldn't draw or paint when I first came to Death Row. Over the years, art has become my life-line, my therapy, and my greatest pleasure. It's how I handle 'doing time.' It is a wonderful escape for me, and I hope it speaks to others in some way. My dream, aside from escaping execution, is to someday obtain legitimate gallery representation in the free world, to 'make it' as a professional artist."

Louis Osei Cotton is an artist, writer and poet, and the editor of <u>Caged Freedom</u> [Audenreed Press]. Mr. Cotton has been recognized for his talents and leadership as Chairman of the Fine Arts Society by wardens of both state and federal prisons, as well as by the Governor of Kansas. "This system screams out for law and order, bellowing at Society, 'Lock 'em up and throw away the key for they are animals, unfit and without feeling, compassion or concern.' Society must accept even the least of us. We are their brothers, husbands, sons, uncles and nephews...And all of us are God's children."

Domingo is a Native-American who is awaiting trial on capital murder charges. His picture was drawn in a Texas jail and given to another inmate for use in this book.

Billy G. Hughes Jr. has been on Death Row at Huntsville, Texas for 20 years. A farrier and horse trainer by trade, he has published the periodical <u>Horseman's Travel Guide</u> from prison and continues to write and draw for horse lovers nationwide. In addition to being a writer and artist, Mr. Hughes, since coming to Death Row, has earned two college degrees, become a Certified Paralegal, takes courses in Bible Studies and numerous other subjects and is training to be a Certified Braille Transcriber with the Library of Congress. "The men and women on Death Row don't have to give up; they can better themselves and do so much to help others."

Anthony Papa received a 15-years-to-life sentence for a non-violent first-offense drug possession. He began to draw and paint after his incarceration. During his years in prison, Mr. Papa's work has been exhibited several times in New York, and he has been the subject of several newspaper articles. "Art has actually saved my life, helped me maintain my humanity. Art for me now is a means of strict survival." After almost 12 years in Sing Sing Correctional Facility, Mr. Papa received Christmas Clemency from the Governor of New York and was released in early 1997.

Jesse Roberts, incarcerated in Canon City, Colorado, has been teaching himself how to create "this 'n that" for about 10 years. "I guess the 'Seeds' concept states my opinion more clearly than words. Add to this my long held belief that art as symbolism must have a life of its own unattached to stigma, labels and preconceptions which flood into and behind the eyes of the audience, when they learn of the creator."

David S. Schofield is a 57 year old, college-educated lifer doing time for the 1977 shooting death of his wife. He continues to assert his innocence regarding this first offense charge-conviction. He became a published writer/artist in the early '90s. "There is no place for systematic executions in the modern age. Two wrongs still don't make a right."

Christian Snyder is serving a 5-15 year sentence in New York State. Since his incarceration, he has launched a career as a freelance magazine and editorial cartoonist, and plans to continue this profession upon his release. "The justification of executing a confessed or convicted killer can come from many perspectives. The act of sparing his or her life comes from only one—mercy."

Royalties from the sale of **Frontiers of Justice, Volume 1: The Death Penalty** are donated to Murder Victims' Families for Reconciliation.

MVFR provides information about the needs of victims' families and the concerns of victims' families who are opposed to the death penalty in all situations.

MVFR knows first hand of the deep hurt and pain that occur when a loved one is murdered. MVFR knows that, in spite of that pain, vengeance is not the answer. The taking of another life by state killing only continues the cycle of violence.

MVFR believes that all life is sacred, and that no one has the right to take another life. MVFR knows that we can make a difference in the struggle to abolish the death penalty.

MVFR works with organizations such as Amnesty International, the National Coalition to Abolish the Death Penalty, CURE, American Friends Service Committee, Southern Christian Leadership Conference and other local and religious groups towards the goal of abolition.

Murder Victims' Families for Reconciliation, PO Box 208, Atlantic VA 23303-0208, 757-824-0948

The following organizations are some of the other national resources that support the abolition of capital punishment:

CURE, PO Box 2310, Washington DC, 20013, 202-789-2126
Death Penalty Information Center, 1606 20th St NW-2nd Fl, Washington DC 20009, 202-347-2531
Equal Justice USA, PO Box 5206, Hyattsville MD 20782, 301-699-0042
The Fortune Society, 39 West 19th Street, New York, NY, 10011, 212-206-7070
National Coalition To Abolish the Death Penalty, 1918 F St NW, Washington DC 20004, 202-347-2411 (publishes The Abolitionist's Directory)

Thanks to Ricky Langley, Death Row, Louisiana State Prison, for his help in collecting resources.

Books on prison issues available from Biddle Publishing Company:

Caged Freedom, Osei Cotton, Ed., $8.50

Dead End, by Gary E. Goldhammer, $10.95

Frontiers of Justice, Volume 1: The Death Penalty,
    Ed.s Claudia Whitman and Julie Zimmerman, $15.95

Going to Prison? 3rd Edition, by Jimmy Tayoun, $7.95

Iowa on the Inside, by Vincent Johnson, $6.00

Shall Suffer Death, by A.J. Bannister, $15.00

Trapped Under Ice: A Death Row Anthology, Ed. Julie Zimmerman, $8.00

The Warden Wore Pink, by Tekla Dennison Miller, $11.95

Catalogs are available on request

Orders only, toll free - 1-888-315-0582, 9-5 ET.
(Please add $2 shipping for first book, .50 each additional book.)

Frontiers of Justice is a series whose goal is to promote humane and effective criminal justice policy. Further volumes will address adult and juvenile offender prison and alternative programs. Volume 2 is tentatively scheduled for release in early 1998.

INDEX